Institutional Economics

Why is it that some countries become rich while others remain poor? Do markets require regulation to function efficiently? If markets offer an efficient way of exchanging goods, why do individuals even create firms? How are economic transactions organized in the absence of a state that could enforce contracts and guarantee property rights? Institutional economics has allowed social scientists to answer many fundamental questions about the organization and functioning of societies. This introduction to institutional economics is concise, yet easy to understand. It not only caters to students of economics but to anybody interested in this topical research area and its specific subfields. Both formal and informal institutions (such as customs, habits, and traditions) are discussed with respect to their causes and consequences, highlighting the important part they play for economic growth and development.

Stefan Voigt is Chair of Economic Analysis of Law at the University of Hamburg and Director of its Institute of Law and Economics. He is also a fellow with CESifo (Munich). Voigt is one of the editors of *Constitutional Political Economy* and a member of various editorial boards, including those of *Public Choice* and the *International Review of Law & Economics*.

T0382942

Institutional Economics
An Introduction

Stefan Voigt
University of Hamburg

CAMBRIDGE
UNIVERSITY PRESS

University Printing House, Cambridge CB2 8BS, United Kingdom

One Liberty Plaza, 20th Floor, New York, NY 10006, USA

477 Williamstown Road, Port Melbourne, VIC 3207, Australia

314–321, 3rd Floor, Plot 3, Splendor Forum, Jasola District Centre,
New Delhi – 110025, India

79 Anson Road, #06–04/06, Singapore 079906

Cambridge University Press is part of the University of Cambridge.

It furthers the University's mission by disseminating knowledge in the pursuit of
education, learning, and research at the highest international levels of excellence.

www.cambridge.org
Information on this title: www.cambridge.org/9781108473248
DOI: 10.1017/9781108573719

© Stefan Voigt 2019

First published 2019
Reprinted 2019

Printed in the United Kingdom by TJ International Ltd. Padstow Cornwall

A catalogue record for this publication is available from the British Library.

Library of Congress Cataloging-in-Publication Data
Names: Voigt, Stefan, author.
Title: Institutional economics : an introduction / Stefan Voigt, University of
    Hamburg.
Description: 1 Edition. | New York : Cambridge University Press, [2018] |
    Includes bibliographical references and index.
Identifiers: LCCN 2018030131| ISBN 9781108473248 (hardback) |
    ISBN 9781108461085 (pbk.)
Subjects: LCSH: Institutional economics.
Classification: LCC HB99.5 .V65 2018 | DDC 330–dc23
LC record available at https://lccn.loc.gov/2018030131

ISBN 978-1-108-47324-8 Hardback
ISBN 978-1-108-46108-5 Paperback

Brief Contents

Detailed Contents

Figures

Tables

Preface

The new institutional economics is an impressive success story. Within just a few decades, this young subdiscipline has attracted some of the brightest scholars around, several Nobel prizewinners among them.

The book is aimed at familiarizing anybody interested in the new institutional economics with its most basic concepts. No prior knowledge in economics is needed. I have attempted to use plain language and avoid economic jargon. As the new institutional economics continues to develop at high speed, it was impossible to do justice to every branch of its research program; instead, this book summarizes the state of the art from a subjective point of view.

A German-language predecessor, *Institutionenökonomik*, was published in 2002 by Wilhelm Fink publishers. A comparison between that edition and the current one reveals how much, and how quickly, new institutional economics has progressed: some chapters had to be completely rewritten to reflect the progress made during the last 15 years.

I was extremely lucky to have a group of very gifted – and highly critical – collaborators. We discussed every single page of this introduction to the field. Thanks to Marek Endrich, Dr. Jerg Gutmann, Dr. Stephan Michel, and Konstantinos Pilpilidis for critically – but also constructively – reading the first draft of this edition. Dr. Sang-Min Park and Mark Pegors helped make my English readable. Many thanks to them, too.

Introduction

Why do a few hundred million people enjoy a very high income while billions suffer from malnourishment and struggle to survive? Why do certain types of constitutions – ones that have proved very successful elsewhere – often not have their intended results, for instance, high incomes for the populace and a stable political system? Why is it that development programs introduced with the best intentions by the World Bank or the International Monetary Fund (IMF) often do not induce development, but instead sometimes even make the poor worse off? Is there a systematic relationship between individual freedom and per capita income? In the case of formerly socialist societies, is there indeed only a single silver bullet, namely, to privatize as fast and comprehensively as possible?

These are among the many questions that concern institutional economists. Institutional economists do not claim to be able to answer these questions comprehensively, but they do claim that their methods of investigating these questions can lead to more convincing answers than those offered by traditional economists.

The core hypothesis of institutional economics is that *growth and development are decisively shaped by the prevailing institutions*. The willingness as well as the ability not only to specialize, and thereby contribute to a deeper division of labor, but also to make long-term capital investments depends on the security of private property rights. Chapter 1 shows that property rights are an essential component of the institutions we are about to analyze. The form and content of private property rights, as well as possible costs of their enforcement, are crucial determinants in explaining why growth and development unfold – or do not. Douglass North, who was awarded the Nobel prize for his achievements regarding institutional economics, writes that "the inability of societies to develop effective, low-cost enforcement of contracts is the most important source of both historical stagnation and contemporary underdevelopment in the Third World" (1990a, 54).

Another pioneer of institutional economics, Mancur Olson, asks why some nations are rich while others are poor. After having gone through the usual suspects (such as different access to knowledge, different access to capital markets, differences regarding population size in relation to arable land or the abundance of natural resources, differences in human capital, etc.), he concludes that none of them is particularly convincing and continues: "The only remaining plausible explanation is that the great differences in the wealth of nations are mainly due to differences in the quality of their institutions and their economic policies" (1996, 19).

To most non-economists, the relevance of institutions might appear so self-evident that it is difficult to understand why a still fairly young research area in economics puts that relevance center stage and even calls it "new." The answer lies in the fact that mainstream economics has long neglected institutions, albeit usually benignly. For many decades, growth theory tried to explain differences in growth across countries without explicitly taking into account the underlying institutions, looking instead at changes in labor and capital goods supply.

Over the last couple of decades, however, an increasing number of economists have become interested in how institutions might influence economic development. Among them are a number of Nobel laureates, including Ronald Coase, Friedrich Hayek, Douglass North, Elinor Ostrom, Herbert Simon, and Oliver Williamson. The new institutional economics is not marginal anymore: it is an amazing success story.

This brief introduction to the new institutional economics is aimed at a wider audience than just economists or students. Economics does not have a happy reputation; indeed, it is often referred to as the "dismal science." Many non-economists view economics as a soulless science completely divorced from real people and real life. Scientists in other disciplines often claim that economists abstract from so much relevant context that their results are meaningless. The new institutional economics takes these criticisms seriously, while still remaining "economic" in nature, taking some comfort from the fact that some have crowned economics as the queen of social sciences. In truth, economists have always inquired into constraints on human behavior when explaining individual choices. Traditionally, the main focus has been on the laws of nature as well as on budgetary constraints.

The new institutional economics takes the less-traveled path of explicitly acknowledging that both proscriptions and prescriptions influence human behavior and, further, that these proscriptions and prescriptions are not only state imposed and enforced (e.g., speed limits) but are also found in the norms of a society (e.g., in many countries, if one wants to board a bus, one must stand in line to do so, with deviations being sometimes quite severely punished by others in the queue).

Indeed, norms, customs, traditions, and mores can channel behavior just as much, sometimes even more, than laws. Whereas laws can be changed radically and swiftly, such is not the case with norms, customs, traditions, and mores. Thus the second core hypothesis of new institutional economics is that *the possibility of implementing institutions conducive to growth and development is constrained by the cultural imprint of the respective society*. Or, as Douglass North puts it: "Although formal rules may change overnight as the result of political or judicial decisions, informal constraints embodied in customs, traditions, and codes of conduct are much more impervious to deliberate policies" (1990a, 6).

If it is true that growth and development are determined by both formal and informal rules, the interdependencies between them must be explicitly taken into account. A general hypothesis is that the enforceability of formal rules ultimately depends on their compatibility with informal ones (Weingast, 1995; Voigt, 1999a, ch. 5). This is not especially good news for politicians and their advisors whose carefully designed programs optimistically intend to turn entire countries around within just a hundred days and set them on a path to growth and prosperity. Institutional economists view such optimism skeptically and more cautiously hope for a sequence of incremental improvements.

Conventional textbooks usually present the (more or less) solid knowledge of the respective field in a didactically sophisticated fashion. I have opted for a different approach in this book. I frequently point out that our knowledge regarding the effects of specific institutions is quite limited (yet). Every chapter ends with a section entitled "Open Questions." My hope is that these questions will inspire curiosity in readers, even leading some to become researchers themselves. If this book manages to make institutional economics seem exciting and valuable, it will have achieved its goal.

Just a word on my use of references. In each chapter, I quote from or cite those publications that have been seminal contributions to a particular topic. However, I realize that such references might be somewhat daunting to a reader just beginning to become acquainted with the topic. Therefore, the further reading recommendations at the end of the chapters were selected to be more accessible; surveys – either in the form of papers or books – were given priority.

1 The Basics

To deal with specific research questions and the results of a rather novel research program, some groundwork needs to be laid here in Chapter 1. First, we take a brief look at the standard behavioral model of economics utilized by the majority of economists today. We also look at extensions of this standard behavioral model proposed by representatives of the new institutional economics (NIE). Second, we cope with the problems of defining institutions. After briefly considering several different ways of doing this, we develop a taxonomy of our own, one that we then use in all subsequent chapters. Third, we present a systematic overview of the research questions with which representatives of NIE are concerned. The structure of all subsequent chapters in the book is based on this systematic presentation of these research questions. Fourth, we describe instruments and methods employed by institutional economists to shed light on these research questions. Fifth, and last, we locate NIE within the landscape of economics by taking a look at the differences between NIE and neoclassical economics. We then consider differences and similarities between NIE and other related research traditions, such as public choice, constitutional political economy, and the economic analysis of law or law & economics, as it is also called.

1.1 The Standard Behavioral Model of Economics – and a Few Modifications Made by New Institutional Economics

To explain and predict human behavior, we need a behavioral model – and we have one. However, the standard behavioral model of economics – that of the *homo economicus* – is not without its detractors.

The standard behavioral model of economics: the homo economicus

Many regard it as too simple, arguing that a behavioral model that leaves out so many relevant details necessarily produces inaccurate predictions. Consequently, any policy recommendations based on the standard behavioral model will also be less than optimal. In this section, we briefly present the standard behavioral model before considering a few modifications to it proposed by representatives of NIE.

Let's begin with a very basic question: What is economics?

Modern economics is defined by its approach, not by its subject matter

Traditionally, economics was defined via its subject matter, the economy. In recent decades, however, economics has become defined via its approach (see, e.g., Becker, 1976). Economists have realized that their approach can be applied to a variety of subjects, many of which are completely unrelated to "the economy." Following this delineation, economics can be used to analyze any decision that involves scarcity. For instance, there is an economic approach to marriage and fertility, an economic approach to segregation, to crime, even to teeth brushing. The economic approach can also be utilized to analyze politics (public choice) and law (law & economics).

A key assumption of the economic approach is that all actors aim to maximize their utility.

Definition

In economics, **utility** is defined as the contribution of a good to the fulfillment of individual needs.

However, the means for attaining utility are scarce. Moreover, utility does not only involve monetary aspects but can also refer to non-pecuniary aspects. For instance, one's utility can be increased by being liked by one's neighbors. The traditional economic approach also assumes that actors' preferences are constant, but that constraints – that is, restrictions on behavior – are not. **Preferences** are defined as an expression of how alternative goods are valued relative to each other: for instance, A is preferred over B. **Restrictions** encompass not only laws of nature and an actor's resources, but also man-made laws, the violation of which can incur sanctions (which raise the "price" of illegal behavior). Further restrictions include norms, customs, and traditions (these, too, raise the price of certain, nonconforming actions), temporal constraints (one can only work 24 hours per day), and informational constraints (one cannot desire a good without knowing about it).

Definition

Models are purposefully simplified depictions of reality that can help in understanding specific important aspects of reality.

In many economic models, it is assumed that actors are rational in their pursuit of maximizing utility, subject to given restrictions. As a whole, these assumptions are subsumed as the *homo economicus* model. It is important to remember, however, that this is a *model* – and thus it does not claim to describe reality completely or even necessarily correctly.

Nevertheless, the *homo economicus* model can help explain human behavior and predict how such behavior will change when restrictions change. Changes in behavior are never ascribed to changes in preferences, as that would not be an explanation but, rather, a reformulation of the problem.

Homo economicus: rational, utility-maximizing agent with stable preferences

Furthermore, economics is based on the assumption of **methodological individualism**; that is, it is only individuals who act, not collectives, such as firms or governments.

Definition

Methodological individualism is based on the assumption that only individuals can be actors and implies that all outcomes – even at the macro level – must be explained by referring to individual behavior.

When we observe results on a collective level that are the consequence of the interactions of many people and yet these results were not intended by any of the involved actors, it is the task of social scientists, including economists, to explain how the interplay of individual action unintentionally produced this collective result.

It seems fair to say that by now, most economists work with these assumptions. What, then, are the **contributions of NIE** that distinguish it from more traditional economics? There are two main differences between the two approaches:

1. Their subject matter.
2. The assumptions made.

With regard to subject matter, traditionally, rules that help structure interactions were thought of as part of the **reference data** used in decision-making. In other words, they were assumed to be given. By employing the economic approach, it is possible, however, to investigate the **choice of rules** and changes thereof over time. With regard to the assumptions made, institutional economists promote two modifications to the traditional behavioral model. The first is to assume bounded rationality instead of perfect rationality.

The second is to consider the costs of economic exchange. Traditionally, economists assumed that such exchange is costless. Institutional economists emphasize that economic exchange entails information costs, search costs, negotiation costs, and fulfillment costs, the level of each depending on the type of institutions in effect. These costs are called **transaction costs** and in economics they were usually assumed to be zero. The concepts of bounded rationality and transaction costs are closely related to each other.

The distinctive features of institutional economics: bounded rationality and transaction costs

1.1.1 From Perfect to Bounded Rationality

Traditionally, it was assumed that individuals attempt to maximize their utility in a perfectly rational manner. This implies that they can predict every possible state of the world and that they are able to choose from all available courses of action the one that delivers the highest individual utility. In this far-from-the-real world, individuals are capable of evaluating the consequences of all possible actions immediately and without cost. Or as Kreps (1990, 745) put it, completely rational individuals possess "the ability to foresee everything that might happen and to evaluate and optimally choose among available courses of action."

Uncertainty, that is, a situation in which actors are not capable of computing expected utility because they are not able predict all possible states of the world, was introduced to economics by Frank Knight (1922). He distinguishes between uncertainty and **risk**. In the face of risk, actors are able to assign probabilities to a finite number of possible states of the world. Thus, in a risky situation, actors are able to compute expected utility, meaning that established decision theory is applicable. However, once we move from a situation with risk, that is, one in which consequences are relatively predictable, to a situation with uncertainty, that is no longer possible.

Herbert Simon (1955), recognizing that the assumption of perfect rationality is inappropriate given an environment characterized by uncertainty, introduced the notion of **bounded rationality** into economics. He replaced the assumption of individual utility maximization with **satisficing** behavior, which involves individuals defining realistic acceptability thresholds. Only when those thresholds are not met, do individuals begin to consider courses of action different from their routinely chosen ones. It has been demonstrated that in a situation with uncertainty, it can be rational

Boundedly rational individuals attempt to satisfice acceptability thresholds

to utilize rules in deciding how to behave (Heiner, 1983). This type of rationality is often called "rule rationality," and it is a way for actors to rationally cope with uncertainty.

1.1.2 Transaction Costs

Transaction costs were introduced into economics by Ronald Coase (1937). He defines them as the costs of using the market. Ignoring transaction costs (or setting them to zero) is equivalent to assuming markets that function efficiently and costlessly. However, when markets function efficiently and without costs, there is no reason for firms to exist. Why? Let us assume that firms are primarily characterized by interactions not being organized via voluntary exchange (like in markets) but via commands issued from higher-ranked to lower-ranked members of a firm. Relying on instructions and hierarchy entails various costs: those receiving the instructions might not be motivated to complete them to the full satisfaction of their bosses; a costly need to monitor their behavior might arise, and so forth. Let us call the resulting costs "organization costs." Now, if using hierarchies (firms) is costly whereas the use of markets is costless, there is no reason for firms to exist. Coase now explains the existence of firms by saying that – for some activities – the costs of using the market (i.e., transaction costs) are higher than the costs of using hierarchies like firms. Carl Dahlman (1979, 148) describes transaction costs as "search and information costs, bargaining and decision costs, policing and enforcement costs."

Imagine that temperatures begin to fall and you are thinking about buying a winter coat. Since it is already quite cold outside, you decide to shop online. You want something that is fashionable and well-made and to buy it from a store that has a good reputation not only for quality but for customer service, too. And, of course, you would like to pay as little as possible. Finding a coat that meets all these requirements will cost you some time and this cost is here subsumed under search and information costs. Suppose that you finally find a coat that you would really like to have, but not at the price currently shown. So, you use a search engine to locate a better price and you even try to find webstores that allow you to make an offer. But now you need to assess the reliability of some of these offers. Will that store in East Asia really deliver the original product? Do you trust it enough to give out your credit card information? Dahlman calls the costs of this type of activity "bargaining and decision costs." You take the plunge and buy the coat. You are delighted when the coat arrives before the first snow falls, but this feeling quickly turns to disappointment when you discover that the coat keeps you neither warm nor dry. You search the store's webpage and eventually find the fine print regarding its returns policy. Packaging up the coat and taking it to the post office costs you additional time and money. Much to your chagrin, the store never sends you a replacement coat, nor does it even acknowledge, much less reimburse you for, the return of the first coat. By this time, you are so angry you are even thinking of taking legal action. You have now incurred what Dahlman calls "policing and enforcement costs."

The assumption of nonzero transaction costs is a logical consequence of bounded rationality, whereas perfectly rational individuals, by definition, face no transaction costs. An individual with perfect knowledge does not have to incur costs of collecting information, negotiating, or enforcing the terms of a transaction.

Close relationship between bounded rationality and transaction costs

The significance of transaction costs not only for the existence of firms, but for economic development in general, should now be clear. Generally, the higher the transaction costs, the lower the number of transactions. And a lower number of transactions implies a lower degree of specialization and, at the end of the day, less income.

Transaction costs and bounded rationality in economics

Both transaction costs and bounded rationality have found their way into other subdisciplines of economics. Information and search costs, as one important component of transaction costs, play a central role in what is called "information economics," which deals with the peculiar properties of information such as how easily it spreads but how difficult it is to verify. Information asymmetry, the situation in which one actor in an interaction has better or different information than another actor, will be discussed in Chapter 3.

Behavioral economics is a subdiscipline of economics that is interested in how real people really behave – not in how they would behave were they fully rational. In a sense then, the limited – or bounded – rationality of real people is the starting point for behavioral economics.

The concept of transaction costs is not restricted to the economy. For example, analysts of political markets employ the same idea, and call these costs **political transaction costs** (North, 1990b, 1993). Given that political markets are subject to much more inefficiency than traditional goods markets due to the difficulty of quantifying the goods to be exchanged or committing to binding promises regarding the services to be rendered, the relationship between a politician and his or her electorate can be viewed as a barter exchange. Votes are exchanged for promises to enact certain policies. However, after the election, voters have very few, if any, means of forcing politicians to keep their promises. New institutional economists are actually not the first to realize this. Jean-Jacques Rousseau, for example, said: "The English people think they are free, but they are greatly mistaken. They are free only at the moment when they elect members of Parliament, and once those are elected, the people are slaves, they are nothing." The first German chancellor after its unification in the nineteenth century, Otto von Bismarck, wrote that "[p]eople never lie so much as after a hunt, during a war or before an election." And finally, American writer H. L. Mencken quipped "[e]very election is a sort of advance auction sale of stolen goods." Applying the concept of political transaction costs to this situation, it follows that these costs, in the form of monitoring and enforcement costs, are high.

Alternative delineations of transaction costs

It is frequently the case that terms central to a novel research program are defined very differently by different scholars, and the term "transaction costs" is no exception. Doug Allen (2011, 19), for instance, defines them as *"those costs necessary to establish and maintain any system of rules and rights."* Whereas our preferred definition focuses on the costs that participants to an interaction situation incur individually, Allen's definition focuses on the overall costs necessary to maintain functioning institutions. His definition is thus not concerned with the costs incurred by individuals but in those incurred by society as a whole.

In the *Encyclopedia of Law and Economics,* under the topic "Transaction Costs," Allen (2000) distinguishes between a neo-classical definition that focuses on the costs of trading in a market and a property rights definition that centers on the costs of establishing and enforcing property rights. Allen presents a very detailed survey not only of the various definitions of trans-action costs, but also of the history of the term, as well as the difficulties in measuring transaction costs and the possible implications of this difficulty.

In our preferred definition of transaction costs, information costs are at the root of transaction costs. This view is not uncon-tested. Yoram Barzel (1977), for example, argues strongly in favor of strictly separating information from transaction costs. As definitions cannot be true or false, the most appropriate definition might well depend on the specific research question being investigated.

1.2 Institutions: Functions, Types, and Interrelationships

Two cars approach each other on a street so narrow that they cannot pass each other without reducing their speed. Each driver wonders what the other will do. Two strangers would like to exchange goods, the quality of which is not immediately obvious. Under what conditions will the strangers agree to the exchange? Two students decide to found a firm. How can either of them ascertain that the other will not cheat? These are three examples of interaction situations in which there is **strategic uncertainty**. Strategic uncertainty is present when the result of an action depends not only on one's own behavior, but also on that of another actor. This is different from **parametric uncertainty**, in which the result of an action depends on the realization of some exogenous event, for instance, on whether it rains or snows. One possible consequence of strategic uncer-tainty is that some exchanges simply do not occur. For example, with regard to the interaction situations described above, it is possible that the good will not be traded or the firm will not be founded.

Two types of uncertainty

As soon as two real people interact, there is strategic uncertainty. If the interacting individuals are unable to form expectations con-cerning the actions of each other, long-term interactions are unlikely to take place. Trade relations, for example, will tend to be restricted to simultaneous exchanges and the extent to which labor specializes and division of labor is worthwhile will be limited.

Ultimately, living standards will be low. This suboptimal environment can be improved, however, if strategic uncertainty can be reduced by behavioral restrictions. And this is one of the main functions of **institutions** – to **reduce uncertainty**, thus lengthening the time horizon of actors and providing incentives to specialize, which leads to a higher degree of division of labor. In short, institutions can help to improve living standards.

Consequences of strategic uncertainty

To this point, the concept of institutions has been presented from a functional perspective. However, if we are interested in explaining the development of institutions, we must be careful not to commit a functionalist fallacy, which occurs when the existence of some phenomenon is explained by its positive effects. For example, a law should not be assumed to pass because it can be expected to have positive effects on welfare, but because certain actors expect to gain from it. Within the framework of methodological individualism, we can explain the origins of institutions only if we understand the incentives of the actors involved in their establishment.

1.2.1 Definitions of Institutions

NIE is a young research program and has not yet arrived at a universally accepted definition of institutions. According to North (1990a, 3), "[i]nstitutions are the rules of the game in a society or, more formally, are the humanly devised constraints that shape human interaction. In consequence they structure incentives in human exchange, whether political, social, or economic."

In this book, we propose a definition that is more similar to that of Ostrom (1986) but fully compatible with the one proposed by North. We think it is important to distinguish between two **components** of institutions: the rule component and the sanction (or enforcement) component. We can then define institutions as *commonly known rules used to structure recurrent interaction situations, such rules being endowed with a sanctioning mechanism in case of noncompliance*. This definition is explained in greater detail in Voigt (2013).

Institutions as rule plus sanction

1.2.1.1 Characteristics of Rules

Following Ostrom (1986, 5), we define *rules* as "*prescriptions commonly known and used by a set of participants to order*

Definition: Rules

repetitive, interdependent relationships. Prescriptions refer to which actions (or states of the world) are required, prohibited, or permitted. Rules are the result of implicit or explicit efforts by a set of individuals to achieve order and predictability within defined situations." Two characteristics of this definition are of particular note:

1. A rule is **commonly known**. This does not mean that every individual of a society knows all the rules by heart. Such would not be possible. Instead, "commonly known" means that purely private rules not shared by other members of society are not rules.
2. Rules are the result of human action, but not necessarily the outcome of deliberate human design, as their origins can be traced to both explicit and implicit attempts of individual actors to structure interaction.

Result of human action, but not of human design

A rule can emerge over time due to the actions of individual actors even though those actors did not intend to create the rule. Take, for instance, rules of speech, which have emerged from human action without anyone designing them. The Nobel prize winning economist Friedrich A. Hayek often used the expression "result of human action, but not of human design" in order to point out the evolutionary component of rule development. He credits Adam Ferguson (an eighteenth-century Scottish moral philosopher) as source for this idea. Ferguson, for his part, attributes the idea to Jean François Paul de Gondi, Cardinal de Retz (Ferguson, 1995 [1767])

Rules can take one of two forms: (1) commandments that prescribe specific behavior or a range of allowed actions or (2) prohibitions that disallow one or more specific actions.

1.2.1.2 Types of Enforcement

Five types of rule enforcement

Rules are without consequence unless they can be enforced. There are several archetypal forms of rule enforcement. First, there are some rules that are in one's self-interest to comply with because noncompliance would make you worse off. Such rules are referred to as **self-enforcing**. From a game-theoretic perspective, interactions governed by this type of rule can be described as **pure coordination games** in which rule compliance is the dominant strategy for all players. The most commonly cited example of a self-enforcing rule is the one that requires all drivers in a country to drive on the right side of the road; an individual rational driver will in no way benefit from not complying with this rule.

(1) Self-enforcement

   A second way to enforce rules is **self-commitment** by the actors. What distinguishes this form of monitoring from self-enforcement is that in this case actors are likely to have internalized certain **ethical rules.** Suppose you intend to always follow the golden rule but then a situation arises that makes you contemplate deviating from it. But then you begin to think how bad you are going to feel about yourself if you act against your principles. In the end, you might well decide to follow the golden rule even in this instance.

(2) Self-commitment

Definition

Internalize: to give a subjective character to; specifically: to incorporate (as values or patterns of culture) within the self as conscious or subconscious guiding principles through learning or socialization (Merriam-Webster)

When internalized rules involve culturally handed down modes of conduct, they fulfill the criterion of being commonly known. Via the shared beliefs and opinions of a social group, these rules induce observable behavioral conformities, regardless of specific personal situations. Take, for instance, someone visiting a beach who is sure that no one is watching him and who never plans to return to the beach. Even so, he might incur the "cost" of walking over to the next trashcan to throw away his garbage instead of just leaving it on the beach.[1]

   Not every interaction situation lends itself to a self-enforced rule or self-commitment by the actors. Some types of interactions are governed by rules that require enforcement via explicit sanctions by other actors and thus may involve a **collective action problem.**

---

[1] Behavior and behavioral constraints can also be religiously motivated. The beach visitor in our example might believe that God would see him leaving trash on the ground. In such a case, behavior is induced not via self-commitment, but via the belief that one should act according to the rules of some supernatural being.

> **Note**
>
> Collective action problem: When all actors potentially could
> benefit from a certain action – in this case a particular sanction –
> frequently none of the actors will take that action, hoping that
> the other actors will do so

(3) Spontaneous societal enforcement

The collective action problem of sanctioning rule breakers becomes relevant with regard to **spontaneous societal enforcement**. This involves an unknown number of persons informally monitoring compliance with societal rules. Supposedly, every member of the group has an interest in rule breakers being sanctioned. But since sanctioning is connected with disutility and, hence, costly, every member of the group hopes that some other group member will do the costly sanctioning. If, ultimately, nobody does the sanctioning, the rule is likely to erode. A somewhat indirect sanction for non-compliance is to inform others about the rule breaking and thus damage the rule breaker's social **reputation**. If a poor reputation makes it more difficult to interact with others in the future, the threat of losing one's reputation might be sufficient to ensure compliance with the rule.

(4) Organized private enforcement

(5) Organized state enforcement

There are two other types of enforcement that are different from the ones just discussed in that they are organized: organized private enforcement and organized state enforcement. An example of **organized private enforcement** is private arbitration courts. State courts are an example of **organized state enforcement**. The two types differ in that organized state enforcement, in contrast to organized private enforcement, contains an element of hierarchical order in that private actors are subordinated to state control.

To better understand the concept of institutions, consider the following two points:

1. The first component of an institution (in our definition) is a rule. This rule always constrains behavior. However, not every behavioral constraint is a rule; for example, constraints due to natural laws (e.g., the law of gravity) are not rules. Second, promises as such are not institutions. Contracts contain mutual promises to act in specific ways and they do constrain future behavior. But they are not rules in the sense of commonly known prescriptions. In other words, most contracts are not

Table 1.1. Types of internal and external institutions

Rule	Form of enforcement	Type of institution	Example
1. Convention	Self-enforcement	Internal type 1	Grammatical rules
2. Ethical rule	Self-commitment	Internal type 2	The Ten Commandments, the Categorical Imperative
3. Custom	Spontaneous informal societal enforcement	Internal type 3	Rules of social conduct
4. Formal private rule	Organized private enforcement	Internal type 4	Private arbitration courts
5. Rules of man-made law	Organized state enforcement	External	Private law, criminal law

Source: Voigt and Kiwit (1998, 86).

institutions but they may be, and often are, based on institutions if they are framed within the boundaries of the relevant contract law.[2]

2. Institutions provide information and thus help reduce strategic uncertainty. Other phenomena also provide information, such as newspapers, news broadcasts, or prices, without necessarily reducing strategic uncertainty. But none of these involve a rule or an enforcement mechanism and, hence, do not qualify as institutions.

Table 1.1 provides a summary of what we have thus far covered. We suggest distinguishing between five types of institutions. We propose to classify institutions that are not enforced by the state as **internal institutions**. Institutions that are enforced by the state are classified as **external institutions**. This typology is based on a *conceptual distinction between state and society*. Thus, internal institutions are those for which noncompliance is sanctioned from within society, and external institutions are those for which noncompliance is sanctioned by the state – external to society.

Society vs. state ↔ internal vs. external institutions

---

[2] This view has to be somewhat relaxed when considering contracts that take effect beyond the purely private realm, such as labor agreements or contracts between states.

Values and norms   The values and norms shared by a significant part of a society's members are particularly represented in internal institutions of type 2 and type 3. Values can be defined as "conceptions of the desirable, influencing selective behavior ... Values are not the same as norms for conduct ... Values are standards of desirability that are more nearly independent of specific situations. The same values may be a point of reference for a great many specific norms; a particular norm may represent the simultaneous application of several separable values" (Darity, 2007). Thus, justice could be a shared value, but what is "just" in a specific situation is determined by the norm of justice. Societal justice norms can be enforced via self-commitment by actors (type 2), but also by members of society sanctioning rule breakers (type 3).

Definitions, again

As mentioned earlier, there is no shortage when it comes to definitions of "institutions." In this box, I briefly discuss the relationship between the definition suggested here and other frequently used definitions. North (1990a) distinguishes between formal and informal institutions, using the rule component as the criterion, and I thus refer to this distinction as one between formal and informal rules. Sometimes, however, rules emerge spontaneously and become ever more formalized over time. It is unclear how formalized a rule must be before it qualifies as a formal rule. Does it need to be written down somewhere? Does it need to pass some formal legislative procedure? The distinction between external and internal institutions suggested here is based on who does the sanctioning in the event a rule is violated. If it is the state that sanctions rule breaking, the enforcement is external to society and is called "external" here; if rule breaking is sanctioned by members of society, the institution is called "internal." One can also think of this as "public" versus "private" sanctioning.

Acemoglu et al. (2005a) propose distinguishing between economic and political institutions. Economic institutions "determine the incentives of and the constraints on economic actors" (Acemoglu et al., 2005a, 386). Similarly, political institutions "determine the constraints on and the incentives of the key actors, but this time in the political sphere" (Acemoglu et al., 2005a, 390). According to Acemoglu et al., political institutions allocate *de jure* political power. Political institutions determine economic institutions and the authors thus think of these institutions as hierarchically structured. However, it is not always easy to precisely differentiate between the political and the economic spheres. For example, how would one classify institutions constraining state-owned enterprises? Whereas North (1990a) emphasizes the difference between formal and informal rules, the distinction between economic and political institutions uses the kind of interaction as a classification criterion, and I emphasize the difference between internal and external sanctioning of rule breakers.

Greif (2006) proposes a very broad definition designed to encompass many previous definitions, many of which he mentions and briefly evaluates. He proposes to define institutions as *"a system of rules, beliefs, norms, and organizations that together generate a regularity of (social) behavior"* (2006, 30, italics in original) and points to some advantages of his proposal. I prefer not to use Greif's definition because it has some disadvantages. His definition does, indeed, encompass both the rules of the game and the outcome of the game. If there is no regularity in behavior, no institution exists. Economists are interested in discovering how institutions influence economic results such as growth and income. If the definition of an institution is already based on the outcome, then a cause–effect relationship is difficult to establish. The conflation of at least four elements – (1) rules, (2) beliefs, (3) norms, and (4) organizations – in a "system" seems to make exact measurement almost impossible. Moreover, how exactly are these ingredients transformed into behavioral regularities?

1.2.2 Interactions between Internal and External Institutions

Institutions come in all sizes and flavors; they differ not only with regard to their enforcement, but also with regard to the content of the rule component. As the rule components of institutions have various origins and hence are likely to set conflicting incentives for behavior, we are interested in the interactions between institutions of different types. It is easy to imagine that the incentive effects of some external institution might be corroborated by some internal institution. By the same token, it is possible that internal institutions counter or neutralize the effect of external institutions. Interactions like these should play a significant role in how well an

20   The Basics

institution is able to reduce uncertainty. Logically, there are four kinds of interaction between institutions:

Internal and external institutions can mutually reinforce, but also mutually weaken, their incentive effects

1. Institutions can be characterized by a **neutral relationship**. This is the case when the institutions in question involve unrelated domains of human behavior.
2. Institutions can be **complementary** when they constrain human behavior in a similar or equal manner and rule enforcement is organized via the state *as well as by* private actors.
3. Institutions can be **substitutive**. This is the case when they affect human behavior in the same or similar manner, but rule enforcement is organized *via* the state *or* privately.
4. Institutions can be **in conflict** when compliance with the internal institution implies noncompliance with the external institution and vice versa.

Note that these four kinds of relationships are possible not only between internal and external institutions, but also within different kinds of internal ones and even within single types.

Predictions about human behavior based on the simple model of the *homo economicus* have often proven wrong. In the standard behavioral model of economics, changes in behavior are induced by changes in restrictions, while preferences are assumed to be constant. Rather than completely abandoning this approach, it could be worthwhile to investigate the relevant restrictions in more detail. Institutional economists assert that the quality of behavioral predictions can be substantially improved when restrictions that are based on internal institutions – such as habits, traditions, ethical rules, and so on – are accounted for to a greater extent than in the case under more traditional approaches.

1.3 Research Questions

In the chapters to follow we distinguish between two levels of analysis:

Exogenous variables are variables determined outside the model Endogenous variables are determined within the model

1. On the **first level of analysis, institutions** will be assumed to be **exogenously given**. We then look at how these institutions affect economically relevant variables. By comparing various types of institutions, we can discover whether different institutions lead to different outcomes. Indeed, institutional economists argue that the large variance in observed institutional systems is a crucial factor in differing growth rates of GDP. The second part of the book (Chapters 2–5) deals with this level of analysis.

Table 1.2 Identification of research fields

	Effects of institutions	Origins of institutions
External institutions	1	3
Internal institutions	2	4

Definition

Variance measures the spread of a set of numbers. If all numbers have the same value, the variance is zero

2. On the **second level of analysis, institutions** are **endogenized,** allowing us to investigate the **origins** of institutions, which is important in light of the large variance in existing institutions. In the third part of the book (Chapters 6–7) we present existing approaches to explaining the origins of and change in external and internal institutions.

The 2 × 2 matrix of Table 1.2 is based on the typology of external and internal institutions introduced earlier.

These four research fields are all located within the realm of positive, as opposed to normative, research. The point is not to discuss which institutions are optimal and should, hence, be implemented, but to find out how certain institutions develop (cells 3 and 4) or what effects certain institutions have on economic outcomes (cells 1 and 2). In the following paragraphs, we utilize this simple matrix to describe some of the research questions with which institutional economics is concerned. *(Positive vs. normative)*

The effects of exogenously given external institutions (cell 1) are interesting for a number of interaction situations:

(a) How do institutions affect voluntary exchange of goods between private actors? Specifically, which goods are exchanged? What is the method of payment? This is the topic of **Chapter 2.** *(Structure of the book)*

(b) How do institutions affect the way private actors structure repeated transactions? **Chapter 3** deals with such questions.

(c) **Chapter 4** looks at how institutions affect the incentives for collective action. Here, the focus is on the behavior of state representatives, but we also investigate the possibility of providing certain public goods – for example, clean air – voluntarily, that is, without recourse to government action.

(d) Finally, how do institutions affect GDP growth and economic development? **Chapter 5** reviews results from the literature.

Research questions (a)–(c) are at the level of microeconomics, whereas question (d) involves the macro level. Note that question (d) will be answered based on insights gained from answering questions (a)–(c).

The questions just posed fit in cell 2 of Table 1.2. The third part of the book deals with cells 3 and 4. **Chapter 6** addresses the question of how we can utilize the economic approach to explain change in external institutions. The question of how change in internal institutions can be explained with the economic approach (cell 4) is investigated in **Chapter 7**.

If there is more than one course of action open to a policymaker, the question arises as to which of the possible courses of actions *should* be chosen. Answering this question requires a normative theory. Thus, **Chapter 8** presents extant normative approaches. **Chapter 9** takes a look at what consequences NIE has for public choice theory and actual economic policy. The final chapter of the book, **Chapter 10**, contains an exploration of potential new pathways in NIE.

1.4 The Toolkit of Institutional Economists

We now present the tools that can be used to answer the questions just posed. Broadly speaking, we need tools that help us systematize our thinking and generate conjectures regarding potential effects of institutions as well as possible drivers of their change. We here discuss only one such tool because it is particularly well suited for dealing with strategic interactions, namely, game theory (1.4.1). No matter how convincing our theories might sound, as economists, we want to put them to the test, that is, we want to see whether they truly explain what happens in the real world. In institutional economics, empirical tests are usually based on comparative institutional analysis (1.4.2). The central idea here is to see how well different institutions realized in different countries – or at different times – that essentially serve the same function do in comparison with each other. There are various ways of doing this. One way is to use laboratory and field experiments (1.4.3), another way is to draw on case studies, of which economic history is a particular application (1.4.4). The most established and most frequently used way is to engage in econometric analyses (1.4.5). Comparative institutional analysis plays a special role here. Some NIE scholars argue that since both transaction costs and bounded rationality are now "mainstream," NIE's distinctive feature is comparative institutional analysis. Viewed like this, laboratory and field experiments, just like econometric analysis, can be considered as specific ways to implement comparative institutional analysis. We begin our *tour d'horizon* of the toolkit with game theory, which is clearly not exclusive to NIE but can be used very profitably in NIE.

1.4.1 Game Theory: A Tool for Analyzing Strategic Interaction Situations

One of institutions' chief functions is to reduce strategic uncertainty. However, not every interaction situation is the same: sometimes, actors can achieve higher payoffs by coordinating (coordination games); sometimes, one actor's loss is another actor's gain (zero-sum games); and some situations involve a mix of coordination and conflict (mixed-motive games). Game theory reduces a large variety of interaction situations to their essential components and thus helps predict the behavior of rational actors in such situations. Although even a short introduction to general game theory is beyond the scope of this book, game theory has become an essential element of economic reasoning across the entire field of economics. Thus, we briefly present two important game types: coordination and mixed-motive.

A game can be completely described with six components:

1. The **players.** Here, we distinguish between two-player and multiple-player games, although most of the focus will be on two-player games.
2. The **rules.** The rules describe the menu of actions available to each player at each point of the game. In some games, players choose their action simultaneously; in others, actions are taken sequentially. Whether being the first to decide is an advantage or a disadvantage depends on the game's structure.[3]

---

[3] In the *mixed-motive game* "battle of the sexes," a boy and his girlfriend want to spend the evening together. However, their preferences regarding the location diverge. He prefers to meet at a soccer game, she prefers meeting at a club. Whoever of the two is faster to commit to a course of action ("I already bought our tickets to the soccer game, honey"), secures a *first-mover advantage.* In contrast, in a game of "rock, paper, scissors" where players decide sequentially, the one who moves first has a disadvantage.

3. The **strategies**. A strategy is a complete description of all possible actions that a player can take in all possible states of the game.
4. The **information set**. Assuming **complete information** is equivalent to assuming that the players know the rules of the game, the strategies available to all other players, and the payoffs associated with all possible states of the game. **Perfect information** implies that a player knows all relevant actions of the other player up to now.
5. The **payoff functions**. These describe how the players value the possible states of the game.
6. The **results**. Here, the concept of (Nash) **equilibrium** is of particular importance. Such an equilibrium is achieved when, given the other players' action, none of the players can benefit by unilaterally deviating from that action.

There are different ways of depicting games. Here, we use a **reduced form**, which is a way of depicting a game with all its payoffs depending on the combination of actions of the players. The first payoff refers to the row player, the second payoff refers to the column player.

1.4.1.1 A Coordination Game

Picture two cars approaching each other on a narrow street. Let us call the drivers Laurel and Hardy. When they meet, each can steer either left or right (Matrix 1.1). It is in both players' interest to coordinate their behavior with the respective other because failure to do so will result in a crash, which is not desirable for either. This type of game has two equilibria in pure strategies: both players steer left or both players steer right (there is also a mixed-strategy equilibrium in which both players steer left or right with the same probability). Simply looking at the structure of the payoff matrix does not provide many clues as to how the drivers will behave, that is, which equilibrium will result. If the drivers are able to communicate beforehand, they could promise to both steer left (or right). Such promises are credible when no player can expect to benefit by unilaterally deviating. Solutions of this kind are called **conventions**. Conventions, in principle, do not require external enforcement, such

Conventions are   as by the state. Conventions as solutions to coordination games fall
self-enforcing   into the category of internal (or self-enforcing) institutions of type 1.

Matrix 1.1 The coordination game

		Hardy	
		Left	Right
Laurel	Left	0	−2
		0	−2
	Right	−2	0
		−2	0

Note: The four cells contain the payoffs for all strategy combinations. Within each cell, the lower left payoff is Laurel's, the upper right is Hardy's. Higher values indicate higher levels of utility. The equilibria are shaded.

1.4.1.2 A Mixed-Motive Game: The Prisoner's Dilemma

The prisoner's dilemma is probably the most commonly analyzed game in game theory. In this game, two criminal suspects – Bonny and Clyde – are arrested and put in separate cells. The police strongly suspect that Bonny and Clyde have committed the crime in question but they do not have enough evidence for a conviction. Bonny and Clyde are interrogated separately. Both are given two options: testify against the other or remain silent. If neither testifies, they will both be sentenced to one year in prison on a lesser charge. If they both testify, each can be sentenced to eight years in prison. If one testifies while the other remains silent, the one who testifies is sentenced to only three months in prison while the other is sentenced to ten years. This situation translates into the payoff situation depicted in Matrix 1.2.

Matrix 1.2 The prisoner's dilemma 1

		Clyde	
		Silence	Testify
Bonny	Silence	1 year	3 months
		1 year	10 years
	Testify	10 years	8 years
		3 months	8 years

Matrix 1.3 The prisoner's dilemma 2

		Clyde			
		Silence		Testify	
Bonny	Silence		3		4
		3		1	
	Testify		1		2
		4		2	

Obviously, Bonny has an incentive to testify if Clyde remains silent because three months in prison is preferable to one year of incarceration. The previously discussed coordination game has two pure strategy equilibria; the prisoner's dilemma has only one equilibrium: both players testify against each other. In this game, testifying is a **dominant strategy** because it always obtains a higher payoff than remaining silent, given the other player's strategy. What makes this game so interesting is that individually rational behavior leads to a collectively non-rational result: if neither Bonny nor Clyde testifies, they will both be sentenced to one year in prison, but in equilibrium, both face a sentence of eight years.

Matrix 1.3 depicts the prisoner's dilemma in a more general form, where the prison sentences have been replaced by ordinal payoffs.

Ordinal scales

Ordinal scales indicate an order of rank. Interval scales also indicate an order but additionally indicate the numerical distances between values

---

Higher values correspond to a higher level of utility. This – or something very similar – is the most frequently encountered form of the prisoner's dilemma game. It is easy to see that individually rational behavior leads to collectively irrational results: Bonny and Clyde will each end up with a payoff of 2; if they were able to coordinate, they could each attain a payoff of 3.

At first glance, one would not think economists would be much interested in this game and yet they find it highly intriguing. Why? Economists argue that many daily interaction situations have the same structure as the prisoner's dilemma. Remember the two strangers who try to exchange goods without being sure of the goods' quality? Assume that both could be better off with the exchange. However, the seller can realize a gain by selling a cheap imitation instead of the real (and expensive) good. The buyer can realize a gain by paying with counterfeit money or a bad check. This situation is, in fact, a form of the prisoner's dilemma: for both players, cooperation is dominated by defection. From a societal perspective, cooperation among suspected criminals may not be desirable but, in many cases, cooperation between parties to an exchange is definitely desirable. Thus, from a policy standpoint, one of the tasks of NIE is to *propose institutions* that transform the prisoner's dilemma into a game in which it is *rational for both players to keep their ex ante promises.*

Use of game theory is sometimes criticized by proponents of NIE. Some of this criticism revolves around NIE's distrust of assuming perfect rationality, which is an underlying assumption for many games. Furthermore, new institutional economists point out that actors' strategy sets, that is, their possible courses of action, are often not exogenously given. Instead, strategy sets often depend on a specific cultural context or even on an actor's imagination. Even payoff functions need not be exogenously given. All of this implies that explicit integration of transaction costs into games, for example, by subtracting them from the gross payoffs generally offered, constitutes a tremendous challenge and might well prove impossible. Despite these criticisms, however, game theory is a very useful tool for the economic analysis of institutions because institutional economics is concerned with situations of strategic uncertainty, which is exactly the realm for which game theory was developed. Using the prisoner's dilemma as an example again, the game shows that without institutions – regardless of whether they are external or internal – a suboptimal equilibrium is likely to be the outcome. In such a setting, establishing an institution that helps individuals coordinate on another equilibrium might well increase overall welfare.

1.4.2 Comparative Institutional Analysis

The term "comparative institutional analysis" was coined by Ronald Coase (1964), and involves identifying and comparing the effects of alternative institutional arrangements on variables of interest to economists. Comparative institutional analysis is exclusively concerned with *comparing actually realized institutions with other actually realized institutions*. Thus, comparative institutional

analysis is a definite departure from the more traditional sort of
comparative analysis, in which an empirical result is compared
with a theoretically derived optimal result. Typically, the empirical
result fares badly in such comparisons, often resulting in justifications for government intervention.

*Institutional
economists are
interested in
feasible
institutions*

Representatives of NIE are interested in the coordination costs
associated with, and the results caused by, different institutional
arrangements. One obvious way of measuring the quality of an
institution is to measure the cost of implementing that institution
or, in other words, transaction costs. Different institutions are
associated with different transaction costs and are evaluated
accordingly.

1.4.3 Experiments in the Laboratory or the Field

*Laboratory
experiments allow
precisely
controlling the
conditions under
which choices are
being made*

The *homo economicus* behavioral model is a very simple one that
allows for precise predictions. It thus seems logical to test these
predictions in the laboratory, where test conditions can be precisely
controlled. Indeed, the frequency of such tests has increased over
the last years, with the not uncommon result that some behavioral
predictions are consistently falsified. Experimental subjects regularly deviate from theoretically predicted behavior, deviations that
are to some degree systematic, at least on average and over time.
These findings imply that the experimental results can be used to
predict behavior in similar decision situations (for an overview of
this rapidly growing field of research, see Plott and Smith, 2008;
Falk and Heckman, 2009). These experiments are relevant to NIE
because many of the behaviors observed in the laboratory can be
explained by internal institutions, for example, socially shared
values. Thus, laboratory experiments can be employed to assess
the *relevance of internal institutions.* Social norms most likely
depend on cultural context. NIE hence finds it interesting to repeat
the same game with experimental subjects from different cultural
backgrounds. By doing so, differences in observed behavior can be
attributed to differences in social norms, that is, internal
institutions.

Laboratory experiments have been a great success because the
conditions in the lab can be controlled precisely. However, they are
also subject to criticism, chiefly in regard to the possibility that
their results are not externally valid, that is, they might not hold
outside the lab. The context in which real choices occur is often

infinitely more complex than any situation created in a lab. This is why field experiments have gained in popularity over the last couple of years. Some of these merely replicate in a real-life context games previously played in the lab and so are, in a sense, artifactual (the term is credited to Harrison and List, 2004, who distinguish between artifactual, framed, and natural field experiments). On the other end of the spectrum are natural field experiments where subjects are not even aware that they are participating in an experiment. This implies that they are unlikely to modify their behavior as a consequence of being observed. Whereas field experiments may have higher external validity than laboratory experiments, they may have less internal validity than laboratory ones because the factors possibly having an influence on the outcome cannot be completely controlled for in the field.

Validity

Validity refers to the extent to which a conclusion corresponds with the real world. A conclusion is internally valid if it is warranted. It is externally valid if it can be generalized to other situations.

In a way, large-scale social experiments were a precursor of the current wave of field experiments. Such experiments can be employed as small-scale tests of new institutional rules that have not yet been implemented. Experimental testing for the effects of institutional innovation should result in improved predictions regarding the effects of implementing an institutional innovation on a large scale, particularly in regard to unintended consequences. One of the first of these was an experimental study on the negative income tax published as a dissertation in 1970. The experiment set out to test the incentive effects that accompany a negative income tax, an idea introduced by Nobel laureate Milton Friedman in 1962 (the experiment is described in more detail in Levitt and List, 2009, 5).

1.4.4 Case Studies Including Economic History

Case study research involves analyzing a small number of cases in great detail. A typical example is to study how specific institutions, perhaps even only one, emerged during a particular period in a particular country. When such research refers to past periods, it can also be called economic history. Many NIE scholars are economic historians, Douglass North certainly the best-known one. Within NIE, economic historians are interested in the causes that led to the creation of specific institutions, for example, technological progress or changes in resource endowment. Economic historians are also interested in the effects brought about by (changed) institutions. For example, Greif (1992) makes the astounding claim that the Commercial Revolution, which occurred between the eleventh and fourteenth centuries, was not due to any substantial change in production technology or resource endowment, but was a consequence of new (or modified) institutions.

This tool (i.e., the case study) has the advantage of being able to handle a great deal of detail; this is also its greatest weakness. It is often unclear if the explanation attributed to the particular case can be generalized. Based on their study of economic history, NIE scholars have contributed some important insight into the role played by institutions. For example, they have demonstrated that gains from trade can be made without state-secured property rights or even without the state – in the present sense – existing at all (Milgrom et al., 1990). They have shown that some institutions that are usually frowned upon (e.g., the merchant guild) actually perform a welfare increasing function (Greif et al., 1994), thus illustrating that NIE can discover counterintuitive results.

1.4.5 Econometric Tests

Econometricians test economic models with quantitative data. Therefore, if institutions can be quantified, both their determinants and their effects can be tested and compared using econometric methods, which allows testing for the consequences of external as well as internal institutions. For instance, aggregated investment stocks or per capita incomes could be regressed on the security of property rights. Chapter 5 illustrates the use of this method for investigating the growth effects of institutions.

At the beginning of this section, I mentioned the special role of comparative institutional analysis for NIE. In a sense, both experiments and econometric estimates can be viewed as ways of comparing institutions. Recently, there has been some talk about "mixed methods," including the argument that, for instance, econometric models that focus on rather large numbers could be usefully complemented by case studies focusing on single cases but adding a wealth of institutional detail. Only time will tell whether such an approach will produce useful insight.

1.5 NIE's Common Ground with and Differences from Other Research Programs

To date, there is no consensus, even among proponents of NIE themselves, as to whether NIE is just another branch of traditional economics or whether it is a new paradigm that stands alone. The first position is taken by those representatives of NIE who are interested in broadening existing research questions: that is, instead of assuming institutions to be exogenously given, they are interested in explicitly analyzing the choice of institutions. Proponents of the second position argue that this is not sufficient and that there needs to be a clear and definite step away from traditional economic thought. They argue that simply modifying an assumption here and there poses a risk of *inconsistent models* (Furubotn and Richter, 1998, ch. 10). One of the founders of NIE – Douglass North – shifted from the first position to the second over time. For example, his hypothesis on the relevance of intentionality as a result of social learning and as the foundation of institutional development (North, 2005) is at odds with the assumptions of neoclassical economics.

The word "new" in "new institutional economics" implies that there is an "old" institutional economics. And, indeed, there is. This so-called old institutional economics blossomed in the first half of the twentieth century and its most famous practitioners are Thorstein Veblen, John Commons, and Wesley Mitchell. New institutional economists criticize this research program for being *atheoretical* and *purely descriptive*. While most research programs in economics developed towards deductive thinking, old institutional economics was characterized by **inductive thinking**. In recent years, there has been a certain renaissance of old institutional economics (for a comparison of old and new institutional economics, see Hodgson, 1998; Rutherford, 1994).

> | **Definition** |
> |---|
>
> **Inductive**: leading from the specific to the general. Opposite: deductive

Both **transaction cost economics** as well as **property rights** Precursors of NIE **theory** can be viewed as precursors to NIE that are now components of it. Transaction cost economics investigates the consequences of transaction costs for the organizational structure of firms; its most well-known representative is Oliver E. Williamson. This research program is looked at in more detail in Chapter 3. The theory of property rights can also be thought of as ancestor of NIE. Its representatives look at the economic consequences of differently defined property rights. They study the idea that economic exchange primarily involves exchanging property rights. The theory of property rights is covered in Chapter 2.

Based on the observation that (correct) information is valuable because it allows actors to make choices resulting in higher payoffs, the subdiscipline of **information economics** emerged. The central problem regarding information is that we are often uncertain whether we can trust a particular piece of information or not. As the main function of institutions is to reduce uncertainty, and uncertainty always implies uncertainty of information, the connection between information economics and NIE is straightforward. **Contract theory** can be considered a subfield of information economics as it studies the design of contracts under asymmetric information. It can also be seen as belonging to the economic analysis of law which will be mentioned shortly.

Traditionally, **constitutional economics** analyzed justifications for the existence of government and governmental action. In recent years, however, researchers in this field have evinced an interest in applying economic thinking to (a) the consequences of different constitutional rules and (b) the reasons why different societies choose different constitutional rules in different situations (for an overview, see Voigt, 2011). Given this new focus, constitutional economics can be viewed as part of NIE, in that it analyzes a specific set of institutions, that is, constitutional rules.

Public choice theory takes an economic approach to analyzing politics. The difference between public choice and constitutional economics is that in public choice, institutions are assumed to be exogenously given whereas they are endogenized in constitutional economics. In the **economic analysis of law** (or law & economics), both the determinants and the effects of legislation are analyzed based on an economic approach. Traditionally, scholars in law & economics have maintained a closer tie to traditional welfare economics than have scholars in either NIE or constitutional economics. In the past, informal rules – which are important in NIE – were either ignored or considered of secondary importance in the law &

Table 1.3 Related research programs

Research program	Central question	Relation to NIE
Transaction cost economics	Consequences of positive transaction costs (also with regard to political processes)	Precursor that became a component of NIE
Property rights theory	Consequences of different property rights arrangements	Precursor that became a component of NIE
Information economics	Interested in identifying ways to deal with situations of uncertainty	In both, uncertainty plays a central role
Constitutional economics	Legitimation of the state Consequences of alternative constitutional rules, determinants of constitutional rules	The normative variant is an addition to NIE The positive variant is a part of NIE
Public choice	Economic analysis of politics	Analysis of the incentive effects of exogenously given rules
Law & economics	Economic analysis of law	Analysis of the incentive effects of exogenously given rules (primarily concerning private and criminal law)

economics field, but this began to change several years ago (see Jolls et al., 1998; Korobkin and Ulen, 2000).

Researchers working with these different approaches to understanding the links between economics and institutions tend not to communicate much with each other, preferring to emphasize the differences between the programs instead of their similarities. We find this unfortunate. So, even though the chief focus of this book is NIE, when appropriate, we will discuss interesting and important insights from related research programs. Table 1.3 sums up this discussion of NIE and related research programs.

1.6 Open Questions

One of the central assumptions of the behavioral model of economics is that preferences are given and time invariant. However, humans are not born with a specific preference for most goods and institutions. Thus, one open question, and not only in NIE, involves the origins and change of preferences. NIE is particularly interested in exploring whether the emergence and change of preferences are dependent on context and culture.

In the context of bounded rationality (and positive transaction costs), it is posited that it could be rational to maximize utility not over each and every action, but merely over a sequence of actions with the help of rules (like rules of thumb; see Heiner, 1983). But if we are merely boundedly rational, is it plausible that we are rational enough to rationally set utility maximizing rules? Thus, there is a need for research on the role of learning and the functions of trial-and-error-processes, and into whether the concept of adaptive behavior might be more appropriate than that of rational choice (see Vanberg, 1994, ch. 2).

QUESTIONS

1. In a famous paper, Milton Friedman (1953) argued that the correspondence between a model's assumptions and the conditions found in the real world did not really matter as long as the predictions produced on the basis of the model were true. What are the implications of this approach, both positive and negative?
2. Why is the assumption of positive transaction costs closely related to the assumption of bounded rationality?
3. What role do transaction costs play in the search for apartments? To what other situations could you apply the concept and how?
4. Explain the difference between individual decision rules (such as rules of thumb) and collective rules as institutions. Use examples.
5. Consider the taxonomy of institutions introduced in this chapter. For each type of institution, name an example and state the rule component as well as the enforcement mechanism for it.
6. Explain why a private contract is not an institution, and yet the private law it is based on is.
7. International law consists of rules to which sovereign nation-states have agreed. Connect international law to the taxonomy of institutions developed in this chapter.
8. Can the different instruments described in this chapter be reasonably combined? If so, what are the benefits and drawbacks of using them simultaneously?

FURTHER READING

The most important book on institutional economics published in recent decades is *Institutions, Institutional Change and Economic Performance* by Douglass North (1990a). *New Institutional Economics: A Guidebook*, edited by Eric Brousseau and Jean-Michel Glachant (2008) contains 21 stand-alone chapters enabling quick access to particular aspects of NIE.

Daron Acemoglu and James Robinson have been among the most influential institutional economists of the last 15 years or so. We refer to their work frequently throughout this book. If you are interested in an easily accessible and popularized version of some of their findings, *Why Nations Fail* (Acemoglu and Robinson, 2012) is a good starting point.

The behavioral model of economics is given a very thorough and concise treatment in *Homo Oeconomicus* by Gebhard Kirchgässner (2008).

Ekkehard Schlicht (1990) critically discusses the concept of bounded rationality. Kreps (1998) discusses the difficulty of incorporating bounded rationality in formal economic models. The starting point of behavioral economics is bounded rationality. Some fascinating insights from that research program are popularized in Daniel Kahneman's (2011) *Thinking, Fast and Slow*. *Nudge* by Richard Thaler and Cass Sunstein (2008) is similarly popular. The authors advocate far-reaching policy designs based on findings about how real people really behave. Their plea for libertarian paternalism is controversial, with many critics arguing that it is nothing but an oxymoron.

Thinking Strategically is a well-written introductory book on game theory by US economists Dixit and Nalebuff (1991). The relevance of game theory for NIE is discussed in Pénard (2008). Examples of how game theory can be used to study economic development are found in Wydick (2007). Smith (1994) lists seven prominent reasons why economists conduct experiments and also deals with the question of what economists have learned from experiments. Greif and Laitin (2004) deal with institutional change relying on repeated game theory. Their paper can also be read as an enlightened defense for the use of game theory in NIE. A website that lists many field experiments is maintained by Chicago economist John List and can be found at www.field experiments.com/. The Massachusetts Institute of Technology runs a

Poverty Action Lab that has conducted many so-called randomized field experiments. Their website is at www.povertyactionlab.org/. Alston (2008) argues in favor of case studies. If you are interested in a survey summarizing and evaluating the most important contributions to NIE from economic history, I suggest Nunn (2009).

Finally, quite a few scholars in NIE have been awarded the Nobel prize in economics. The Prize lecture that is given when they actually receive the prize in Stockholm is usually an easy-to-comprehend summary of their work as they speak to a non-specialist audience. In the recommendations at the end of the chapters, I will therefore frequently refer to these lectures. The website www.nobelprize.org contains additional information such as videos from the lectures, the slides shown during the lecture, bibliographical information on the recipient and more. It is definitely worth a look. Ronald Coase received the prize for "his discovery and clarification of the significance of transaction costs and property rights for the institutional structure and functioning of the economy." He is clearly a founding father of NIE and his prize lecture (1992) can be read as an introduction to the whole topic of NIE.

2 Simple Transactions

Who exchanges which goods with whom, in what quantity and how often, is determined by whether a transaction is expected to be profitable for all sides participating in the transaction. Potential exchange partners must take many factors into consideration when determining whether a theoretically possible exchange, once realized, actually benefits all partners. In this chapter, we discuss several of these factors. Whether buying some good is beneficial for me depends on what I can do with that good after having purchased it. For example, can I modify a house without restraint or I am bound by some legal rules (for instance, laws concerning landmarked buildings)? Am I able to exclude others from the use of my good (for instance, tourists passing through my property)? Is it possible for me to legally exclude others from the use of my good, but factually too costly to do so (for instance, passersby who steal apples from my tree)?

In the following, we deal primarily with simple transactions. We delineate them as *exchanges* that are *not* set out to be *repeated frequently*. This helps us distinguish simple transactions from (1) long-term contracts (e.g., contracts concerning provision of water or electricity), on the one hand, and (2) transactions within hierarchies on the other hand (e.g., within firms; these will be dealt with in Chapter 3).

Chapter Highlights

- Learn why property rights are important for transactions.
- Understand that internal institutions can also be important for transactions.
- Reflect about how property rights and internal institutions can reinforce each other – or be mutually exclusive.
- Attempt to estimate the development of transaction costs in the long run.

What are the
incentive effects
of property
rights?
In the course of this chapter, the concepts of transaction costs – which you already encountered in Chapter 1 – and property rights play a central role. We assume that laws (external institutions), as well as norms and customs (internal institutions), are exogenously given and ask how they channel the behavior of the actors in question. We proceed as follows: First, we introduce the concept of property rights and discuss how external institutions impact simple transactions. Second, we ask how internal institutions, such as norms and customs, might influence the extent and intensity of simple transactions. Third, we ask how the interplay between external and internal institutions affects the extent and intensity of simple transactions. Finally, we present an empirical study that attempts to estimate the development of economy-wide transaction costs over a period of 100 years.

2.1 The Relevance of External Institutions for Simple Transactions

The concept of
property rights
We can think of at least three ways in which laws might influence economic exchange:

1. With regard to the scope of rights and obligations that are associated with the exchanged good (design of **property rights**).
2. With regard to the possibilities and limits of trading goods with others (design of **freedom of contract**).
3. With regard to the costs associated with enforcing one's rights in case of noncompliance of the exchange partner (design of **procedural law**).

Economic
exchange as
exchange of
property rights
Traditionally, economic exchange is depicted as the physical exchange of goods, for instance, exchanging a good for money with which one can buy other goods. A research program emerged in the 1960s that depicts economic exchange as exchange of property rights, aptly called **property rights theory**. It states that the value of a good depends on the specific design of the relevant property rights. Four components are traditionally identified:

1. The right to use a good (*usus*).
2. The right to modify a good (*abusus*).
3. The right to enjoy the fruits from the use of a good (*usus fructus*).
4. The right to transfer property rights of a good to other persons (*venditio*).

Typically, if everything else remains constant, the price for a good will be higher when the rights attached to that good establish a higher degree of exclusivity.

Frequently, legislation in the form of regulation constrains the **freedom of contract**. For instance, the government prohibits exchange of certain goods or limits exchange on Sundays and holidays. In the USA, for example, there are still hundreds of "dry counties" that prohibit the sale of alcohol. Whoever violates such prohibitions and precepts might face sanctions. Whether such disallowed exchange is still privately beneficial depends on the probability of detection, the expected profit, and the size of the fine in case of detection.[1] By relying on such regulations, the government intentionally inflates the price of exchanging certain goods. To stick to the example: finding someone willing to sell alcohol in "dry counties" will not be as easy as elsewhere as search costs will be higher. In other words: *The transaction costs are increased intentionally.* Common sense tells us that higher transaction costs result in less frequent economic exchange because the gains from trade are lower.

Finally, whether an exchange is expected to be profitable for all sides depends on how costly it is to use **procedural law** to enforce one's rights in case of breach of contract. When court proceedings are expected to be very costly and prolonged, an exchange might appear less attractive *ex ante*. Likewise, a court ruling is not very useful if it is not immediately enforceable, thus making a potential exchange less attractive. As we can imagine, high transaction costs can have a meaningful impact on the extent of economic exchange. Later in this chapter, we present empirical estimates of the aggregate level of transaction costs.

Costly and prolonged court proceedings can impede economic exchange

Ronald Coase's essay (1960) on the problem of social cost simultaneously explores the concepts of property rights and transaction costs and is central to the development of both NIE and law & economics. When property rights are well defined in the sense of

---

[1] For a very long time, it was assumed that criminal – and other – offenses were not amenable to the economic approach. Gary Becker (1968) challenged that conventional wisdom and laid the foundations for what was to become the economic analysis of crime. A rational individual is likely to commit an offense if the expected benefits outweigh the expected costs. Expected costs are the product of the likelihood of being caught and the severity of the sanction. This insight is highly relevant for policymakers as it implies that a low number of policemen can be compensated for by draconian sanctions. Of course, there might be very good reasons not to make sanctions extremely draconian.

exactly delimiting who is allowed to do what with a good and the exchange of goods is free of transaction costs (i.e., they equal zero), the resulting allocation of goods and rights will be Pareto-optimal, irrespective of the initial allocation of property rights.

| **Definition** |

Pareto-optimality: A Pareto-optimum is defined by the fact that it is not possible to raise one individual's utility without decreasing the utility of another. The concept was developed by the Italian economist and sociologist Vilfredo Pareto (1848–1923).

Put differently: It is essential that property rights are well defined, but the initial allocation of property rights is irrelevant for achieving the optimal allocation as long as transaction costs are zero. This insight has been dubbed the **Coase theorem**, based on Coase's (1960) essay, which is one of the most cited papers in economics. We will now take a closer look at this theorem.

2.1.1 The Coase Theorem

A producer of burglar alarm systems (P) emits loud noises while testing its alarm devices. The only resident who lives in the vicinity (R) is very bothered by this, resulting in a reduced utility of living in his house. R repeatedly asks P to reduce the noise emissions, but P does not comply, as that would be associated with additional costs (e.g., the cost of buying noise filters). When the utility of one actor R is lowered by the actions of another actor P, economists say that the action of P has an **external effect** or **externality**. One can distinguish between positive and negative external effects. A positive externality is given when we are able to enjoy the music of a nearby open air concert free of charge. The same externality can be negative if we are bothered by it.

The firm that produces and tests burglar alarms (P) reduces the utility of resident R and thus produces a negative externality. In welfare economics, the standard approach to such problems is to introduce Pigou taxes (named after British economist Arthur Cecil Pigou, 1877–1959). According to this approach, the producer of a negative externality pays a tax in the amount of the difference between the private and social costs of his or her activity. The tax is equivalent to the damage imposed on others. On the other hand, the producer of a positive externality receives a subsidy in the amount of the difference between private and social costs. The expected outcome is that actors will produce fewer negative externalities, or conversely, actors will produce more positive externalities. The Pigou tax is thus an intervention which is supposed to improve the suboptimal outcome that results if market forces remain uncorrected. Even though we can hardly imagine how to correctly measure the relevant social costs and benefits, policymakers have time and again attempted to apply the concept of a Pigou tax. Examples include the protection of emerging industries against foreign competitors by setting import tariffs and providing subsidies for research and development.

Definition

Private vs. social costs: whereas private costs are only those costs borne by the individuals involved in some economic activity, the social costs reflect the total costs of that activity. Social costs might be higher than private costs if some costs, like pollution, are not borne by those involved in the activity.

Ronald Coase doubts that the existence of externalities requires government action in the form of taxes or subsidies. Assume that the present value (i.e., the sum of all future profits discounted to their current value) of the profits that producer P can attain is €15,000. Let us also assume that before P started its production the house of R was worth €150,000, now it is worth €120,000. The production of P is associated with a destruction of social value: The sum of P's profit and the reduced value of R's house (€135,000) is lower than the house's value without P's production (€150,000). Thus, it would be socially optimal if P stopped its production – at least for this particular location. Finally, let us assume that there is no regulation prohibiting P to produce and test burglar alarms in this location. Is there anything R could do? R could try to pay P an amount of money such that P is at least as well off as if it were still producing. Any amount between €15,000 and €30,000 is possible. Suppose it is €16,000. This would be mutually beneficial: P benefits because the compensation payment is higher than its anticipated profits from production. R benefits because the value of his house minus the compensation payment (150,000 − 16,000 = €134,000) is higher than the value of the house if P were producing (€120,000).

Let us alternatively assume that P expects profits to the amount of €50,000, due to an upward shift in demand for burglar alarms.

Now, the sum of the reduced value of R's house and the expected profits of P (120,000 + 50,000 = €170,000) are higher than the undiminished value of the house (€150,000). Furthermore, there are now legal restrictions regarding noise emissions such that R could sue P for the emission of noise. In this changed situation, P could now benefit from paying compensation to R such that R refrains from suing. P can feasibly pay an amount between €30,000 (the difference between 150,000 and 120,000) and €50,000 (P's profit). Thus, the punchline of the Coase theorem is that *resources will always be allocated towards their highest valued use, independent of the initial allocation of property rights*, given the assumptions of zero transaction costs and well-defined property rights. Note that absence of transaction costs here implies that the various payoffs – under production and under non-production – are known to all participants (game theorists would say they are "common knowledge").

In Figure 2.1, we can see that the Coase theorem is not only applicable to situations with discrete choices (produce vs. not produce), but also to cases with continuous choices (produce a little bit more or a little bit less). Figure 2.1 corresponds to the case in which P is not liable for the damage its production causes (i.e., the

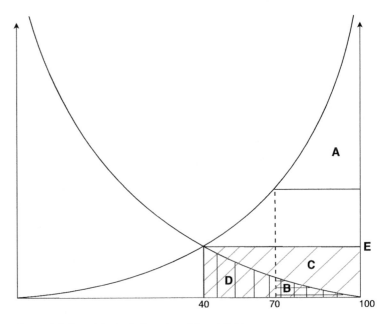

Figure 2.1 Bargaining solution when P is not liable.

decrease in utility of R). We assume that the level of utility loss for R depends on the level of emitted noise from producer P. The curve originating in 0 that is upward sloping to the right is the marginal damage R has to bear. In our example, the damage is equivalent to the loss in the value of R's house. The more noise P emits, the greater the damage suffered by R. We also assume that the costs for lowering noise emissions increase the more P reduces noise emissions. The first filter P buys leads to a substantial reduction in noise, the second such filter already has less of an effect and so on. The marginal cost of noise reduction originates with 100 on the horizontal line since the costs for not reducing noise are assumed to be 0. If P wants more noise reduction, the curve gets steeper, because each additional filter has less of an effect.

If P is not liable for the noise emitted, P has no incentive to invest in noise reduction and we assume P emits noise at level 100. If the level of emissions was reduced to 75, R could avoid damages in the amount of the shaded area A. It would cost producer P an amount of B to avoid that much noise. Since the size of B is only a small fraction of the area A, the benefits of this decrease in noise clearly outweigh the costs. We have, thus, identified a possibility for both parties to make themselves better off: R can offer P a sum that is higher than P's costs of noise avoidance but lower than the increase in P's utility gain. Continuing this line of reasoning, we can easily see that the "optimal" level of noise emissions is at 40; to the left of this level, the marginal costs of avoiding noise are higher than the marginal utility loss.

Assuming that R and P are able to bargain and agree upon noise level 40 and that R compensates P with a price E for each unit of avoided noise, then P's revenue from this transaction is 60 times E which is equivalent to the shaded area C. P's costs for avoiding 60 units of noise are, however, only the area below the marginal cost curve (denoted as D in the figure) implying that P makes a profit equivalent to area C–D from the agreement. Based on the two cost curves displayed in the figure, it is easy to see that a noise emission level of 40 is optimal. Reducing the noise emissions even further would cost more in terms of noise reduction than would be gained in terms of the value of the house. Rational parties would, thus, agree on the noise level 40.

The second case, in which P is liable for the externality, can be solved analogously. We refrain from showing the corresponding figure here but encourage you to draw it yourself as an exercise.

In the absence of transaction costs, the initial allocation of property rights is irrelevant for the final outcome However: Transaction costs are almost always substantial

If the assumptions of the Coase theorem were fulfilled, there would always be *optimal resource allocations without the need for government intervention.* However, how realistic is it to assume transaction costs to be zero AND property rights to be well defined? This seems rather implausible. Even in our original case with merely two actors we could assume that bargaining might take some time. Furthermore, the parties would have to spend resources to monitor whether the respective other party sticks to the agreement. Now imagine that P's production facilities are located in a residential area such that 200 residents are bothered by the noise emissions. Then the 200 households would first need to organize themselves, which is in itself associated with costs. What if the producer was a Japanese nuclear power plant that emits contaminated waste which eventually affects people living in the USA? In this constellation, millions of US Americans would need to negotiate with millions of Japanese and solutions via private bargaining seem very unlikely.

But suppose transaction costs were not substantial. The Coase theorem still might not apply because property rights were not well defined or tradable. Rights might be, for example, inalienable, that is they cannot be sold or traded. This is the case for all basic human rights, as well as for the right to vote. And this is also frequently the case for emission levels, whose regulation is administered via public law. Public law, in turn, cannot be bypassed by drawing on private contracts.

Thus: The initial allocation of property rights is very important!

The core statement of the Coase theorem is that – *given zero transaction costs and well-defined and tradable rights – bargaining will result in an efficient allocation of resources, irrespective of the initial allocation of property rights.* Given these assumptions, the specific delineation of property rights is irrelevant. Why, then, within the NIE do we have a specific theory dealing with the allocative consequences of alternative delineations of property rights? Because transaction costs are usually not zero. *Since rights are typically not tradable without costs, their specification is quite important.*

The Coase theorem has become one of the cornerstones not only of NIE but also of law & economics. As noted earlier, the paper in which Coase first described his groundbreaking ideas is one of the most-cited papers in economics of all time. Small wonder then that it has not remained without criticisms. Here, we mention only two specific **criticisms:**

1. The Coase theorem neglects **strategic behavior.** For instance, producer P could announce *ex ante* that it will be producing a

great deal of noise, in order to receive a higher compensation for reducing its emissions. It could even be profitable to specialize in these kinds of announcements to receive compensation payments for not following through.

2. Coase emphasizes that the specification of property rights is irrelevant for the resulting allocation. However, the resulting wealth or income **distribution** clearly depends on whether we initially have the right to emit noise or not. This implies that the Coase theorem is only applicable when the distributive consequences are not expected to influence the resulting allocation.

2.2 The Relevance of Internal Institutions for Simple Transactions

By now, it should be clear that external institutions – such as state-enforced property rights – influence the extent of economic exchange since their exact delineation has an impact on the potential gains from trade. The relevance of internal institutions should also be apparent. For example, when a social group follows the rule that contracts should be complied with and sanctions rule breakers by informing all members of the group about the breach, any individual actor within that group has an incentive to comply with contracts as they would anticipate not being able to find transaction partners after noncompliance.

How do internal institutions affect the extent of economic exchange?

Norms are not only relevant in explaining whether contracts are concluded, but also in explaining the content of contracts. We can easily imagine contract modalities that might be in perfect compliance with the external institutions of a society, but not in compliance with that society's internal institutions. Consider, for example, transactions involving pork or alcohol in a Muslim society governed by the external institutions of a colonial power. Although legally possible, such transactions are likely to be frowned upon by one's fellow Muslims. Instead of attempting to give a complete and systematic account of how internal institutions can affect contract modalities, let's consider two examples.

2.2.1 Example 1: Norms of Cooperation and the Ultimatum Game

The ultimatum game was introduced by Güth et al. (1982) and has led to intense discussions about the fundamental behavioral assumptions in economics. In this game, a metaphoric cake has to

be split between two players. The first player has the right to
propose a specific split; the second player can then either accept or
reject the proposal. In case of acceptance, the cake is split according
to the proposal. In case of rejection, both players receive nothing.
Compared to a situation with a payoff of zero, a rational – and
selfish – second player would accept even a minuscule offer.
A rational first player would anticipate this and offer only a minuscule amount to the second player, keeping the rest for himself.

Homo economicus
prediction is not
confirmed in the
ultimatum game

We cannot possibly summarize all the literature that has
developed around this game. Two results are of particular importance for the NIE and are worth stressing as they show that the
traditional *homo economicus* assumptions are not met when two
people play this game in the laboratory. These results are:

1. Fairly equal splits of the cake often emerge.
2. Proposals that offer a third or less of the cake to the second
   player are often rejected.

These results hold even when the payoffs involved are quite substantial. For instance, Cameron (1999) played the game with Indo-
nesian students for whom the size of the cake corresponded to the
value of three average monthly incomes.

A common but far from universally accepted explanation for
these results is **justice and fairness norms** of the actors. Let us
assume that such behavior can be explained by societal values and
norms, that is, by internal institutions. Such institutions are far
from uniform around the globe. It is, thus, of interest to play the
same game in alternative cultural environments. Ensminger (1998)
and Henrich (2000) were among the first to do just that. When
Henrich played the ultimatum game with subsistence farmers living
by the Amazon River, he found that proposals made there were
substantially lower than in developed countries and that proposals
were very seldom rejected. Ensminger (1998) conjectures that
*justice and fairness notions are a consequence, not a cause of
institutional development.* In Henrich et al. (2001), Henrich and
his co-authors – all very experienced field researchers – played
the ultimatum game and other games in 18 small-scale societies
that are characterized by great variety in both economic and cultural conditions. They find considerable differences in the way the
game is played in these societies around the world. One general
result is that the more prevalent market exchange is in a particular
society, the higher the level of cooperation in experimental games.

If the prevalence of market exchange is based on institutions, then these institutions seem to induce higher levels of cooperation.

2.2.2 Example 2: Fairness Notions and Price Formation

While the above insight is highly interesting, it has the limitation of being based on experimental evidence. We cannot be sure that the experimental evidence remains valid beyond the conditions of the experiment. Our second example is, therefore, based on real-world observations and deals with insights concerning price formation. Traditionally, we assume that the marginal willingness to pay for a good corresponds to the marginal utility the consumer expects from it. This implies that the identity of the seller (a fancy luxury restaurant or a run-down grocery store) should be irrelevant. It further implies that the profit made by the seller should also be irrelevant. But there is plenty of evidence that both traits do matter.

Peak-load pricing is a strategy for suppliers to channel highly volatile demand levels. Prices are high when demand is high; prices are low when demand is low. Though economically rational, such a strategy is often condemned by consumers. For instance, many consumers simply do not accept higher prices for flowers around a holiday although the quoted price is below what they are willing to pay (their "reservation price" in more formal terminology). Some consumers are even willing to accept additional costs to prevent paying higher prices. When the gas stations of large chains raise their prices during summer holidays, we can observe very long queues at alternative gas stations not bound by the price hike of the large chains. Apparently, consumers are willing to accept high opportunity costs (in terms of lost time) in order to not pay the additional 2 to 3 cents per liter of gasoline because their fairness norms are violated. If this is the case, Frank (1988, 167) predicts: "*People will sometimes reject transactions in which the other party gets the lion's share of the surplus, even though the price at which the product sells may compare favorably with their own reservation price*" (italics in original; further examples can be found in Frank (1988) and Kahnemann et al. (1986)).

Both of our examples show that *exchange prices and other contract modalities can be influenced by fairness and justice notions*. If we fail to account for these factors in an analysis of, for example, price formation, the resulting predictions will probably be less precise. Thus, accounting for internal institutions can increase the predictive accuracy of economic models.

Accounting for justice and fairness notions can improve predictive accuracy

2.3 The Relevance of Interplay between External and Internal Institutions for Simple Transactions

In Chapter 1, we mentioned four possible ways in which external and internal institutions might be related:

1. neutral,
2. complementary,
3. substitutive, and
4. in conflict.

In this section, we ask how simple transactions are influenced by the fact that these simple transactions can be arranged via external as well as internal institutions.

2.3.1 Conflicting External and Internal Institutions

Internal and external institutions are in conflict when a certain behavior in an interaction situation is allowed or even encouraged according to the external (internal) institution, but prohibited according to the internal (external) institution. If both institutions prescribe a certain behavior, then irrespective of which institution an actor decides to adhere to, he or she has to anticipate a sanction. When a colonial power attempts to enforce its "home grown" set of external institutions in a colony without modifications, conflicting institutions are very likely. The consequences of conflicting external and internal institutions with respect to economic development are apparent. Under such circumstances, it is often beneficial for individual actors to conduct economic exchange in secrecy. This in turn can have negative consequences for business development. Optimal firm size cannot be achieved, marketing cannot be exploited, and external financing is hard to come by and very expensive.

Conflicting institutions can impede economic development

2.3.2 Complementary External and Internal Institutions

We defined external and internal institutions as complementary when they restrict human behavior in a similar manner implying that *rule enforcement is organized both privately and by the state.* Someone who signs a contract with someone else and then does not stick to the terms of the contract is not only likely to lose in court but also to see his reputation damaged as soon as it becomes publicly known how he has acted. Such informal shaming is based on internal institutions and can significantly increase the "price" of breaking the law. While the price of losing in court might be a rather modest sum of money, losing my reputation as a reliable business partner might cost me dozens or even hundreds of contracts in the future.

If it is true that internal institutions are much less subject to directed change than external institutions, but both complementarily fulfill the function of stabilizing expectations, there is very little scope for successfully changing external institutions. Importantly, *the complementarity of internal and external institutions is a necessary, but not sufficient condition for the economic success of a society.* The reason for this is that complementarity as a formal criterion leaves open the specific content of institutions. Thus, when internal and external institutions are complementary, but both encourage behavior that impedes economic development, the prospects for economic development are low.

Complementary institutions reduce the costs of state sanctions

2.3.3 Substitutive Relationship between External and Internal Institutions

When institutions are substitutive, they steer human behavior in a similar fashion, but *rule enforcement is organized either by the state or privately.* Here, we only deal with two combinations of internal and external institutions that are suitable to illustrating this relation, the interaction between external institutions and internal institutions of type 3 and 4 respectively (customs and formal private rules respectively. Reminder: you can find our typology of institutions in Table 1.1 on p. 17).

Imagine a situation in which there is a conflict between two actors due to rule-breaking behavior and there are three possible ways to proceed:

An example

1. Private conflict resolution between the two parties involved, as a borderline case of a type 3 internal institution.
2. The involvement of a private arbitration court, thus a type 4 internal institution.
3. Resorting to a state court (external institution).

Many business people who feel that their contract partners have not lived up to their contractual obligations face exactly these three choices. Turning to private arbitration usually implies that

the case will not be moved to a state court, hence the either/or of
Invocation of a a substitutive relationship. Many businesses prefer arbitration
private over state courts because *arbitrators* are selected directly by the
arbitrary court conflicting parties. Often, arbitrators are familiar with the conventions of the industry to which the conflicting parties belong
and their decisions are more likely to be accepted by all parties
than those of generalist state judges. Also, the arbitrator has an
incentive to achieve a successful resolution, as her reputation
might suffer from a failed arbitration. Because a solution by
arbitration is usually characterized by some form of compromise,
it tends to allow the involved parties to *save face* more than in
state court proceedings.

State dispute   It might appear that state enforcement is universally less prefer-
resolution able than private enforcement. This is a deceptive impression, not
only because the invocation of a state court is more appropriate for
some cases, but also because the influences of external institutions
extend far beyond the narrow scope of court proceedings (Galanter,
1981). Although judges only rule in concrete cases, their decisions
provide information that is relevant for private dispute resolution
(Galanter, 1981, 13). Thus, private conflict resolution is influenced
by the state if it invokes a state court ruling. The decisions of
private arbitral courts, however, are often not made publicly available, limiting their ability to fulfill this societal function. What's
more, the possibility of state court involvement might be what
causes the conflicting parties to look for a resolution outside of
court, in order to avoid the costs of a court procedure. Thus, the
relevance of the decisions made by state courts cannot be disputed
even if they consider only a relatively low number of conflicts.

The relationship between state adjudication and private dispute
resolution can also run the other way: Private dispute resolution
affects state adjudication (Galanter, 1981, 24). The interpretation of
indeterminate legal concepts presupposes an understanding of the
relevant cultural context. In this manner, private notions of what is
a just resolution to a conflict might have a direct effect on a state
court judge's rulings.

2.3.4 Empirical Results on the Relationship between External and Internal Institutions

Having considered several hypothetical examples in an effort to
shed light on the different types of relationships between internal

and external institutions, we proceed to briefly discuss some empirical work in this area. Assume that actors can choose how to resolve a conflict, either by resorting to formal law (external institutions) or by invoking customs (internal institutions). By analyzing the institutional arrangements chosen in specific situations, we can learn a great deal about the actual relevance of different institutions. Ellickson (1986, 1991) provides an example of such an empirical study. Ellickson asks whether the famous example discussed by Coase (1960), in which there is a conflict between a cattle farmer and a grain grower, possesses empirical relevance. The conflict arises when stray cattle enter the grounds of the grain grower and destroy part of his crops. Coase claims that the manner of conflict resolution is determined by the specific design of the legal framework. Our previous example relied on this claim to assert that the initial allocation of property rights determines the resulting level of noise emissions. Ellickson (1994, 97) claims that this assessment cannot be confirmed for most rural areas in which neighboring farms are subject to such conflicts. The author empirically investigates how conflicts between farmers and growers are resolved in Shasta County, California. This county was chosen because cattle farmers are liable for damages caused by stray cattle in only a few municipalities. In most municipalities, the grain growers are responsible for protecting their crops. Ellickson shows that the manner of conflict resolution is not dependent on the legal rule that is in place in a specific municipality, i.e., that the design of the legal framework does not affect which form of dispute resolution is chosen. The result of this study is that internal institutions can – under certain circumstances (here: repeated interactions) – crowd out external institutions, even in highly developed regions such as California.

> The form of dispute resolution chosen by neighboring farms is independent of the specific legal rule in effect

Many African countries tried to formalize property rights in land by giving titles to land that was documented in registries. One goal was to reduce the compartmentalization of customary landownership. From the point of view of traditional economics, this makes perfect sense. If I hold a formal title to land, I can use it as collateral with a bank. The bank is more likely to lend me money which I can invest in agricultural machinery. At the end of the day, agricultural productivity should be higher. In a fascinating study, Ensminger (1997) shows that this almost never happened because long-run privatization plans almost always failed in Africa and, sooner or later, people returned to their customary rights. She reasons that these attempts failed because the newly passed external institutions did not fit the customary internal ones. Her observations illustrate how this rings true. Specifically, the idea to consolidate land into single but much larger units failed because farmers preferred having smaller plots in different areas to serve as insurance against one (or more) of their crops failing. She also observed that for irrigation purposes, it seems important to have family members as neighbors rather than some other business entities. Farmers simply ignored that titling was only possible for tracts of land that achieved a minimum size. The same holds true for the maximum number of heirs established by the external institutions (which was originally set to five in Kenya, the country that occupies center stage in Ensminger's study). *De jure*, most registered plots were registered with men. *De facto*, women play a very important role in agriculture. Due to the bad fit of external institutions with internal ones, titling never reflected *de facto* landownership.

The study of Stone et al. (1996) examines the relevance of external and internal institutions for business people in two countries: Brazil and Chile. At the time the study was conducted, Brazil was characterized as being interventionist with very detailed regulations. Chile, on the other hand, had implemented systematic reforms to roll back government interventions into markets and introduce rule-based competition laws (Stone et al., 1996, 100). The authors examine two situations in which private business people interact with government representatives (start-up of a firm and regulation of firms) and two situations in which private business people interact with customers (orders and sales on credit). They conducted interviews with representatives of 42 textile firms in the region of São Paulo (Brazil) and the region of Santiago (Chile). The results are surprising. Even though it is much more difficult to start a firm in Brazil, the Brazilian textile representatives rarely complained. The explanation offered by the authors is the development of a specialized professional known as a *despachante* that has evolved as a reaction to the complicated legal structures and overflowing bureaucracy.[2] Start-up firms do not attempt to tackle the legal hurdles of obtaining all permits for their new business by themselves, but rather delegate this task to a *despachante*. The total

---

[2] *Despachar*: Spanish for to process, to take care of. *Despachantes* are specialized in taking care of the administrative paperwork required by government authorities.

costs for starting up a firm amount to $640 in Brazil and $739 in Chile. The average time for registering a start-up is 1.6 months in Brazil and 2 months in Chile.

These studies offer somewhat surprising results concerning the relevance of the relationship between external and internal institutions. Ellickson shows that in some situations internal institutions dominate external institutions, while Stone and co-authors show that dysfunctional external institutions can in part be counterbalanced by functioning internal institutions.

Regulation often causes unintended consequences

We might use a different approach to analyze the relational relevance between internal and external institutions. Assume that the external (internal) institutions that different social groups use to structure their interactions are identical, but there are observable differences in outcomes such as per capita income, growth, and so on between the groups. In such a case, it would make sense to ask whether the outcome differences are correlated with differences in internal (external) institutions between different social groups. An obvious candidate for an analysis of this type is Italy. While the external institutions – at least *de jure* – are identical everywhere, the manner in which interactions are structured differs widely between regions. In particular, one can observe stark differences between the north and the south, implying that internal institutions also differ widely.

Differences in outcomes within a country can be explained by differences in internal institutions

Putnam (1993) shows that the number of voluntary, non-hierarchical associations (such as sports clubs, but not the Catholic Church) at the end of the nineteenth century is an excellent predictor for the quality of local governments today! Putnam argues that **voluntary associations** do not represent idealistic altruism, but rather serve to make **practical reciprocity** possible, enabling members to reduce risks in a quickly changing society. He emphasizes the importance of organizational features for social cohesion and by no means claims that the south of Italy is apolitical or asocial. However, the south is characterized by a much lower degree of functioning civil society ("civicness") due to the more vertical nature of social structures. A vertical organization is a sign of dependency and exploitation. Putnam claims that horizontal organization, such as can be observed in the north of Italy, has helped solidarity to develop.

Italy as an example of a country with heterogeneous internal institutions

Putnam uses the concept of **path dependency** to describe the different ways the two regions of Italy have developed (Putnam, 1993, 177–180). The north is characterized by a stable social equilibrium with high levels of cooperation, trust, reciprocity, and so forth. In contrast, the south is characterized by a likewise stable equilibrium in which defection, distrust, opportunism, and so on seem to be the dominant strategy. At this point, we abstain from delving deeper into the concept of path dependency; we will return to it in Chapter 6.

2.4 On the Estimation of Transaction Costs

One obvious indicator of quality for a set of institutions is how much it costs to conduct transactions. Thus, one can attempt to measure the quality of institutions in different countries by comparing the transaction costs required to carry out a transaction. Comparing different levels of transaction costs might then allow us to comparatively assess the quality of alternative sets of institutions.

A heuristic is a systematic instruction on how to gain new insights

For a long time, institutional economists did not even attempt to quantify transaction costs empirically. Transaction costs were classified as conceptual or heuristic and the lack of empirical testability was not considered a problem. More recently, however, estimations of the level of transaction costs have been published. Before looking at the results, let us discuss a few of the challenges associated with an empirical measurement of transaction costs. Benham and Benham (2000) give four reasons why there are only a few empirical studies:

1. There is no universally accepted conceptual definition of transaction costs.
2. The estimation of transaction costs is difficult, because they often occur in unison with transformation costs.
3. When transaction costs are prohibitively high, the transaction is not carried out, making it impossible to measure them.
4. The "law of one price" is not applicable to transaction costs because they occur individually. Transaction costs are subject-specific and cannot easily be operationalized.

Transformation costs

Transformation costs are costs that are necessary to transform resources (inputs) into products (outputs). Often, this category of costs is also called production costs. "Law of one price" describes the tendency of prices for identical goods, after accounting for transportation costs, to equalize. When there are unequal prices, there is an incentive for arbitrage, leading to an equalization of prices.

Wallis and North (1986) are more interested in tracing the development of transaction costs over time on an aggregate level. They are aware that transaction costs comprise subjective components. For that reason, they do not attempt to measure the sum total of transaction costs in an economy, but rather the size of the **transaction sector**. Wallis and North attribute to this sector any activities concerning initiation and execution of economic exchange, such as the activities of lawyers or real-estate agents. The transaction sector can be distinguished from the **transformation sector**, which primarily comprises the production of goods, and from the **transport sector**, which can be interpreted as the spatial dimension of the transformation sector. According to Wallis and North, there are three main components to the transaction sector:

1. **Transaction industries**, which are mainly concerned with enabling transactions. They can also be called intermediaries and include all resources spent in the fields of finance, insurance, real estate, wholesale and retail trade.
2. Even within the **transformation industries**, many workers engage in procuring input factors, distributing products, processing information and so on. The labor costs for these employees are also attributed to the transaction sector. They include firm owners, managers, supervisors, lead workers, inspectors, lawyers, accountants, judges, notaries, and police and security personnel.
3. Many of the duties conducted by the **public sector** are aimed at protecting private property rights. In this respect, they fundamentally enable the division of labor. This is why Wallis and North include public budgets for defense, education, transport, and municipalities.

Wallis and North estimate that the transaction sector of the US economy in 1870 amounted to around 26 percent of gross domestic product (GDP). By 1970, the size of the transaction sector had more than doubled to 54.7 percent. This estimate, however, has several critics. Davis (1986), for example, points out that the result is very sensitive to the exact delineation between production and

There seems to be a positive correlation between the transaction sector and economic development transaction activities. At the end of the day, many jobs contain elements of both production and transaction activities.

The results of this longitudinal study should not be taken to mean that the quality of the relevant institutions in the USA has steadily declined in the course of the 100-year period being analyzed. Rather, the analysis shows that a higher degree of division of labor is associated with a higher portion of the labor force dealing with the execution of the increasing number of transactions. The fact that, during the same period, per capita incomes have risen many times implies that the productivity gains in both the transformation and the transport sector must also have been substantial. Put quite simply: the cost of single transactions might be going down, which is expected to lead to more transactions. As a consequence, the sum of all transactions costs – or, as delineated by Wallis and North – the size of the transaction sector might go up.

2.4.1 Estimations of the Size of the Informal Sector

The informal sector of an economy includes activities that occur outside formally regulated activities that are documented in official statistics. Thus, black market labor falls into this sector. Another term that is often used in this context is shadow economy. We are now putting forward the hypothesis that *the size of the informal sector is a good indicator for the relative quality of external institutions*. When external institutions create an environment that makes conducting transactions extremely costly, more transactions will be conducted through reliance on internal institutions. It is important to keep in mind that this is a *measure for the relative quality* of institutions. It does not state anything about the quality of external or internal institutions per se, merely about their relation. It is also important to not implicitly assume an exogenously given number of transactions. If neither external nor internal institutions are suited to substantially reducing uncertainty, the total number of economic transactions should be low.

The most influential study in this context is the investigation of three informal sectors in the Peruvian economy by De Soto (1990): **informal housing**, **informal trade**, and **informal transport**. De Soto conjectures that the informal sector is larger when external institutions and internal institutions are less compatible: "We can say that informal activities burgeon when the legal system imposes rules which exceed the socially accepted legal framework – does not honor the expectations, choices, and preferences of those whom it does not admit within its framework – and when the state does not have sufficient coercive authority" (De Soto, 1990, 12). In the parlance of this book, De Soto states that *we should expect a flourishing informal sector whenever the government designs external institutions that are incompatible with the internal institutions of the relevant actors*. The policy recommendation can be made that external institutions should be, by and large, compatible with a country's internal institutions in order to prevent an extensive informal sector.

> De Soto: The shadow economy flourishes when external and internal institutions are incompatible

Even though socially beneficial transactions are conducted within the informal sector and the sector can be quite orderly, De Soto refrains from glorifying its achievements. When discussing informal business, he states that most firms have to *forgo the realization of potential economies of scale*, as it would be impossible to remain informal beyond a certain firm size. He also finds that many firms in the informal sector are at best undercapitalized, that their capital is not accepted by banks as collateral, that they cannot access certain markets such as the stock exchange or fairs, that their transactions are associated with substantial information costs, and that long-term investments are generally not possible.

Note

Ceteris paribus: All other things being equal or held constant. Common approach in economic models, often abbreviated "c.p."

This implies that – *ceteris paribus* – the rate of investment in the informal sector should be lower than in the formal sector.

2.5 Open Questions

Many of the results that were obtained using the ultimatum game as a laboratory experiment are not compatible with the standard rationality postulate that is still common in economics. It is unclear what conclusions can be drawn with regard to the modeling of human behavior. Are we merely faced with special cases that show the need to further generalize the standard behavioral model of economics? Or could it be that we are faced with such fundamental inconsistencies that a completely novel behavioral model is required?

QUESTIONS

1. Does the result of the Coase theorem change when we account for strategic behavior of the involved actors?
2. Come up with further examples for the four different interrelationships between internal and external institutions. How do these relationships affect the manner and extent of transactions? How can conflicting internal and external institutions negatively affect societal development?
3. In the first part of the chapter, we dealt in detail with property rights. How would you classify human rights in this context? What are commonalities with and differences to material property rights?
4. Give reasons why we could assume that the production of art is only marginally influenced by the design of the relevant property rights, such as intellectual property. How would you try to refute such an assumption?
5. The Coase theorem is only valid if the distribution of resources does not affect the resulting allocation. Try to think of ways in which the distribution of resources could have an effect on the ensuing allocation.
6. In the description of the Coase theorem, we only explained in detail the case in which the polluter is not liable for damages from emission. Explain in detail what happens when the polluter is liable using Figure 2.1.
7. Wallis and North (1986) report that the GDP share of transaction costs in the USA has more than doubled in the course of 100 years. How can it be that per capita income has simultaneously multiplied?
8. It is commonly claimed that new developments in modern communication technology are associated with a *decrease* in transaction costs. That would describe a trend opposite to the one observed by Wallis and North (1986). Discuss.

FURTHER READING

An early contribution to the theory of property rights is Furubotn and Pejovich (1972). Alessi (1980) mainly surveys empirical studies. Pejovich (2001) has compiled two volumes for the "International Library of Critical Writings" containing some of the most important original contributions.

A well-written introduction to the Coase theorem can be found in Cooter and Ulen (2012). Over the years, the Coase theorem has been criticized by many scholars from all sorts of angles. One nicely written example is Deirdre McCloskey's piece on "the so-called Coase theorem" (1998). By producing a small and accessible volume, Coase (1988) not only clarified some of his original ideas but also answered a number of his critiques. Allen (1998, 108) claims that by defining transaction costs as "the costs of establishing and maintaining property rights," the Coase theorem can be defended against some standard criticisms.

Oosterbeek et al. (2004) survey the vast literature surrounding the ultimatum game. A more recent survey is by Güth and Kocher (2014). Henrich et al. (2005) contains an overview of results for 15 small, non-industrialized societies. They confirm what we conjectured above: the higher the level of market integration in a society, the higher the incidence of pro-social behavior.

Schneider and Enste (2007) contemplate alternative possibilities to estimate the extent of the informal sector. Based on data collected by the World Bank among firms around the world, Kovač and Spruk (2016) have recently proposed a new measure for transaction costs. They find that higher transaction costs slow down economic growth.

Massell (1968) studies the case of several Islamic countries that became part of the Soviet Union in the 1920s, in which inhabitants started to resolve conflicts without recourse to the formal legal system when said system was perceived to be illegitimate.

Voigt and Park (2013) ask whether businesses resort to private dispute resolution when state dispute resolution is thought to be of poor quality. They find that state and private dispute resolution are not substitutive but rather complementary.

3 Repeated and Long-Term Transactions: On the Choice of Governance Structures with Given Institutions

3.1 Introductory Remarks

In Chapter 2, we analyzed how internal and external institutions influence simple transactions. In this chapter, we consider the effects of given institutions for transactions that are repeated and intended to be long-term. We speak of "given" institutions to indicate that they are not created by the actors directly involved in the transactions, but that they have been "given" to them by others, most likely lawmakers.

In 1937, Ronald Coase asked why firms exist at all when other economists posited that markets are efficient. You know the answer already: markets cannot be used without costs. In many cases, hierarchies are able to manage transactions at a lower cost than horizontally structured markets, thereby reducing positive transaction costs. However, coordination via hierarchies, such as firms, is also characterized by costs, so-called **organization costs**. These comprise the costs for procuring inputs as well as those spent on managing and monitoring personnel. This simple observation already allows for a prediction regarding firm size: *A firm will stop expanding when the additional transaction cost savings are lower than the additional required organization costs.*

Optimal firm size depends on the ratio between organization costs and transaction costs

When two friends pool resources in order to jointly produce and sell something, a long-term contract might be required. Frequently, it is extraordinarily difficult to determine the value of different individual inputs that go into the production of a good. Accordingly, it can be very difficult to observe whether both friends are putting an appropriate amount of effort into joint production or whether one of the two is trying to free-ride on the other's effort. One could also envision a situation in which a buyer places an order for a large amount of the produced good. In order for the producer to confirm the order, the firm needs to extend its production capacities requiring a significant investment. But what if, before the investment has fully amortized, the purchaser decides to switch to a different supplier?

> ## Chapter Highlights
>
> - Understand some of the incentives of people making up a firm.
> - Hear about the various problems caused by asymmetric information.
> - Get acquainted with the view of the firm as a team – as well as a collection of assets.
> - Learn about the connection between transaction characteristics and governance structures.
> - Think about the relevance of internal institutions for firms.

In this chapter, the new institutional economics of the firm are discussed. The main issue revolves around the incentives that drive the behavior of actors within the firm (owners, managers, employees). If these are understood, it might be possible to set up governance structures that help to increase the overall performance of the firm. Firms themselves are not institutions, they are organizations. North (1990a) refers to organizations as the players of the game – as opposed to institutions that define the rules of the game. According to him, firms – just as other organizations – are "made up of groups of individuals bound together by some common purpose to achieve certain objectives" (North, 1994, 361). But firms are based on external institutions, e.g., the corporate law of a country. At the same time, firms usually create their own (internal) institutions that are used to coordinate behavior of people within the firm. The external institutions on which a firm is built impact its running costs. For instance, whether a firm is a limited liability company or an unlimited liability corporation is relevant for the costs of borrowed capital. If I am liable for a loan with my entire wealth – including my private wealth entirely unrelated to the firm I own – banks might grant me better conditions for a loan than in the case in which I am only liable up to a specified amount, say €30,000. Thus, while firms are not institutions, they are constrained by institutions.

Firms are organizations, not institutions

In Chapter 1 we distinguished organizations from institutions without defining organizations. Following North (1990a, 4), we define organizations as *groups of individuals that are united in the pursuit of a common objective*. While institutions can be called the rules of the game, organizations can be called the (collective) players of the game.[1] The founding of organizations is influenced by the constraints and possibilities that a game offers for potential members of an organization to increase their (individual) utility. In firms, resources – i.e., property rights – are pooled among their owners and behavior is frequently coordinated by a mix of rules and commands.

In reality, we observe (a) a large variety of given institutions on which organizations can be based and (b) a great diversity of organizational forms within a given institutional framework. It therefore seems straightforward to assume that optimal organizational forms will differ depending on the concrete circumstances the organization is facing.

Traditional microeconomics differentiates between household theory (supply of input factors and demand for goods) and the theory of the firm (demand for input factors and supply of processed goods). Usually, the firm is depicted as a production function, that is, a functional relationship between input factors and outputs. Topics that are not addressed by the traditional theory of the firm include processes within firms, incentives of alternative salary schemes, and information problems associated with increasing division of labor. Thus, it seems a bit pretentious to talk of a "theory" of the firm. Critics often refer to the firm as a **black box**: in the black box, input factors are transformed into output goods, but traditional microeconomics tells us very little about how exactly this transformation occurs.

The firm as production function?

Transaction cost economics is a subdiscipline of the NIE that deals with exactly these topics. Business administration also deals with these kinds of topics, and rightly so. Indeed, many institutional economists consider the usual distinction between economics and business administration to be artificial. After all, representatives of both disciplines draw on the toolkit of modern economics described in Chapter 1.

The remainder of this chapter is divided into six sections. In Sections 3.2 to 3.5, we consider different aspects of how institutional economics addresses a theory of the firm. In Section 3.6, we deal with the relevance of internal institutions for repeated and long-term transactions. In Section 3.7, we formulate open questions.

---

[1] Organizations, as such, cannot act. Strictly speaking – and in line with the concept of methodological individualism that we introduced in Chapter 1 – it is, hence, not organizations that act, but rather the individuals who are part of an organization.

3.2 From a Black Box to the Firm as a Team

In their groundbreaking essay from 1972, Armen Alchian and Harold Demsetz describe the firm as a team, shifting the theory of the firm away from the traditional view as a production function towards a view of the firm as an organizational structure. In the framework of Alchian and Demsetz, owners of resources pool their resources because the *output* from joint production is larger than the sum of *outputs* from individual production. In essence, when owners pool their resources, they create a team. All such teams are characterized by one common problem; as soon as joint production starts, it is difficult to measure the (marginal) contribution of each team member to the joint output. The consequence is that each team member has an incentive to exert less than optimal effort with respect to the joint objective, hoping that the remaining team members will carry the burden. In other words: Each team member tries to **free-ride**. This incentive exists for all team members. A careful reader will see that the underlying interaction situation is that of a prisoner's dilemma.

Incentive problems in teams …

In this case, the game is not played between two actors, but between one team member and the rest of the team. In order to keep the notation simple, we will utilize a common trick. By assuming that all other actors have the exact same range of options available, we can depict them as a single actor (see Matrix 3.1). The rows represent the available actions of the single team member, while the columns represent the possible actions for the rest of the team.

The highest possible payoff for the single team member is achieved when he exerts no effort, while the rest of the team does (lower left cell). But when the rest of the team also exerts no effort, free-riding will not be associated with a high payoff (lower right cell).

Matrix 3.1 The prisoner's dilemma within a team

		Rest of the team	
		Exert effort	Exert no effort
Single team member	Exert effort	3	4
		3	1
	Exert no effort	1	2
		4	2

From this matrix, it can be inferred that because all team members are subject to the same incentive structure, no one will exert effort. On balance, individually rational behavior leads to socially suboptimal results. Thus, each team member would be better off if the team were able to implement a mechanism that brings all team members to exert effort, or in the language of game theory, to cooperate instead of defecting.

... and a possible solution   Alchian and Demsetz (1972) suggest a solution to this problem. Team members assign one person to coordinate their activities. This person is not only authorized to monitor all team members, but also to hire new team members and fire existing team members. This would solve the incentive problem of the team. However, there might be an incentive for the coordinator to exert no effort, which would imply that free-riding would still be the outcome of the game. Thus, an additional mechanism is required to create the right incentives for the coordinator: The coordinator is given the right to appropriate the **residual income** – that is, the profit – from joint production. Because a high firm profit correlates with a high payoff for the coordinator, there is an incentive for the coordinator to coordinate the team's activities optimally.

Definition

The **residual income** is what remains from a firm's revenues after paying off all contractual obligations, such as wages

Two factors stand out when considering the firm as a nexus of contracts:

1. The coordinator – we could also call him entrepreneur – enters into bilateral contracts with all team members as a group. In this manner, he can economize on negotiation costs. If for any reason there is a breach of contract, or a change in team composition, and the entrepreneur had to renegotiate with each team member individually, the resulting costs would be high.[2]
2. The better durable capital goods belonging to the firm and used to produce the goods the firm intends to sell are taken care of, the longer their lifespan and the higher the return on investment.

---

[2] One reason for the inefficiency of worker governed firms and many cooperatives is that many decisions are made jointly, which is associated with high decision-making costs.

Because the entrepreneur is endowed with control rights, he has an incentive to invest in the maintenance of capital goods. If the entrepreneur contributes a large part of the firm's real capital, it makes sense that he should also be given the control rights for the capital goods, as this leads to the proper incentives.

The theory of the firm proposed by Alchian and Demsetz was criticized, but also further developed, by a host of authors, including both Demsetz and in particular Alchian (see Alchian, 1984; Alchian and Woodward, 1988). Barzel (1987) proposes the **measurement cost approach**, which emphasizes that there are high costs associated with the entrepreneur measuring his own *inputs*. Barzel's conclusion is that the person whose contribution to team production is the hardest to determine is the entrepreneur.

Having discussed the origins of the institutionally founded theory of the firm, we turn to a problem that is prevalent not only in many firms, but also other relationships: asymmetric information between a supervisor (more general: a principal) and his or her employee (more general: an agent).

3.3 Problems Associated with Asymmetric Information: The Principal–Agent Theory

In their 1976 paper, Michael Jensen and William Meckling introduced what would later be referred to as principal–agent theory. At its core, principal–agent theory is concerned with the *consequences of asymmetric information between partners to a contract*. The principal assigns a certain task to an agent. However, the principal cannot perfectly (or costlessly) observe the agent's actions, nor can the principal evaluate the performance of the agent's contractual task in complex situations. Thus, the agent possesses some degree of discretion that she can use to maximize her own utility – which may not be congruent with the principal's utility. The main research interest of principal–agent theory is the *optimal design of contracts given the assumption of asymmetric information*. In its applications, the contribution of Jensen and Meckling is not limited to the theory of the firm. Many other relationships can be analyzed using this theory. This includes the relationship between voters and politicians, between department head and department staff, between creditors and debtors, and so on.

The classic example is the incorporated company. The shareholders – the principals – have at their disposal a different level of information than the managers – the agents. Shareholders have an interest in signing contracts with managers that lead to the maximization of their expected profits. Two crucial preconditions for such contracts have been identified, namely:

1. The agent is at least as well off by entering into the contract as she would be if she didn't (this is called "participation constraint" in contract theory).
2. The agent takes actions that maximize her own expected utility within the respective contract (this is called "incentive compatibility constraint" in contract theory).

The costs that arise from asymmetric information are called **agency costs**. These include all costs borne by the principal in order to restrict agent behavior that is not in the principal's interest.

Asymmetric information can occur ex ante and ex post

By assumption, information is asymmetrically distributed between principal and agent. To keep measurement costs low, the principal will resort to easily observable variables when trying to evaluate the productivity of agents. Productivity, however, is only imperfectly observable, e.g., when hiring new employees. Because there is discrepancy between the attributes the principal would like to observe and the attributes the principal can observe, certain problems can arise. Two of these problems are **adverse selection** and **moral hazard**. Let us look at these in a little more detail.

In general, adverse selection implies that a buyer cannot distinguish between high quality and low quality products before buying a good. The inability on the buyer's side to distinguish between high and low quality implies that her willingness to pay will be rather low. Formulated differently: were she able to distinguish between low and high quality goods, she would be ready to pay more for the high quality good. The inability to distinguish between different qualities means that average prices will be rather low. This, in turn, implies that the potential sellers of high quality goods might prefer not to sell at all. In extreme cases, this process can lead to a complete stop of any exchange in such markets. This story was first told by George Akerlof (1970) with reference to used cars. Here, the inability to distinguish between various qualities on the side of the buyer leads to adverse selection in the sense that the average quality offered on such markets is likely to decrease over time.

Adverse selection is also a problem if a firm wants to hire agents with high productivity. The principal might simply be unable to ascertain the quality or productivity of the agent. This situation is often referred to as *hidden characteristics*. Hidden characteristics refer to stable attributes of an agent that cannot be observed by the principal *ex ante* (i.e., before a contract is concluded) but will be revealed *ex post* (i.e., after the contract has been concluded). An agent may be a hard worker, but not very skilled at completing a task. Thus, the problem is relevant before entering into a contract with a potential agent. For firms, this problem occurs primarily in the process of hiring. While potential new employees might have a good idea about their own productivity, firms try to measure productivity either by using costly methods (also referred to as *screening*) or by resorting to other ways of obtaining information that might correlate with productivity (*signaling* where the potential agent tries to credibly signal his qualities). It is crucial that signals are hard to fake, i.e., that only those with the desired attributes can send them. In economic parlance: signals must be costly. One example for the latter is a college degree with good grades. Although a good college degree does not directly measure productivity, a highly productive individual is more likely to complete college with a good degree. Some business consultants hire people with a degree in the natural sciences. Knowledge in biology or chemistry is often only marginally useful in consulting. It seems that these graduates are hired because their degrees signal their ability to perform well in a demanding environment.

Ex ante ...

In general, moral hazard refers to a situation in which one person takes a high risk because he does not have to bear all of the consequences of the behavior. Moral hazard, hence, involves a negative externality. The problem of moral hazard is present when the principal is able to observe the agent's productivity (no information asymmetry here), but cannot ascertain to what degree the resulting outcome is due to the agent's actions or due to exogenous factors. Thus, while the problem of *adverse selection* occurs before entering into the contract, the problem of *moral hazard* occurs after entering into the contract. For instance, shareholders (the principals) have a hard time determining whether their firm's decreasing profits are due to bad management decisions or to unanticipated exogenous shocks that might have counteracted the otherwise good work of management.

... and ex post

> **Exogenous shocks**
>
> **Exogenous shocks** are unanticipated events that are beyond reach, hence exogenous. The event of a natural disaster could be such a shock. By destroying the better part of a crop, it causes prices to increase.

Naturally, agents are aware of these problems and have an incentive to blame poor firm performance on exogenous shocks. Moral hazard is often differentiated into *hidden information* and *hidden action*. *Hidden information* describes a situation in which the principal does not possess the expertise to adequately evaluate the agent's actions. *Hidden action* describes a situation in which the principal simply cannot observe the agent's actions. Both types of information asymmetries are associated with moral hazard problems.

In Section 3.4, we discuss several approaches for mitigating problems caused by information asymmetries.

3.4 Transaction Cost Economics

As a student of Ronald Coase, Oliver E. Williamson continued to explore Coase's inquiry into why firms exist and developed a unique approach to transaction cost economics. In Williamson's approach, the question is not merely why some transactions are carried out via markets and others via hierarchies (his 1975 anthology is entitled *Markets and Hierarchies*), but also which type of transaction is carried out using so called **hybrid governance**. Hybrid governance refers to forms of governance somewhere between the two "pure" forms of governance, namely markets and hierarchies. *Joint ventures* and *franchising* are just two examples of such hybrids. More specifically, Williamson investigates how the optimal type of contract (or governance) is affected by various characteristics of a transaction (behavioral assumptions, specificity of investment, transaction frequency, and so on).

Individuals are assumed to be boundedly rational and opportunistic

Williamson assumes that the actions of individuals are characterized by **bounded rationality**. He also assumes that individuals are **opportunistic**, that is, they will proceed with an action that makes them better off, even if that action has a negative effect on another individual. If potential transaction partners are not able to utilize or develop institutional mechanisms that prevent opportunism, then many transactions that otherwise might be mutually beneficial will not be realized. Again, we can see that an adequate institutional framework is important for the number and the value of transactions in a market economy. Opportunistic behavior is particularly prevalent when a specific *ex ante* investment by one party is required in order for a transaction to be realized. As soon as that investment is made, however, the value of the next best use for that investment good is much lower than the value that can be obtained within the contract. Suppose the investment is a factory for producing smart phones. If, all of a sudden, no smart phones are to be produced there but notebooks, the return to the investment is likely to be lower. Williamson refers to this phenomenon as **asset specificity** or specific investment. Note that specificity can refer not only to real capital and human capital, but also to the location of a firm. It is important to realize that the incentives before entering a contract (*ex ante*) are very different from the incentives after having agreed on a contract (*ex post*). Before making specific investments, a supplier is not tied to a particular buyer. After having made that specific investment, the situation is that of a bilateral monopoly. For Williamson, this change in incentives is so important that he also talks of it as the "fundamental transformation."

Imagine a railroad network installed according to the specific requirements of the buyer, e.g., a railroad company. If for some reason the railroad is no longer used, one could uninstall the rail tracks, install them elsewhere, or simply melt them to regain the steel. Re-dedicating the use of the railroad network is associated with significant costs. The part of these costs that cannot be recovered – for instance by selling off remaining parts and materials – is called **sunk costs**. Once costs have been sunk, contracting partners are locked to each other, as switching partners would imply writing off the sunk part of the investment. This is called **lock-in**. The difference between the value of the first best use and the second best use of a good is called **quasi rent**. A buyer tries to recoup as much of the quasi rent as possible.[3] Despite the assumed bounded rationality, many suppliers will anticipate this, such that many potentially beneficial transactions will not be realized. Think back to the example we introduced at the beginning of this chapter: A buyer orders a large quantity of a good. The supplier is only able to supply this large quantity after investing in additional capacity.

---

[3] This strategic situation is called **hold-up**. The buyer figuratively attempts to "hold up" the supplier for a part of the quasi rent.

However, after this investment, the buyer has an incentive to try to renegotiate the price. If the supplier anticipates this, he might not carry out the required investment in the first place. One possible solution to this problem is for buyer and supplier to merge into a single firm since under joint profit maximization, the problem of opportunism does not arise.

Williamson shows how variations in the assumptions regarding bounded rationality, opportunism, and specific investment affect the optimal type of contract (1985, 31).

Planning   When perfect rationality, opportunism, and specific investment are given, actors can use their perfect rationality to anticipate all relevant eventualities and deal with them in respective contract clauses. In other words, contracts are complete in the sense that all possible events (even events with an extremely low probability of occurring) are explicitly dealt with in the contract, and there is never scope for an *ex post* dispute regarding their correct interpretation. The type of contract under these assumptions is referred to as "planning" or "mechanism design" by Williamson.

When we assume bounded rationality and specific investments, but actors are not opportunistic, contracts cannot be complete because the consequence of bounded rationality is that we cannot
Promise   possibly foresee all future states of the world. Promises to pursue a common goal, however, would be credible and thus sufficient. In the absence of opportunism, such a contract is self-enforcing, such that third-party enforcement is not required. The optimal type of contract under these assumptions is called "promise" by Williamson.

If we assume that actors are boundedly rational and opportunistic, but specific investments are absent, goods can be re-dedicated at any time without significant loss. Under this assumption, markets function as they should according to neoclassical theory:
Competition   Competition will lead to efficient results and Williamson refers to the implicit type of contract here as "competition."

Finally, let us assume that all three assumptions are given. Then, the contracting parties will not resort to any of the previously
Governance   mentioned contract types, but rather create a **governance structure** of their own. This could, for instance, have the form of a joint venture. There are two further alternatives in the presence of bounded rationality, opportunism, and asset specificity: First, the transaction is not realized at all. Second, the transaction is realized, not via the market, but within an organization. In our example, that would imply a merger between the buyer and the supplier. The

creation of a governance structure is associated with the need for contractual safeguards against opportunistic behavior.

Let us posit for now that it makes sense to assume bounded rationality, opportunism, and asset specificity. A consequence of operating under all three assumptions is the prediction that actors will try to create a specific governance structure in order to realize mutually beneficial transactions. The logical corollary question is: Which factors determine which specific governance structure is optimal for a given type of transaction? We now discuss this question in detail.

Williamson distinguishes three characteristics of transactions:

Factors that are relevant for the choice of a governance structure

- the degree of asset specificity,
- the degree of uncertainty, and
- the frequency with which a transaction is repeated.

Regarding asset-specificity Williamson proposes to distinguish between (1) non-specific assets, (2) assets of an intermediate degree of specificity, and (3) idiosyncratic specificity. Regarding the frequency with which transactions are repeated, he makes a distinction between "occasionally" on the one hand and "regularly" on the other. If we were to combine these two dimensions by drawing a table we would thus get a table with six cells.

The distinction between transactions that are carried out occasionally and ones that are carried out regularly is probably self-explanatory although it might not always be crystal-clear how to group a specific transaction. With regard to the characteristics of the investment good, that is, the extent of asset specificity, some explanation might be required. If the investment is non-specific in character, the value of its second best use is nearly as high as the value of its first best use. Hence, sunk costs are hardly relevant here. At the other end of the spectrum, there are idiosyncratic assets. By this, Williamson means an investment good with unique characteristics. Such goods require a high degree of specific investment.

Williamson now argues that different transaction characteristics lead to different optimal governance structures. To characterize these governance structures, he goes back to a 1974 essay by Ian Macneil. According to Macneil, **classical contracts** are characterized by a strong reliance on external institutions and formal documents. Because bounded rationality prevents actors from anticipating all possible future contingencies and including them in the contract, the effort to take care of all eventualities that might occur in the future leads to a quick escalation in negotiation costs for long-term contracts. "Classical contracts" are governed by relying on markets. This type of governance is best suited for goods that are non-specific, no matter whether exchanged regularly or only occasionally.

Neoclassical contracts can be interpreted as a middle ground between attempting to anticipate all possible contingencies on the one hand and accepting the fact that contracts are necessarily incomplete on the other. In this constellation, the solution involves the establishment of arbitration mechanisms and resorting to external arbitrators that are respected and trusted by all parties involved. Therefore, the governance structure underlying neoclassical contracts is also referred to as "trilateral governance" and it is most appropriate for goods with an intermediate degree of specificity that are exchanged only occasionally.

Finally, the concept of **relational contracts** views individual transactions as part of an ongoing business relationship that is made up of a large number of such transactions, the extent and frequency of which is impossible to anticipate *ex ante*. Given such a conception of contracts, it is not necessary that the mutual account is in balance after every single transaction. Under such contracts, it is not uncommon for one party to advance funds in the expectation that this will be compensated for in the long-term business relationship. When the goods to be exchanged are idiosyncratic and this occurs regularly, a unified governance structure (such as a single firm) is expected to be most appropriate.

Policy consequences

Transaction cost economics can have far-reaching consequences for competition policy. Here is just one example: In traditional economics, vertical mergers (that is, mergers between firms at different levels of the value chain) are seen rather critically. However, given the insights of transaction cost economics, a re-evaluation might be in order. What if the (expected) transaction cost savings of such a vertical merger are higher than the (expected) additional organization costs? Then, prohibiting such a merger would prevent a more efficient organizational structure. This is why transaction cost economists take a stance on antitrust policy that is markedly different from more traditional approaches.

3.5 The Firm as a Collection of Assets

During the second half of the 1980s, a group of economists began to think more deeply about the effects that vertical integration, i.e., unified governance, would have on the incentives of all the affected actors. In order to develop a theory of the firm that is able to say something meaningful about the boundaries of the firm, the extent to which a firm is vertically integrated is crucial. Sanford Grossman, Oliver Hart, John Moore, and Jean Tirole were among the economists thinking about these issues. Since their conceptualization of the firm relied heavily on property rights, it is also called the **property rights approach to the firm**. More generally, their approach is known as incomplete contract theory and they view the **firm as a collection** of assets.

Suppose there is a contract between a buyer and a seller that specifies many – but not all – contingencies. Contracts cannot be complete because some information is observable (to the contracting parties) but not verifiable (in front of a neutral third party, such as a court). Ownership of assets now implies that the owners possess **residual rights** of control over the respective assets. According to property rights theory as introduced in Chapter 2, ownership implies the right to transfer the rights to use or modify an asset. But when contracts are incomplete, not all potentially valued rights can be perfectly transferred. The term "residual right" refers to the right of an owner to proceed with her asset as she sees fit as long as no particular contract or general law stands in her way.

This view of the firm includes all kinds of **nonhuman assets** (from machines and inventories, buildings and client lists to patents and copyrights). Human assets are explicitly excluded because they can neither be bought nor sold. In essence, the theory claims that the identity of the asset owner matters for how assets are used, for the relative bargaining power of the contractual partners vis-à-vis each other, for how they divide a potential surplus, and, at the end of the day, for how much investment will take place.

These assumptions are then used to identify the boundaries of the firm. Hart (1989, 1770) summarizes the main findings:

- Highly complementary assets should be owned in common; a minimum size of the firm is the likely consequence.
- As the firm grows, the value created by some activities at the periphery is unlikely to be specific to the assets at the center; at that stage, a spinoff is in order to reduce the danger of hold-up of the periphery by the center.
- In the absence of significant lock-in effects, nonintegration is always better than integration; coined differently, in the absence of lock-in, relying on markets is better than relying on firms.

- Transfer of ownership of physical assets has incentive effects for the owners of human assets; quite simply, it is in my self-interest to cater to the interests of the new asset owner as that will improve my bargaining position in relation to her.

The property rights approach of the firm has had a huge impact. Some shortcomings that have been criticized are that the propositions are nearly untestable (Whinston, 2003) and that it is a theory of the firm without managers (Gibbons, 2005). Another critique might be considered the cornerstone for yet another theory of the firm. As pointed out, the theory confines itself to nonhuman assets. An alternative theory of the firm focuses explicitly on human assets and emphasizes that firms, as governance structures, have advantages in the creation of firm-specific knowledge. In explicit contradistinction to Williamson, organization costs decrease with human asset specificity. This view of the firm has been developed by Richard Nelson and Sydney Winter (1982).

In this chapter we have retraced various steps in the development towards an "institutional theory of the firm" including principal-agent theory as well as transaction cost economics. Given the observation that different legal forms of firms are prevalent (thus entrepreneurs do not always opt for the same legal form), we can conjecture that some institutional arrangements are more suited for certain business objectives than others. Within the scope of this text, we can only discuss this matter very briefly. A short discussion of the advantages and disadvantages of different legal forms from the perspective of institutional economics can be found in Eggertsson (1990, 177–188). A more detailed discussion, albeit without institutional focus, can be found in any introductory textbook on business administration (such as Schermerhorn, 2012).

The choice of legal form depends significantly on the respective feasible production techniques on the one hand, and tax implications on the other hand. Capital intensive production with a high degree of fixed costs is usually not feasible in sole proprietorship.

The basic differences between sole proprietorship (the sole proprietor is liable fully and solely) and other legal forms of partnership (nontrading partnership, general partnership, limited partnership) and a joint stock company (incorporation, closed corporation) are probably known to you. For certain objectives, the legal forms of cooperative society or foundation might be optimal. These various legal forms differ significantly with respect to their liability consequences. Liability, in turn, impacts possibilities for and costs of funding.

We would like to stress here that different legal forms are associated with different incentives for employees. This applies not only to the incentives to exert effort, but also to the incentives to invest in one's own human capital and specialize. The problem of *ex post* opportunism is relevant here too. A firm might need a worker who is highly specialized. However, if the value of the second best use for his specialized human capital is much lower outside his current workplace, there is an incentive for his employer to lower his salary as a consequence of his specialization! Anticipating this, the worker will refrain from making productivity enhancing investments into his human capital absent an institutional solution that gives the employer an incentive to raise the worker's salary after such a specific investment in human capital. On the other hand, an employer might make a considerable investment in training a new employee, which increases the trainee's market value considerably. To prevent a highly qualified trainee from simply being headhunted away after finishing his training, many trainee contracts include a clause requiring the trainee to stay with the company for a minimum number of years.

Legal form influences employee incentives

3.6 The Relevance of Internal Institutions

In Chapter 2, we saw how internal institutions might restrict the way in which simple transactions are carried out. Here, we discuss how and in what situations they can have an impact on repeated and long-term transactions. Again, we do not aim for a full discussion, but rather discuss two examples of how internal institutions can affect such transactions.

3.6.1 Example 1: Corporate Culture: On the Coordination of Interaction Situations within Firms

Employees interact with each other in many different ways within a firm. Similar to the example of Laurel and Hardy in Chapter 1, employees prefer to coordinate their behavior. The sum of conventions used by employees to coordinate their behavior has been coined **corporate culture** by Kreps (1990). "This is how we do it," is an instruction often given to new employees that are not yet familiar with a firm's corporate culture. Corporate culture is not necessarily limited to a set of conventions (that is, type 1 institutions), but can also include other institutions. For instance, employees who break a certain rule could be scolded by their colleagues (based on custom, i.e., a type 3 institution). This can involve the *spontaneous formation of behavioral rules* which can be very costly for, or even impossible to change by top management. Entrepreneurs are also interested in cultivating certain aspects of corporate culture. For example, if there are corporate norms that lead employees to informally sanction colleagues who try to steal office supplies, the control costs of preventing such theft will be lower for management. Conversely, entrepreneurs will want to abolish corporate norms that use social exclusion as a sanctioning mechanism for "over-eager" colleagues.

The difficulties in realizing theoretically possible synergies after two companies have merged are commonly known by now. An explanation that suggests itself is that incompatible corporate cultures can be a major impediment. A number of empirical studies on this topic are available with somewhat contradictory findings. In mergers taking place within countries, different organizational cultures reduce the profitability of mergers, as expected. In cross-country mergers, however, different national cultures tend to have the opposite effect. Any insight that can be gained from the study of merging firms promises to be relevant for other areas too: When different administrative bodies within an international organization have to cooperate, different (corporate) cultures can clash. As such, there might be some coordination failures at the EU in Brussels due to national administrative cultures. This notion can also be applied to the "fusion" of societies or states.

3.6.2 Example 2: On the Relevance of Reciprocity in Labor Relations

Quite a few experimentalists started their careers as labor economists. As a result, their primary interest was employee–employer relationships. Small wonder, then, that some of the early experiments dealt with exactly this relationship. One example is the study by Fehr et al. (1997) which examines an "experimental labor market." Participants were either employers or employees. For an employer, the ideal employee puts a lot of effort into her work but does not demand a high wage. For an employee, the ideal job is not very demanding in terms of necessary effort but highly paid. In the experiment, the employer offers a labor contract that specifies a certain wage combined with a desired effort level and a contract is made with the first employee who accepts the offer. The employee receives the agreed upon wage no matter how much effort she has put into her work. There is no way for the employer to punish the employee if she puts in less than adequate effort.

In theory, this game has a straightforward solution: the employee would put in a minimum level of effort. The employer, anticipating this, would only offer a wage level sufficient to provide him with an employee. In actual plays of the game, however, employers often offered high wages combined with high levels of effort. The employees, rather than taking advantage of this by answering with a low level of effort, often reciprocated with high effort levels. As a consequence, both employers and employees were often better off than suggested by the theoretical solution.

Now, if the experiment ended here, we could conclude that employees are strong reciprocators. But we could not say anything about employers, after all, their generous offers meant higher profits for them, so their behavior could be rational profit-maximizing. To learn more about the behavior of employers, Fehr and his co-authors extended the experiment and gave employers the possibility to reward or punish employees, but at a cost. The game was not repeated, so the actors did not have the opportunity to develop a reputation as "tough" or "effort rewarding" or whatever else. In theory, no employer would spend a single cent on punishing or rewarding any employee since he would not reap any benefits by such behavior. In the experiment, however, employees were often punished or rewarded depending on their level of effort. These findings have been confirmed in other experiments (see, for instance, Fehr et al., 2009 or Gächter et al., 2011). If these findings also hold outside of the lab, they would prove that internal institutions that sanction employees who do not reciprocate play an important role in employer–employee relationships.

3.7 Open Questions

In this chapter, we have formulated multiple hypotheses that have not yet been thoroughly investigated empirically. Even the *implications of the Internet for governance structures* cannot be fathomed. In a similar vein, the agency and measurement costs that occur in virtual societies also remain unexplored.

QUESTIONS

1. Think back to the definition of institutions. Could (a) share-holder agreements, (b) labor contracts, and (c) corporate and labor law be thought of as institutions?
2. In the view of Alchian and Demsetz (1972), what is the solution to the incentive problem of "simple" team members and the coordinator (the entrepreneur)?
3. Explain the problem of moral hazard using the example of fire insurance.
4. Illustrate the problem of adverse selection using the example of an insurance company that sells automobile insurance by determining the premium based on the actuarial value.
5. Discuss incentive problems pertaining to collectively organized cooperatives, taking into particular consideration the view of the firm as a nexus of contracts.
6. Discuss to what degree outsourcing decisions can be explained with Williamson's approach.
7. In Section 3.4, I use many words to describe things that can be easily depicted as tables. Go back to that section and try to produce a table regarding optimal contracts and another one showing optimal governance structures taking into account both the degree of asset specificity as well as the frequency in which transactions occur. I would have liked to reprint the tables from Williamson (1985) but the copyright holder set a prohibitive price, which is why the tables are not included here. Instead, you can compare your tables with those that are on pages 31 and 79 respectively in Williamson (1985).
8. What category of contract would be appropriate if neither bounded rationality, nor opportunism, nor asset specificity is assumed to be present?
9. Try to come up with yet another example for the relevance of internal institutions in employer–employee relationships considering possible implications for the design of labor contracts.
10. Use incomplete contract theory to explain why mergers and spinoffs are often part of the lifecycle of the firm.

FURTHER READING

Paul Milgrom and John Roberts (1992) have written a very good textbook on the theory of the firm from an institutional economics point of view. Williamson received the Nobel Prize in economics for "his analysis of economic governance, especially the boundaries of the firm." In his prize lecture (2010), he gives an account of how transaction cost economics progressed over time.

Friedman (1991) gives a short introduction into the life and research of Ronald Coase. An evaluation of his impact on economics is Shirley et al. (2014).

An overview of contract theory can be found in Bolton and Dewatripont (2005). An introduction to principal–agent theory can be found in Sappington (1991).

One of the crucial contributions to the theory of adverse selection is "The Market for Lemons" by George Akerlof (1970) in which he shows that asymmetric information can even lead to the complete collapse of the market for a good. Incidentally, lemon does not refer to the fruit but rather to cars of low quality. The argument of Akerlof can be applied to all goods for which potential buyers cannot immediately ascertain the quality. This contribution is one of the reasons why Akerlof received the Nobel Prize for economics in 2001.

Baker et al. (2002) give an introduction to the concept of relational contracts.

Hart (1989) provides a very accessible description of the development of the theory of the firm putting major emphasis on the collection-of-assets view. Williamson (2002) offers his take on the theory, including a concise criticism of the shortcomings of the collection-of-assets view. Garrouste and Saussier (2008) explicitly acknowledge the ingenuity of Coase's early (1937) contribution but also mention weaknesses of his early take and compare his theory to more recent theories of the firm. Aghion and Holden (2011) survey the relevant theoretical literature on incomplete contracts in a very accessible way.

Shelanski and Klein (1999) is an overview that surveys the literature on empirical estimates of transaction costs in firms. The essay by Macher and Richman (2008) is not only more recent, but also wider in its applications, as it also includes transaction cost estimates for areas such as legislation, health policy, and agricultural policy.

The effects that differences in corporate governance across countries can have on the gains of cross-border mergers have been analyzed by Martynova and Renneboog (2008). If the bidder originates from a country with good corporate governance (regarding, for instance, the protection of minority shareholders or creditors) and the target company with worse governance, then the merger is likely to result in a positive spillover effect, implying that governance structures will improve in the country of the target company.

Kreps (1996) has written an introduction on the topic of corporate culture from the viewpoint of economics. The empirical findings regarding the influence of both organizational and national culture on a merger's success are surveyed by Teerikangas and Very (2006). They also inquire into the reasons for the conflicting findings in the literature to date. Ahern et al. (2015) find strong evidence that three important dimensions of national culture have significant effects on both the number of mergers as well as their realized synergies. These are the degree to which people trust each other, the degree to which hierarchies are commonly accepted, and the degree of individualism. Countries with similar national cultures not only realize more mergers, the mergers also experience higher synergies.

4 Institutions and Collective Action

4.1 Introductory Remarks

We have repeatedly asked why firms exist when the common conception is that goods and factors find their most efficient use through "quasi-automatic" allocation via markets. We have seen that the use of markets is not without costs, and that the choice between using the market (horizontal coordination) and the firm (vertical coordination) depends on the costs associated with the respective type of coordination. In this chapter, we ask a broader question: *If markets (and the firms within them) function so efficiently, why do we need states?* The traditional answer in economics is quite simple. We need states because the private provision of certain goods is not possible due to the specific characteristics of those goods, even though the consumption of these goods is beneficial to most (or even all) citizens. Economists call such goods **public goods**. One of their characteristics is that as soon as they have been provided no one can be excluded from their consumption without prohibitive costs given the available technology. This is called **non-excludability**. Another characteristic of public goods is that one individual can consume them without reducing their utility for other consumers. This is called **non-rivalry**. Consider a dam that protects all farms behind it from flood damage irrespective of whether all farmers in question contribute to the costs. Non-rivalry means that the level of protection for farmer B is not reduced by the fact that farmer A is also protected by the dam. Once again, we can illustrate the underlying structural problem of public good provision by referring to the prisoner's dilemma.

Why do we need states?

The characteristics of public goods

In Chapter 3, we used a simple trick to facilitate the illustration of a multi-person prisoner's dilemma. We again assume that all actors are endowed with the same range of options, which allows us to create one category of "all other actors," and another category of "one actor." The row player is one actor; all other actors are represented by the column player (see Matrix 4.1).

Matrix 4.1 The prisoner's dilemma as N-person game

		All other actors	
		Cooperate (C)	Defect (D)
One actor	Cooperate (C)	3	4
		3	1
	Defect (D)	1	2
		4	2

To "cooperate" here means to contribute to the provision of the public good, for instance the construction of the dam. To "defect" here means not to contribute to the provision of the public good. Those who do not contribute hope that all other actors provide the public good (thus cooperate), making it possible for the defector to benefit from the public good without incurring any costs. The problem with such a "solution" is that all actors have the same incentives in determining whether to contribute to the provision of the public good. Rationally, we have to expect that all actors will defect and the dam will never be constructed based on voluntary contributions. At the same time, we know that all farmers would be better off if the dam were to be constructed. The classical solution to this problem is for the government to provide public goods such that the outcome of the game is not the individually rational equilibrium (D, D), but rather (C, C). *The government is able to provide public goods because it has the power to tax citizens.*

From Chapter 3, you remember the problems associated with team production. We saw that in order for team production to be (economically) successful it is not sufficient to assign one team member to monitor the rest of the team. The monitoring agent needs to be provided with incentives to ensure he or she monitors the team properly. While there are many differences between the problems faced by economic organizations (firms) and political organizations (governments), these organizations share a number of structural similarities. Let us define citizens as members of "team society" who assign a few among them with the task of providing certain goods and services. Again, we need to consider carefully the incentives of the chosen agents, who we now call government instead of entrepreneurs. As soon as we endow some agents with special competencies – in particular the monopoly to use force – the danger arises that those actors might abuse these competencies.

> **Chapter Highlights**
>
> - Understand how politicians behave under given institutions.
> - Familiarize yourself with the dilemma of the strong state.
> - Get acquainted with the public goods game – and how it is played in the laboratory.
> - Learn about possibilities – and pitfalls – to manage common pool resources.

The main goal of this chapter is to explain the behavior of agents who are assigned the task of providing public goods and who are subject to certain institutional constraints. Even when we assume that the average politician is interested in maximizing his or her utility, we still see that there is a wide variety in the behavior of politicians in different countries. Institutional economists propose that an explanation for this variety of political behaviors is differences in institutional constraints, not differences in objective functions.

Politicians' behavior can also be explained via institutions

In the remainder of this chapter, we assume the state – and its constitution – to be given because we want to analyze how the incentives of different constitutions impact the behavior of politicians and other actors. In a subdiscipline of institutional economics – **constitutional economics** – it is common practice to distinguish between a **constitutional** and a **post-constitutional** level. With respect to the state, the constitutional level corresponds to the constitution of a country, while the post-constitutional level corresponds to legislation that is passed based on that constitution. Thus, one potential approach is to consider a state's constitution as a given institutional structure and then to ask what incentives politicians have to pass different laws, given those structures. As always, we define an institution as having a rule and a sanction component. The question here is how politicians are sanctioned when they are noncompliant with the rules governing their behavior.

4.2 Explaining Politicians' Behavior Under Given Institutions

4.2.1 Preliminary Remarks

During the last few decades, representatives of public choice theory have dealt with several questions that we are interested in here.

Giving a comprehensive overview of public choice theory is beyond the scope of this book (Holcombe, 2016 is a brief introduction). We restrict ourselves to naming just a few of the research questions that public choice theorists have been concerned with. These include:

1. What is the effect of different decision rules (i.e., unanimity rule or different forms of majority rule) on the expected outcomes?
2. What is the influence of the electoral system on the number of political parties?
3. What determines the propensity to form coalitions and their stability?
4. Does it matter whether a state is organized federally or centrally?
5. What is the effect of direct democracy on politicians' behavior?
6. How can the behavior of bureaucrats be explained?

To illustrate the general logic of public choice theory, let us consider an example of how different institutional arrangements can lead to different political behavior. Imagine a country A, in which legislation can be passed by a simple parliamentary majority and contrast this with country B, in which legislation can only be passed with the majority of votes from the Lower House, a majority in the Upper House, and a signature of the president (similar to the US system). As soon as different parties control the two Houses, it becomes much more difficult, that is, more costly, to achieve the majorities required for passing legislation. *Ceteris paribus*, we expect a lower number of new laws passed in country B than in country A.

The restrictions in place can also induce political behavior that is not concerned with the provision of socially beneficial public goods, but rather with the maximization of a politician's utility while harming the rest of society. We look at two examples of such behavior: (1) **rent seeking** and (2) **political business cycles**.

4.2.2 Example 1: Rent Seeking

Examples of harmful political behavior   The term "rent seeking" was coined by Anne Krueger (1974). The notion itself goes back to Gordon Tullock (1967). It has nothing to do with payments for a leased good, but can be thought of as that part of a price that is above its production costs. Rent seeking describes activities by lobby groups aimed at using the political process to secure special benefits, such as protection from import competition or simply subsidies. It implies that some actors are privileged and others – in turn – are discriminated against. Politicians who hand out rents thus behave in a way that is not compatible with the rule of law. Although the process of rent seeking wastes resources (any resources that flow into rent seeking cannot be utilized for productive purposes), private agents will spend resources on rent seeking as long as the expected net utility of this behavior is positive. Politicians – the agents of interest here – will grant special privileges when they expect to be better off because they receive something in return like political donations, campaign support, or even bribe money. The demand for and the supply of special privileges should be determined by the institutional structure of a country. If an institution's sanction for accepting bribery implies the end of one's political career, we would expect less bribery than if there is no sanction for bribery. If there are sanctions for supplying special privileges, we would expect a lower demand for such privileges by interest groups, as the probability of gaining special privileges would be rather low. If the expected utility of rent seeking is low, interest groups will invest fewer resources to gain special privileges.

The potential for and the limitations of rent seeking are closely related to the institutions in place

Olson (1982) believes that extensive rent seeking by interest groups is one reason for the economic decline of nations. Becker (1983) emphasizes that as the number of interest groups increases, it is more likely that their ensuing competition will neutralize demands for special privileges. In the latter view, rent seeking is not necessarily associated with economic decline. Buchanan and Congleton (1998) discuss whether it is possible to reduce the extent of discriminatory privileges (which are consequences of rent seeking) utilizing adequate institutional (in this case constitutional) structures. Their answer boils down to the principles of the rule of law. The more general a rule, the lower the potential for it to be abused for rent seeking.

4.2.3 Example 2: Political Business Cycles

Economists believe that one of the principal functions of government is the stabilization of business cycles. Some economists, however, question whether governments are ever able to stabilize business cycles, even when they are assumed to be benevolent. Rather than argue this point, we continue to investigate the incentives of political agents. This investigation leads to a surprising result: *Rational politicians cause business cycles.* Thus, politicians might not be the solution, but rather the cause of the problem.

Politicians are part of the problem

Let us assume that the probability of a government's re-election depends decisively on the level of unemployment shortly before the elections. Further, we assume that fiscal measures can lower unemployment in the short run, while leading to inflation in the long run. High inflation rates, however, are viewed very critically by the electorate, lowering the chances of re-election. Given these assumptions, a rational government has an incentive to use fiscal measures such that the decrease in unemployment (which increases the chance of re-election) occurs just before elections, while the increase in inflation (which decreases the chance of re-election) optimally occurs only after elections. One final assumption is required in order to produce such **political business cycles**, namely that the electorate places a higher value on utility gained today than on utility gained tomorrow. Put differently, with regard to the outcome of today's election, current political success of the government is more important than failures of the past.

Different models of political business cycles have been tested and confirmed empirically again and again for various countries (Mueller, 2003, 430–436, provides an overview of the empirical research). Institutional economists are interested in whether the observed differences in the extent of political business cycles can be explained via the constraints institutions place on politicians. For instance, whether the use of short-term fiscal measures is more limited in some countries than in others. Or whether the degree to which central banks in different countries are free of political influences plays a role in moderating political business cycles. And yes, under certain circumstances, institutionalized constraints on budget deficits can limit the size of political budget cycles. One such example is a constitution with explicitly spells out budget limits. But even with clear constitutional constraints, highly transparent processes for the creation and implementation of the budget are necessary to guarantee that the constraints are honored.

4.2.4 The Dilemma of the Strong State

In Chapters 2 and 3, we looked at ways in which individuals might secure transactions that are beneficial. We saw that external institutions can play a crucial role in this. For example, contracts can be structured allowing for recourse to external institutions or the visible hand of the state. In this chapter, we are dealing with the incentives that representatives of the state encounter. Think of the state as a unitary actor (for instance a dictator who represents all functions of the state). Further, think of a private citizen who considers entering into a voluntary transaction in which the state is a contracting party. There are many examples of this. For instance, when a private citizen works for the state, when a private company supplies the state with goods such as tables or chairs for a ministry, or when citizens lend money to the state. Now suppose that the private citizen on the one hand and the state on the other interpret their contract differently and the private citizen would like to seek redress in front of a state court, i.e., rely on external institutions. There, he will encounter the state in two functions: not only as the defendant against whom the private citizen is airing a grievance, but also as the judge who will provide the ultimate decision. Using a sports metaphor, we can formulate the problem thus: The state faces the problem of being both player and referee at the same time. Given this situation, few private actors will be willing to participate in a transaction with the state.

Problem: The state is a player as well as the referee

In market economies, one function of the state is to protect private property rights and voluntary transfers thereof. Effective protection requires a strong state. However, as illustrated above, the strength required to protect private property rights can also be a significant problem. As Weingast (1993) suggests, a strong state has the discretion to disregard private property rights entirely. We are faced with this dilemma: On the one hand, a strong state is required for a market economy to function well; on the other hand, a strong state can impede the economic development of a market economy. We propose to call this the **dilemma of the strong state**. If representatives of the state are able to credibly promise to respect private property in the future, private actors are likely to invest more and thus contribute to higher economic growth. Governments and representatives of the state can expect higher tax revenues and lower interest rates, allowing for a greater scope of action and easier access to financing for their expenditures. This problem is similar to the problem of moral hazard we discussed in Chapter 3. Here, the citizens are the principal and state representatives are their agents. After having entered into the (social) contract, the agents might choose actions that exert significant negative externalities on their citizens (the principal).

Rational governments want to be able to credibly commit …

Governments could, of course, promise to respect private property in the future in order to induce more private investment. Then, as soon as those investments are made, representatives of the state can attempt to nationalize them or attenuate their value. Private

... but have a hard time making credible promises

actors know that the government has an incentive to make promises *ex ante* but renege on them *ex post*. Acting on this knowledge, rational private actors will, thus, refrain from private investment.

In order for a government to induce private actors to invest in the market, it must be able to convince private actors that it will not renege on its promises. Private actors may resort to several **self-binding mechanisms**, described by Schelling (1960), to convince others that they will keep their promises. Many of these self-binding mechanisms require the presence of an independent third party to sanction breach of contract. The ability of the state to self-bind, however, is limited. If representatives of the state attempt to tie their own hands, there is rarely a third party available to sanction breach of contract.

Separation of powers as one possibility to increase the credibility of promises

The concept of **functional separation of powers** suggested by Montesquieu is an attempt to mitigate the dilemma of the strong state. Laws passed by representatives of the state (the legislators) are more credible if they are implemented by a separate office (the executive) and if a third office (the judiciary) decides how these laws conform to existing contracts (the state's constitution). We can infer that representatives of the state who accept a separation of powers recognize that a voluntary and credible limitation of their competencies can, indeed, strengthen their position. This is an "**as if explanation**" of the functional separation of powers. It does not claim to correctly describe historical developments, because, in reality, the separation of powers has often been the result of intense struggle rather than the action of enlightened rulers. Federalist structures are sometimes referred to as **vertical separation of powers**. These structures can also help to mitigate the dilemma of the strong state as they guarantee a minimum amount of autonomy to the constituting states.

One means to mitigate the dilemma of the strong state

The traditional idea of the separation of powers implies separating the functions of legislating, executing, and judicial decision-making from each other. If legislators promise potential investors (by way of general legislation) that their investments are safe and that they can set prices at their will, can freely transfer profits, will not be taxed very highly, and so on, this may sound attractive to potential investors. Still, they will wonder if such promises are credible. And if they do not believe them to be credible, they will not invest. If, however, there is a judiciary that is independent from the legislature (and the executive), an investor who feels that her property rights have been infringed can turn to the judiciary and have it decide whether government has kept its promises.

A judiciary that is actually independent from government is thus one way to mitigate the dilemma of the strong state. If a country manages to establish an independent judiciary, it is expected to attract more investment and experience faster growth. This is, indeed, the case as shown by Feld and Voigt (2003) and more recently by Voigt et al. (2015).

We have just described a potentially inverse relationship between the powers that politicians have at their disposal and their resulting level of utility. This insight can also be applied to **monetary policy**. If, for example, the government is endowed with monetary policy competencies, it has an incentive to promise price stability, in order to induce moderate (nominal) wage increase demands by trade unions. After the conclusion of collective agreements, however, the government has an incentive to expand money supply, in order to lower the (real) cost of labor and increase employment rates. As trade unions will rationally anticipate this, their expectations that inflation will increase in future will already be accounted for in the negotiated collective agreement (*inflationary bias*). High inflation increases everyone's costs as relative prices are likely to be affected and consumers will incur costs simply to ascertain the current prices of goods they are interested in. Thus, monetary policy under such an institutional frame causes social costs (in the form of increased inflation), while not being able to induce any social benefit (Kydland and Prescott, 1977; Barro and Gordon, 1983). Even a utility maximizing government could be interested in solving its **time-inconsistency problem** by transferring monetary competencies to an independent central bank. Given this, it appears that all members of society – including politicians – would favor the foundation of an independent central bank whose sole mandate is to maintain price stability. And indeed, over the last couple of decades more and more central banks have become independent, at least on paper.

> Independent organizations as another mechanism to mitigate the dilemma

Definition

A decision-maker is subject to **time-inconsistent preferences** when she prefers one policy in advance but a different policy when the time to implement has come. In the example, government has time-inconsistent preferences because it has incentives to announce a tight monetary policy *ex ante* but once the time to implement has come, it has incentives to implement an expansionary policy.

We have mentioned two instruments that representatives of the state might use in order to reduce the problem of self-binding:

1. Traditional functional separation of powers.
2. Delegation of competencies, which is also a separation of powers in a broader sense.

Membership in international organizations as third possibility A third, related, possibility is to submit to the rules of international organizations. If the rules of an international organization are endowed with a sanction, we call them "international institutions" here. An example of such institutions is the World Trade Organization (WTO) rule stating that tariffs cannot be increased unilaterally – except in specific circumstances. If a government breaches its commitment to comply with the rules of the WTO, the country aggrieved by this behavior can initiate highly formalized proceedings against the noncomplying government. The Dispute Settlement Body of the WTO is an international body comparable to a state court in the national setting. It has proven to be a well-functioning body.

A nice illustration of the dilemma of the strong state is offered by Levy and Spiller (1994) using the privatization of telecommunication networks as their point of reference. Politicians (particularly in less developed countries) have an incentive to attract foreign investors to their country. As soon as foreign investors have created the networks, however, domestic politicians have strong incentives to expropriate them. Anticipating this, many foreign investors are unwilling to participate in attractive investment opportunities unless governments are able to demonstrate their promises are credible. All involved actors (government, investors, and the population) are better off when governments are able to commit credibly. Levy and Spiller show that optimal regulation depends on (exogenously given) institutions. In their analysis, they explicitly account for informal restrictions (internal institutions in our terminology). They suggest that governments that are not able to demonstrate a credible commitment fall back on international organizations as funding sources (such as the World Bank). Another possible scenario is to privatize networks so that the shareholders come from a broad spectrum of the domestic population. In this scenario, a government trying to expropriate the rightful owners would expect heavy domestic opposition, making expropriation a very costly option.

Drawing on a particularly interesting case, Voigt et al. (2007) analyze whether membership in international organizations can indeed be beneficial for a country. After attaining independence, several of the former British colonies continued to accept the Judicial Committee of the Privy Council in London as their highest court of appeal, while others switched fully to a judiciary of their own. Even after controlling for miscellaneous differences (for instance, geographical or ideological distance to Great Britain), those countries that kept the Judicial Committee as their highest court of appeal have attracted more foreign investment, have paid lower interest rates on their sovereign bonds, and are characterized by higher economic growth. More recently, Dreher et al. (2015) have shown that governments are able to "buy" credibility by joining international organizations. They find that the theoretical conjecture of Levy and Spiller (1994) can be confirmed and that governments that voluntarily have their discretion curbed by membership in multiple international organizations attract more foreign direct investment. There is, thus, some evidence that the credibility problem of governments can be alleviated not only by domestic institutions, but also by international institutions that are administered within the realm of international organizations.

4.3 Explaining Collective Action Using Internal Institutions

4.3.1 From Non-Repeated to Repeated Games

We referred to the prisoner's dilemma game to illustrate the problems associated with the provision of public goods and the possibilities of collective action. The only Nash equilibrium of this dilemma we have encountered is (D, D). Our conclusion is that the voluntary provision of public goods is not individually rational and that the existence of a state, which provides public goods, can make every individual better off. We then demonstrated that the variance in political behavior with respect to the provision of public goods is due to varying institutional constraints, assuming the institutional constraints (i.e., the constitution) to be exogenously given.

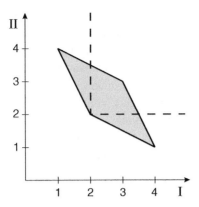

Figure 4.1 A graphic depiction of the prisoner's dilemma
The payoff for player 1 is on the horizontal axis, the payoff for player 2 on the
vertical axis. The corner points of the gray area represent the possible payoff
combinations that you remember from the non-repeated game. In the iterated
game, other (average) payoff combinations within the gray area are possible too.
A player who defects in each round can secure at least two payoff units. Thus,
payoffs below that are not part of the equilibrium area. The areas below the dashed
lines and to the left therefore do not belong to the area of possible equilibria.

For ease of exposition, however, we intentionally oversimplified
the argument and confined it to non-repeated games. But in the
real world, many relevant interactions do occur repeatedly. Once
we allow for the game to be repeated, an entire universe of additional equilibria beyond (D, D) or (2, 2) becomes feasible (the so-
called *Folk theorem*[1]). In Figure 4.1, the gray area depicts all
possible equilibrium payoff combinations of a repeated prisoner's
dilemma. The figure also shows that the strategy combination (C, C)
is a possible equilibrium, albeit only one of many. What we need
now is some type of mechanism that helps us predict what equilibrium is likely to be selected. Game theorists have been working on
this for a long time. However, it seems fair to say that until now,
they have been rather unsuccessful in spelling out mechanisms that
would help people to bring about any specific equilibrium. Here, we
refrain from surveying that literature in any detail and instead
focus on the possibility that internal institutions might affect the
ultimately realized equilibrium.

---

[1] The name stems from the fact that this result used to be commonly known
among game theorists. Fudenberg and Maskin (1986) derived it formally.

When considering the provision of public goods, the existence of equilibria to the northeast of (D, D) implies that provision of public goods without recourse to the state might be possible. Internal institutions might be one key explanation for this outcome. There is a host of real-world examples in which **voluntary provision of public goods** occurs. For example, when citizens voluntarily serve as jury members or lay assessors, or join the fire-fighters or any other non-governmental organization providing public goods. Even when people contribute to Wikipedia either by writing contributions or by donating money, a public good is provided that can be used by anyone. We first present some of the laboratory evidence concerning the voluntary provision of public goods and then discuss several internal institutions that might facilitate voluntary provision.

4.3.2 Evidence from the Laboratory

Based on the framework of game theory, we can conjecture that rational actors will not voluntarily provide public goods in a non-repeated prisoner's dilemma, thus contributing zero. Results from experiments refute this conjecture. Even in non-repeated games, participants contribute an amount significantly larger than zero. There is ample evidence from so-called **linear public goods experiments**. In these games, all participants are given an equal amount of resources, usually in the form of tokens. They then must decide whether or not to contribute (and, if so, how much) to the provision of a collective good. Tokens put into the common pot multiply by a factor larger than one. The common pot can be thought of as the public good. Consequently, the pot is divided among all participants of the game no matter how much they contributed. The group's total payoff will be maximized if all players put all of their tokens into the common pot.

A numerical example of the public goods game

Here is a numerical example of the public goods game: Suppose each member of a group of five is given $10 at the beginning of the game. Each member now decides how much of the money to keep (privately) and how much to transfer into a public account. At the end of the game, each participant receives the sum of what is in the public account (it is supposed to mimic a public good, thus nobody can be excluded from its consumption, even those who did not participate in its provision). The "investments" transferred into the public good are, however, multiplied by a coefficient of, say, 0.4 before being paid out.

With these numbers, the sum of individual payoffs would be maximized if each participant transferred the entire $10 into the public account. In that case, $50 would end up there. After multiplication by 0.4, each participant would receive $20, i.e., twice the original endowment. If all five participants chose to invest their entire endowment, the sum of all payoffs would, thus, amount to $100. However, if I kept the $10 for myself and all of the other participants transfer their original endowment into the public account, I would still be better off. In that case, I would receive 10 + 0.4(40) = 26. All others would then receive only $16 and the sum total would be $90. If everybody tries to free-ride on the others, then no money would end up in the public account and no public good would be provided at all.

However, contributing is not individually rational. Instead, a rational individual will contribute zero. Again, we are confronted with a situation in which individually rational behavior leads to collectively suboptimal results. This game has been played hundreds of times in laboratories all over the world. The most noteworthy outcome is that – contrary to theoretical predictions – many players do contribute significant parts of their original endowment.

Individually rational behavior leads to socially suboptimal results in public goods games

While Davis and Holt (1993), Ledyard (1995), and Chaudhuri (2011) present more comprehensive overviews, Ostrom (2000) offers a seven-point summary of the results found in the laboratory:

1. In non-repeated games, participants contribute between 40 percent and 60 percent of their initial endowment for the provision of the collective good. This also holds for the first round of finitely repeated games.[2]
2. In the rounds following the first, the contributions decrease, but still remain clearly above the predicted zero percent.

---

[2] In theory, finitely repeated games should lead to the same results as non-repeated games: In the *ex ante* known last round, the repeated game is equivalent to the non-repeated game. We would thus expect (D, D) in that round. By extension, the same should hold for the second to last round, and so on. In game theory, this approach is called **backward induction**. It is not without critique (Elster, 1989a, 4–8, provides a concise summary; Kreps et al., 1982 show that cooperation can be rational even in the finitely repeated prisoner's dilemma).

3. Participants who expect other participants to contribute will likewise contribute with greater than average probability.
4. The amount a player contributes decreases with a falling rate the more often the game is played. Ostrom concludes from this that players who have gained a better understanding of the game cooperate more, not less, as was commonly believed for a long time.
5. Allowing direct communication between players increases the contribution rate in all rounds of the game. Thus, non-binding commitments, commonly referred to as *cheap talk*, might not be so "cheap" after all.
6. If allowed, players are willing to use some of their own resources in order to sanction other players who contribute less than average.
7. The contribution rate also depends on contextual factors. These include, for instance, the way in which the game is described (i.e., "framing").

A standard criticism of laboratory results is that they stem from the laboratory, not from real-world interactions. The external validity of laboratory results would, therefore, be questionable. Despite possible challenges to laboratory results, the sheer amount of evidence is impressive. What is of interest to us is an examination of the role played by internal institutions in producing these results. *Limitations of laboratory results*

For a clearer overview, let us return to the table we introduced in Chapter 1, expanding it with relevant examples (Table 4.1).

Conventions are institutions. A convention is the stable equilibrium of a game with two or more stable equilibria (in the traffic example introduced in Chapter 1, two in pure strategies, namely

Table 4.1 Internal institutions and individual contribution to collective action

Rule	Form of enforcement	Type of institution	Example
1. Convention	Self-enforcement	Internal type 1	Traffic rules
2. Ethical rule	Self-commitment	Internal type 2	Fairness norms, Justice norms, Secondary virtues
3. Custom	Spontaneous informal societal enforcement	Internal type 3	Norms of reciprocity, norms of solidarity
4. Formal private rule	Organized private enforcement	Internal type 4	Churches

everyone steers left, everyone steers right, and one in a mixed strategy like drive on the left with probability one half). The non-repeated prisoner's dilemma, however, has only one stable equilibrium, (D, D). In the repeated prisoner's dilemma, (C, C) is also a possible equilibrium. Political scientist Robert Axelrod (1984) showed that there is one strategy which trumps all other strategies, both on average and over time. That strategy is called tit-for-tat. It is a very simple strategy: One cooperates in the first round, but in all subsequent rounds, one mirrors the other player's strategy of the respective previous round. As long as the other player cooperates, (C, C) results. A criticism expressed by some game theorists is that accidental defection (or cooperation that is mistaken for defection) leads to an infinite sequence of non-cooperative strategy combinations. They propose strategies with a higher tolerance threshold, for instance defection might only be chosen after two defections in a row

Axelrod shows that there are certain *conditions* that facilitate the viability of tit-for-tat as a strategy. These include: (1) a low preference for the present (a high preference would imply that payoffs in this round might be valued higher than the loss in payoffs in future rounds) and, (2) the probability of meeting again with the same player, which for its part should be negatively correlated with group size. It is the latter factor that makes it questionable whether tit-for-tat realistically qualifies as a viable convention for an n-person prisoner's dilemma. It is only when the relevant group is sufficiently small, or there is some "natural" division into smaller groups, that the strategy described by Axelrod is viable. The tit-for-tat strategy has little relevance for us, because here we are interested in solutions for very large groups.

When examining how large groups provide public goods, it is much easier to develop arguments from the perspective of ethical rules. For instance, if certain justice or fairness norms have been part of an individual's upbringing, one could well imagine that individual utility is reduced by not contributing a "fair" or "just" amount to the public good. If members of a social group can *ex ante* promise each other to contribute a certain amount to the public good, there is even more scope for ethical rules to apply, for instance the rule to stick to one's promises. Such rules are often referred to as **secondary virtues**.

Customs, the noncompliance of which is sanctioned by third parties, are particularly relevant in our context. Contributing less

Tit-for-tat as a particular strategy to play the prisoner's dilemma

Requirements for tit-for-tat to work

Relevance of ethical rules

Customs enforced by third parties

than what is commonly perceived as fair or less than was promised, could be sanctioned by ostracism, or public airing, leading to loss of reputation. In general, the very sanctioning of non-cooperative behavior carries associated costs. Let us assume there is a norm of cooperation that benefits all members of a social group. This implies that all members of that social group have an interest in upholding that norm and protecting its continued existence. If sanctioning is associated with costs, all group members are interested in not only sanctioning rule breakers, but also in letting other group members carry out the sanction. In other words: *The act of sanctioning is in itself a collective good, the provision of which is not guaranteed.* Guaranteeing the provision of adequate sanctions is more likely, the more precisely the task of sanctioning is allocated to certain group members. Many experiments have been conducted to analyze the conditions under which participants are willing to incur costs to punish those who do not contribute what is perceived as their fair share for the provision of the public good.

Definition

Ostracism as practiced in ancient Athens is the practice of excluding someone from the group. In Athens, it was often used to expel people who were considered potential tyrants. To this day, ostracism is practiced by many groups.

Perverse punishment

Many experiments have shown that people are willing to punish free-riders, i.e., those who do not pay their share for the provision of a public good (Chaudhuri, 2011 gives a nice overview). But the story does not end there. Benedikt Herrmann, Christian Thöni, and Simon Gächter (2008) conducted a fascinating experiment in 15 very different locations ranging from Boston and Melbourne to Samara, Riyadh, and Muscat. These locations were chosen to find out whether cultural differences had a significant impact on how the game was played. The surprising finding of this experiment was that high contributors were frequently punished. How can we make sense of this seemingly perverse punishment? It is possible that this punishment directed at the high contributors is simply an act

Free-rider problem

of retaliation, because the punishers suspect the high contributors are the ones who previously punished them (the game was repeated ten times). Herrmann et al. term this behavior "antisocial punishment." Consequently, societies that punish the pro-social behavior of those who contribute a lot to the provision of public goods are expected to have substantial difficulties in providing public goods. Interestingly, the lowest amount of antisocial behavior was recorded in Boston and Melbourne, whereas the most was found in Samara (Russia), Riyadh (Saudi Arabia), Athens (Greece), and Muscat (Oman).

Formal sanctions by private organizations Finally, one could also argue that sanctions administered by private organizations might be relevant. Let us interpret the voluntary donations of members of a religious group as contributions to the provision of a collective good. There might be a rule that a certain percentage (e.g., the tithe in Christianity or the *zakat* in Islam) of one's income should be donated to the religious group. Sanctions for noncompliance with that rule could range from simple informal reminders by representatives of the religious group to meet the required contribution, to more formal sanctions that might include expulsion from the group.

4.4 The Interplay between External and Internal Institutions and its Relevance for Collective Action

In a previously mentioned essay, Elinor Ostrom (2000, 147) writes this concerning the interplay between external and internal institutions:

The worst of all worlds may be one where external authorities impose rules but are only able to achieve weak monitoring and sanctioning. In a world of strong external monitoring and sanctioning, cooperation is enforced without any need for internal norms to develop. In a world of no external rules or monitoring, norms can evolve to support cooperation. But in an in-between case, the mild degree of external monitoring discourages the formation of social norms, while also making it attractive for some players to deceive and defect and take the relatively low risk of being caught.

Certainly, this is a very striking conclusion. So let us spend some time to see how Ostrom arrived at it.

Common pool resources and public goods share the characteristic of non-excludability. Common pool resources differ from public goods in that their consumption is rival in the sense that one unit consumed by a particular member of the community cannot be consumed by anybody else. If no clear rules regarding the use of the goods exist, the threat of depletion looms large. Here is an example: Assume a lake with many fish. It is individually rational for every fisherman to fish as long as his personal benefits from an additional catch are at least as large as his personal costs. Usually, this implies overfishing, and fishing would soon come to depletion if no institutions regulating fishing are established and enforced. This problem was described by Garrett Hardin (1968) as the **tragedy of the commons**. Besides the lake just used as an example, there are many other common pools in the world; the oceans, the woods, meadows, (clean) air, and so on.

To prevent the depletion of common pool resources, institutions are necessary

Quite often, state ownership has been recommended as a solution. In fact, considerable amounts of development aid have been paid to governments of developing countries to develop and manage their common pools, e.g., water systems on which farmers depend. Alternatively, private ownership with property rights enforced by the state has been recommended. Ostrom (1990, 14) points out that these recommendations share a common assumption that some external institutions must be imposed from above on the individuals affected. Ostrom begs to differ. She points out that those directly affected – such as herders using a particular meadow year after year – might have the most accurate information regarding "their" common pool. Out of self-interest, they might also have the strongest incentives to monitor the compliance with any rules regarding the use of the common pool.

There are, in fact, examples of small-scale communities that have successfully managed their common pool resources over hundreds of years. Examples that Ostrom mentions refer to communal tenure in high mountain meadows and forests in Switzerland and Japan, and to irrigation systems in Spain and the Philippines. But there are also many – probably more – examples in which the communities have not been able to deal with their commons properly. Ostrom sets out to identify the factors that help communities to be successful in dealing with their common pool resources. She suspects that the capacity to communicate within the group and the ability to develop trust are important aspects helping groups in successfully managing their own commons. In her comparative analysis of many communities, she utilizes the framework of the comparative institutional analysis we introduced in Chapter 1.

The commitment problem discussed at length above also plays a central role here: At the time the rules are agreed upon, every user will promise only to take so much water out of the canal but when his or her harvest is in danger at some later time, the incentive not to behave as promised is present. Ostrom argues that commitment is never credible without monitoring. She suggests a commitment can be credible only if there is some systematic monitoring of how much water every farmer takes out of the canal. In her field studies, Ostrom was particularly interested in learning how communities deal with the commitment and monitoring problem. In *Governing the Commons*, she produced a list of seven design principles that characterize all institutions that helped their communities manage their common pool resources successfully (1990, 90ff.). There needs to be:

Design principles for the successful management of common pool resources

1. Clearly defined limits regarding the right to withdraw resource units from the common pool resource; this refers to the precision regarding the rule part of institutions as defined in this book.
2. Congruence between rules defining how much a user can take out of the common pool (so-called appropriation rules) and how much the user is obliged to put in (for monitoring, cleaning, repairing, and so on; so-called provision rules).
3. Ways to modify the collective-choice arrangements. To increase the probability of compliance, it is important that most individuals affected by operational rules can participate in their modification if necessary.
4. Accountability of the monitors to the appropriators; one straightforward way to set up monitoring is to have appropriators do it.
5. Graduated sanctions, implying that during times of severe crises tolerance for rule infractions might be higher than in normal times.
6. Conflict-resolution mechanisms to resolve conflicts on the exact interpretation of the valid rules.
7. Minimal recognition of the right to organize. This brings us back directly to the issue of the relationship between external and internal institutions: if governmental officials insist on their monopoly to define rules, enforcement by locals might be impossible.

Numerous lessons can be drawn from Ostrom's observations. Perhaps most important, ownership or management of common pool resources should not be reduced to either state or private ownership but communal ownership as extensively described by Ostrom should be considered as a possible alternative. Societies that rely primarily on internal institutions for the management of common pool resources are better able to recognize and utilize the existing local knowledge about these resources.

Of course, reliance on internal institutions will only work if government does not insist on monopolizing the creation and enforcement of institutions. In other words, when there is no conflict between external and internal institutions.

Why is this so important? It is not only important to explain why some traditional societies have been successful in dealing with their commons while other traditional societies have not. It is also important because global climate can be thought of as a common pool resource with literally billions of appropriators and – at least potentially – billions of providers. How much the world climate will change depends on how much CO_2 and other greenhouse gases are emitted into the atmosphere as a consequence of billions of individual choices. Scientists from two Max Planck Institutes in Germany asked whether there are ways to encourage contributions to the global public goods and developed a game that added a number of unusual features to the standard game already described above (Milinski et al., 2006). The unusual feature of interest here is the possibility to contribute to the common good – climate protection – publicly. Public-mindedness can, thus, be observed. This, in turn, enables others to reward those who have been behaving public-mindedly and, at the end of the day, such behavior may even turn out to be personally profitable. The authors conclude by stressing the hope that we might be able to design strategies to improve reputational gains from behaving public-mindedly as an important device to reduce climate change.

Ostrom's observations, analyses, and conclusions offer us one way to think about these things. Bruno Frey (1997) has also dealt with the relationship between external and internal institutions. He builds on David Hume's statement: "In contriving any system of government, and fixing the several checks and controls of the constitution, each man ought to be supposed a *knave*, and to have no other end, in all his actions, than private interest" (Hume, 1987 [1777], 42). Frey argues that the apparently required strong distrust between principal and agent can lead to a *crowding out* of intrinsic motivation. The term *crowding out* is more commonly used with respect to governmental borrowing: A credit-financed expansion of governmental demand can lead to a higher interest rate and thus a *crowding out* of private demand. Frey, however, uses the term to emphasize that an *expansion of governmental control might crowd out the private willingness to contribute to public goods*, for instance, to voluntarily pay taxes.

Politicians as principals ...

... and as agents.

If we use the vernacular of principal–agent theory, we notice some interesting asymmetries. Politicians can be agents as well as principals (this is valid for citizens too). Politicians are principals when facing citizens who are supposed to pay taxes. Politicians cannot readily observe before-tax income of citizens, causing an information asymmetry. Politicians are agents when they are providing the bundle of public goods desired by citizens. But here again an information asymmetry exists because citizens cannot readily observe whether politicians are taking adequate action in order to provide the public goods. In another possible scenario, if politicians do not trust citizens to pay taxes and express this distrust by hiring additional tax collectors, some citizens who are intrinsically motivated to pay taxes ("There is a price to good infrastructure; it is only fair that I contribute my share to its financing."), might decide to evade taxes.

Frey argues that crowding out might also work conversely. If citizens express their distrust by an overly detailed constitution with very precise restrictions, a decrease in the intrinsic motivation in politicians might be the consequence. The general conclusion is clear: There are *interdependencies between external and internal institutions*. If these interdependencies are not sufficiently accounted for in the design of external institutions, even a well-intended change in external institutions can induce unintended changes in internal institutions, leading to a possible net loss in social welfare.

4.5 Open Questions

While reading Sections 4.3 and 4.4, you might have noticed that our ability to explain the impact of internal institutions on collective action is limited. It is also difficult to describe the interdependencies between external and internal institutions. We are better able, however, to describe the impact of external institutions on collective action. There are many reasons for this status quo. One reason is our inability to be specific with terms. For example, "public good" can describe a variety of goods; "collective action" can refer to a variety of actions. Future research should be very clear and explicit about this.

Evidence from **behavioral economics** suggests that there is a significant difference between decisions concerning the controlled use of a public good that already exists (such as meadows, fishing stocks, forests), and a collective good that must first be created (such as dikes) through the contributions of group members (Brewer and Kramer, 1986). A reduced usage of common pool resources is often seen as social loss, the utility gained by providing a public good as social gain. One key result of behavioral economics is that *utility reductions induced by loss are valued higher than utility increases induced by gains*. This could imply that it is easier to manage a reduction in the usage of a common pool resource than ensuring the provision of a (yet non-existent) collective good.

So far, we have assumed that a constitution is exogenously given and *de facto* enforced. As we can observe in many parts of the world, this assumption is rather naïve. One can thus ask what determines whether or not constitutional rules are actually enforced. A possible answer might be that it is not only the design of external institutions that matters (remember the separation of powers), but also internal institutions. A rational government will only break constitutional rules if it expects to gain from it. If government members expect broad opposition to such rule breaking, they might refrain from it altogether. *The provision of opposition is equivalent to the spontaneous provision of a public good*: If it is effective, all citizens benefit from it. However, contributing to the provision of opposition is associated with costs. Thus, the spontaneous production of the public good opposition seems more likely if there are appropriate internal institutions. In addition, if such internal institutions are in place, the chance that the *de facto* constitution is in line with the *de jure* constitution is higher than if they are not (a more detailed discussion can be found in Voigt, 1999a). In Chapter 6, we address this matter again.

QUESTIONS

1. In Section 4.2.1, we formulate a number of questions that public choice scholars are concerned with. Think about possible answers.

Hints on the answers are provided in the Further Reading section.

2. Describe the dilemma of the strong state and discuss institutional arrangements that might be able to mitigate it.
3. Think of additional examples of the voluntary provision of public goods and discuss which internal institutions might be relevant in enabling their voluntary provision.
4. Think of additional examples for a crowding out of intrinsic motivation of (a) politicians and (b) citizens due to a very strictly formulated principal–agent contract.
6. Why will private firms underprovide public goods?
7. Which factors make cooperative outcomes in public good games more likely?

FURTHER READING

A number of decision rules and their effects are dealt with in chapters 7 and 8 of Mueller (2003).

It has been argued by Maurice Duverger (1954) that electoral systems relying on majority rule (often also called first-past-the-post) lead to two-party systems whereas those relying on proportional representation lead to multiple party systems. Since the evidence on this argument is very strong, this relationship is also known as **Duverger's Law**. Mueller (2003, 271–276) summarizes the empirical evidence.

Coalitions are often formed quite trivially to reach parliamentary majorities. It is said that as soon as the necessary parliamentary votes are reached in a coalition, additional parties are unlikely to be admitted to the coalition because the members of the coalition would then have to share the spoils of governing with more parties. This notion is called **minimum-winning coalition**. But the idea that any combination of parties, no how matter how far apart ideologically, could form a coalition seems unrealistic. A modified version has been called **minimum-connected-winning coalition**. It is based on the idea that ideologically neighboring parties are more likely to enter into coalition agreements. Somewhat counterintuitively, coalitions with sizable majorities seem less stable than those securing a bare parliamentary majority (Mueller 2003, 281–284).

The economics of federalism is an important branch within public choice. One of the eminent scholars of federalism within public choice,

William Riker, wrote this (1975: 155): "Nothing happens in a federation because of the federal constitutional arrangements that could not happen otherwise in fundamentally the same way." While some scholars doubt that being constituted as a federation – rather than as a unitary state – has important consequences, there is lots of evidence that this does matter. Weingast (2014) is a recent survey of the relevant literature.

Direct democratic institutions can make the agents – the politicians – more accountable to their principals – the citizens – because direct democratic institutions allow the citizens to express their preferences on single issues and politicians do not like to be corrected by their citizens. This is why direct democracy increases politicians' incentives to listen to citizens. Matsusaka (2005) is a good survey of the literature. Blume et al. (2009) is the first cross-country study inquiring into various effects of direct democracy institutions.

William Niskanen (1971) was one of the first to analyze the behavior of bureaucrats from a public choice perspective. Although his model is highly stylized and many assumptions have been criticized, it is still very readable. The subsequent discussion is neatly summarized in Mueller (2003, chapter 16).

The literature on rent seeking has turned into a veritable cottage industry. A two-volume set, edited by Roger Congleton, Arye Hillman, and Kai Konrad (2008), contains the most important contributions to this field over a 40-year period. In a recent contribution, Toke Aidt (2016) deals with the commonalities and differences between rent seeking and corruption. Mueller (2003, chapter 15) summarizes the literature on rent seeking.

More on the application of principal–agent theory to the relationship between citizens and governments can be found in Moe (1990).

The argument that a strong distrust between citizens and politicians might lead to a crowding out of intrinsic motivation is at the core of a monograph by Brennan and Hamlin (2000).

Ostrom (1990) deals in detail with mechanisms that social groups utilize in order to secure the use of common pool resources or provide new public goods. She was awarded the Nobel Prize in 2009 "for her analysis of economic governance, especially the commons." Her prize lecture (2010) nicely summarizes her thinking about how to govern the commons.

Voigt et al. (2015) show that higher levels of *de facto* judicial independence are robustly correlated with higher levels of economic growth.

Hayo and Voigt (2008) connect two of the topics of this chapter, namely the separation of powers and central bank independence. They show that higher levels of *de facto* independence of the judiciary from the other government branches are associated with lower inflation levels.

5 The Relevance of Institutions for Growth and Development

5.1 Introductory Remarks

In Chapters 2, 3, and 4, we discussed the consequences of institutions for individual action. We considered simple and complex transactions, the interrelationships between different types of institutions, and the incentives to act as part of a social group. In this chapter, we look at the consequences of these individual-level actions for the macro level. More specifically, we are asking what the consequences of institutions are for aggregate measures such as economic growth. At the most basic level, we have one conjecture: *The cheaper it is to carry out mutually beneficial transactions, the more frequently such transactions will be carried out, the faster a society's economy will grow, and the higher the resulting income and welfare level of society will be.*

You might think that economists are obsessed with growth. Or you might think that they are boring because in the end, their discussions always revolve around a single topic, growth. I would prefer to call the concern with growth a clear priority rather than an obsession. Why? Depending on how one counts, there are at least one billion people on the planet suffering from poverty. This has terrible implications: insufficient nutrition, inadequate shelter, poor health, lack of education, and so on. The only way to improve the lot of the poor, and for that of most people as well, is economic growth. Economic growth implies that more goods and services are produced and can, hence, also be consumed.

Definition

Economic growth: The gross domestic product (GDP) measures the value of all goods and services produced in one country over a certain period of time (usually one year). Economic growth is the increase of GDP from one period to the next. It is usually measured on a per capita base and thus indicates the change in average individual income between two periods. Current income can be thought of as growth that accumulates over a long period of time.

Now, you might wonder why redistributing wealth from the (few) rich to the (many) poor is not a solution? The simple answer is incentives. The rich whose income is reduced by transferring it to the poor have fewer incentives to keep on producing as much in the future. The poor, who can consume a little more as a consequence of receiving transfers, have fewer incentives to increase their own efforts to get out of poverty. So, at the end of the day, everyone might be worse off. On top of this, administering a global redistribution scheme would eat up an enormous amount of resources. Taking money from the rich will be met by some resistance and will, therefore, be costly. For administering large welfare programs, many bureaucrats are needed. In sum: Redistribution has negative incentive effects for both the rich and the poor and its implementation will eat up a substantial part of the resources.

You might know that traditional **growth economics** explains growth rates based on input factors, particularly labor and capital.

Note
Growth economists attempt to identify the determinants of growth in per capita income.

The so-called new or **endogenous growth theory** further accounts for the fact that the factor labor is neither homogeneous nor exogenously given. In other words, people have different skills and can invest in their skills by attending university or following training programs. Institutions, as we understand them, are not considered in endogenous growth theory. If the basic conjecture that we just formulated is supported empirically, a rethinking of growth economics towards an institution-based theory is in order.

Chapter Highlights
• Discuss potential determinants of economic growth.
• Ask how institutions can be measured.
• Discuss one early measurement attempt in detail.
• Summarize the most important findings regarding the influence of institutions on economic growth.

As in the previous chapters, we deal both with external as well as internal institutions. In Section 5.2, we not only reiterate the central theoretical conjecture that is the foundation of the NIE – namely, that high quality institutions are conducive to growth – but we also discuss briefly two competing explanations. One explanation posits that it is primarily geographical factors that determine income and growth, another one points at the overwhelming relevance of culture. Section 5.3 deals with the question of whether differences in external institutions cause differences in growth rates. To answer that question, reliable measures for institutions are needed. Some attempts to make institutions measurable are presented and discussed. We then summarize the available evidence regarding the effect of institutions on growth. In Section 5.4, we report some evidence on the effects of internal institutions on growth and economic development. In Section 5.5, the relationship between external and internal institutions and the implications of that relationship for economic development are explored.

5.2 Determinants of Economic Growth: Institutions, Geography, Culture?

5.2.1 Institutions

If we look at the year 1750, differences in income levels across countries were fairly small. In other words, no matter where you lived you had to get along with little money and few goods. Around 250 years ago, this situation of fairly equal income levels began to change. A number of European countries started to experience substantial growth rates and some of the (former) settler colonies like the USA and Australia soon followed suit (Figure 5.1). This situation was not a global phenomenon; most other countries did not experience substantial change in growth rates. This difference in the growth paths of countries has led to vastly unequal income levels today. There are still a number of African countries such as Burundi or Malawi where the average income is less than US$1 a day. Just pause for a second and think what that means. This number does not refer to the poorest 10 or 20 percent of the population, it is the average over the entire population. On the other side of the spectrum, there are a number of countries with an average income of above US$50,000 a year. Besides British influenced countries (Australia, Canada, and the USA), this is also the case in most Scandinavian countries (Denmark, Norway,

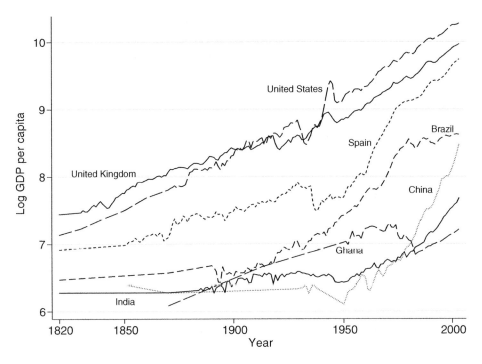

Figure 5.1 The evolution of income in the USA, the UK, Spain, Brazil, China, India, and Ghana between 1820 and 2000.

Source: Acemoglu (2008, 14)

Sweden, and Iceland). This means that the average person in one of the richer countries is 150 times richer than the average person in one of the poorest countries.

Conjecture: Economic growth is determined by institutions

Institutional economists argue that the main reason for some countries "taking off" is that they improved their institutions. The Glorious Revolution of 1688 is considered by many scholars to be one of the important moments in history, because it constrained the discretionary power of the king and made government behavior more predictable (e.g., North and Weingast, 1989). Other countries followed suit, like France in 1789. Reliable institutions that protected property rights were a precondition for technological innovation to occur and spread quickly. When thinking about these stylized facts, at least two questions come immediately to mind: How can we know it is really institutions that led to these radically different development paths? And, if European countries managed to set up growth-enhancing institutions 200 or more years ago, why didn't every other country simply copy them? This chapter deals primarily with the first question. The second question will be dealt with in Chapter 6.

One illustrative example for the enormously important role of institutions is the economic development of Germany. The main power in Imperial Germany (i.e., before 1918) was Prussia which extended over large areas of both the eastern and western parts of the country. Geographical conditions were fairly similar across the entire country and the population was fairly homogeneous in terms of language, religion, culture, and other aspects. Up to World War II, rapid industrialization took place in both the eastern and the western part of the country. After World War II, the country was separated into East (socialist) Germany and West (market oriented) Germany. In the West, private property rights were re-established, a hard currency was introduced, and the country soon began to experience high growth rates after the devastation of the war. East Germany was under the influence of the Soviet Union and private property rights were mostly limited to personal belongings. The consequence was that there were few incentives to be creative and entrepreneurial in the East. Productive technology in the East soon lagged behind the West. Since the country did not produce many goods that could be exported, it did not acquire any foreign currency and its citizens could not even consume simple imported products such as bananas or coffee.

All this clearly shows up in the diverging income levels between the two countries. In 1960, the net disposable income of an East German household was around two-thirds (67 percent) of an equivalent West German household. Over the ensuing decades, that share fell continuously. In the early 1980s, it was only 45 percent of the West. In the late 1980s, it fell to less than 40 percent of the West, and in the end the system simply collapsed. But the story does not end there. In 1990, the countries were reunited and the institutions that had been in place in the West were essentially implemented in the East. Just as the West had experienced after World War II in the 1950s, the East now experienced its own *Wirtschaftswunder* (economic miracle). Between 1991 and 1997, per capita GDP grew by around 60 percent, roughly the same number the West had experienced between 1950 and 1956. Today, disposable incomes in the East are 85 percent of the Western level. If we take into account that consumer prices are still lower in the Eastern part of the country, disposable income in the East is 90 percent of that in the West. The divergent developments that have taken place in North and South Korea after World War II tell a similar story (e.g., Acemoglu et al., 2005a). The German example, however, is even more revealing as it not only shows that different institutions can cause vastly different developments (pre-reunification), but also that substituting high quality institutions for low quality ones can even reverse the previous development (post-reunification).

It is unlikely that other competing theoretical frameworks (namely, geography and culture) can adequately explain the differences in growth rates that occurred in East and West Germany. After all, the East and the West developed more or less in tandem until the end of World War II. Then, the institutions of West Germany were heavily influenced by France, the UK, and the USA, whereas those in the East were created and implemented under the direct influence of the Soviet Union. In other words, the German case is a good example for the relevance of external institutions. But one or even two examples (Germany and Korea) could be exceptions to the rule. This is why we look into this issue more systematically later in this chapter.

Pointing towards the growth-inhibiting and growth-enhancing traits of institutions to explain the vast differences in per capita income levels across countries has convinced most, but not all, people. That is why we are sketching two competing explanations here, namely geography and culture.

5.2.2 Geography

Competing conjecture 1: Economic growth is determined by geography

The French philosopher Montesquieu, who is perhaps best known for his writings on the separation of powers, conjectured that climate has an important effect on how people behave and how productive they are (Montesquieu, 1989 [1748]). Consider this straightforward example of how the climate could have a direct impact on economically relevant behavior. In very mild and temperate areas where nature offers abundant produce regardless of the time of the year, delaying consumption now to be able to consume in the future is of little value. But developing the habit of delaying current consumption so that it is possible to consume in the future is saving, saving is a precondition for investing, and investing is a precondition for economic growth. This is one very simple example of how the environment might shape people's behavior, their attitudes, and their productivity.

Webster's Dictionary defines geography as "a science that deals with the earth and its life" and mentions in particular "the description of land, sea, air and the distribution of plant and animal life including man and his industries with reference to the mutual relations of these diverse elements." When "geography" is named as a potential determinant for incomes around the world today, the term is used to synthesize a lot of quite diverse aspects. We began our discussion of geography by looking at temperature, one of many possible aspects of climate. Climate is closely related to the characteristics of the soil, the ruggedness of the terrain, and so forth. How rugged the terrain is will determine how difficult it is to connect the various parts of the country with streets. The soil, in turn, can be home to a huge variety of natural resources that might also impact upon economic development. If a country is land-locked, both exporting and importing will be relatively more difficult than if it has at least one port. But the climate together with the soil and the ruggedness of a country also determine its disease environment and so on. As this is an introductory text into institutional economics – and not into the economics of geography – we do not aspire to give a fully-fledged summary of all the aspects of geography that could impact on economic development. Instead, we mention a limited number of aspects of "geography" to exemplify the type of argument based on it. We propose to separate arguments making the point that "geography" has a very direct impact upon income levels from those that argue that the impact of "geography" is mediated via institutions. At the end of the section, objections of institutional economists regarding the relevance of "geography" are briefly summarized.

Let us begin by having a quick look at the simplest – and probably also the most important – conceivable geographical variable, namely **latitude**. Latitude measures how far away a particular country is from the Equator. Being located on or close to the Equator implies an unfavorable disease environment and low productivity due to the combination of high temperatures and humidity. The farther away a country is from the Equator implies lower temperatures and humidity and, hence, a higher expected income. In Figure 5.2, the absolute latitude of a country (i.e., its distance from the Equator) has been plotted against its 1995 per capita income in a logarithmic scale. The straight line minimizes the squared distances between the latitude–income combinations of 180 countries and the line itself. Its positive slope indicates that,

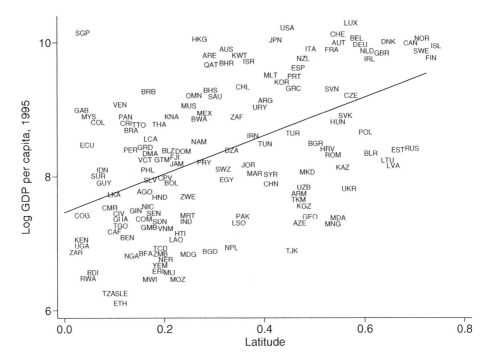

Figure 5.2 Relationship between latitude (measured as the distance of a country's capital from the Equator) and income per capita in 1995.

Source: Acemoglu (2008, 125)

as expected, more distance from the Equator is correlated with higher per capita income. As you can see, a couple of countries are far away from the line, these are commonly referred to as outliers. Singapore (depicted as SGP in Figure 5.2) is one of them. Based on its distance from the Equator, we would expect it to have an income a lot lower than that actually realized. This certainly means that there are other variables that influence current income levels. These could be other geographical traits (in the case of Singapore, for example, having access to the sea), cultural norms (if, for example, people believe that success in life is mostly determined by their own efforts, and not merely by luck), or institutional factors.

The distance from the Equator is easy to measure. However, it is little more than a black box. We can see that there is a close correlation between this distance and current income levels, but the exact channel through which a particular aspect of geography (in this case proximity to the Equator) causes growth to be high or low still needs to be unveiled. In fact, it might be any one of the many aspects mentioned above.

The most coherent argument placing geography at center stage is raised by US American scientist Jared Diamond in a number of popular books, most notably in *Guns, Germs, and Steel* (1998). During the Neolithic revolution (i.e., at the time when hunter-gatherer economies transformed themselves into pastoral production) the inhabitants of Eurasia in general, and in particular those inhabiting the area often referred to as the Fertile Crescent, enjoyed a number of advantages compared to people elsewhere. Among these were the high number of edible plants and domesticable mammals. The East–West orientation of the continent (i.e., small variation of latitudes) also allowed for rapid diffusion of agricultural innovations, because there are likely to be similar climatic conditions across the continent. Contrast that to a North–South orientation (i.e., large variation of latitudes) where one encounters a different climate fairly often, and the diffusion of innovations is correspondingly less likely.

Definition

The Fertile Crescent is the area encompassing the Nile riverbed in the west, spanning across to Mesopotamia in the east. It is fertile in terms of agricultural output, and is often considered to be the birthplace of agriculture, urbanization, writing, trade, and science.

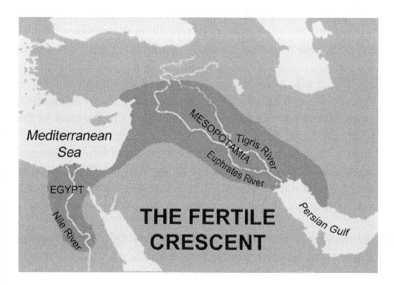

These advantages enabled this region (covering parts of modern-day Egypt, Israel, Jordan, Lebanon, Syria, and Iraq) to prosper more than other regions, to feed a growing population, and to experience an early wave of technological innovations. People from this region enjoyed a head start. Their immunity against many diseases (germs), combined with their technological advances (guns and steel) enabled them to dominate people from other regions (most notably in Latin America) who had not enjoyed a similar geography-based head start. Olsson and Hibbs (2005) tested Diamond's hypotheses empirically and found that the direct effects of geographical conditions on current income levels are remarkably strong. They show that the impact of geography, while perhaps mediated via institutions, is quite direct.

There are other studies that show that geography can impact income levels by affecting the prevalent institutions. Jeffrey Sachs is probably the best-known economist who argues that the disease environment of a country is one of the central factors determining its growth prospects. He focuses on malaria and shows that wherever malaria is prevalent, poverty is high and economic growth is low. He shows that malaria impedes development through a number of obvious channels, e.g., increased medical costs, premature mortality, absenteeism, and lower worker productivity, but also via less obvious channels such as its effect on fertility, population growth, and savings and investment behavior, to name a few.

Malaria – and the disease environment in general – as an important aspect of "geography"

A region's climate and general geography are also key determinants for the crops that are cultivated. In the northern parts of the USA, wheat and potatoes are appropriate crops, whereas in the south, cotton is more prevalent. If we go even further south, say into Latin America, the climate and geographical features may be more conducive to growing coffee. The regionality of crops determines the factors of production. Crops grown in the north use small-scale farming, whereas southern crops rely on plantations and need lots of input from cheap labor. Economic historians Stanley Engerman and Kenneth Sokoloff (2000) argue that it was not a historical accident that slaveholding was much more important in the south than in the north, rather it was a direct consequence of the prevalent geographical conditions or the relevant resource endowment. They establish, in other words, a direct link between geography and institutions. Slavery is here considered an institution because it establishes that human

Institutions a function of geography?

beings can be held as property. Slaves can be bought, owned, and sold according to the relevant property law, which is a set of institutions.

More recently, Alberto Alesina and two co-authors advanced the observation that the degree to which societies relied on the plough in traditional agriculture is a good predictor for today's role of women in society (Alesina et al., 2013). The argument that specific agricultural practices could have an important influence on gender role differences was first advanced by Ester Boserup (1970) and is straightforward: Cultivation of the soil relying on the plough requires a lot of body strength to either pull the plough or control the animal that pulls it, giving men an advantage over women. Agriculture that relies more on the hoe and the digging stick requires less strength and is more labor intensive allowing women to actively participate in farm work. Work with these tools can easily be interrupted and resumed again, a fact that is compatible with child caring, a task performed by women almost everywhere. Relying on information about whether or not the use of a plough is suitable for a particular area (i.e., geography), Alesina and his co-authors show that norms and beliefs about the appropriate role of women in society and participation of women in the workplace can be predicted based on geography. Here, geography has also had a lasting impact on culture by way of influencing the norms and beliefs regarding the proper role of women in society.

It certainly appears that geography has both a direct and an indirect effect on income levels today. Examining only a limited number of geographical factors (the East–West orientation of the continent, the simple latitude variable, or agricultural variables), we can see high correlations between geographical aspects and income levels. It seems that there is little room or even need for an explanation based on institutions. Acemoglu, Johnson, and Robinson (2002), however, stress a number of facts not compatible with this simple view. They ask a simple question – what countries were the richest in the world around the year 1500? (i.e., before the onset of colonization) – and observe that the Mughals (in India), and the Aztecs and Incas (in what is today known as Latin America) were among the richest. Since no income statistics are available for so many years back, they use two proxies for income. They look at urbanization rates and population density based on the assumption that densely populated urban centers could only emerge if

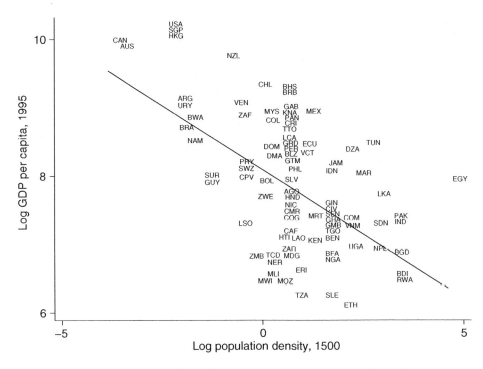

Figure 5.3 Population density in 1500 and income per capita in 1995 among former European colonies.
Source: Acemoglu (2008, 131)

agriculture was sufficiently productive to feed a large population of people who were not active in agricultural production. In addition, they look at population density based on the assumption that more densely populated areas were only possible if agricultural productivity was sufficiently high. So what do they find?

When favorable geographic conditions do not lead to high income: the reversal of fortune   If one plots the regional or national income circa 1500 against the regional or national income today, a negative correlation results (the plot is shown as Figure 5.3). In other words, countries that were rich 500 years ago tend to be poor today and countries that were poor circa 1500 tend to be rich today. Acemoglu et al. (2002) coin this occurrence the **reversal of fortune**. It took quite some time for this reversal to happen. Acemoglu and his co-authors suggest it occurred between 1800 and 1850. So this is a blow against any simple geography-based explanation and the authors go on to show that it was the differences in the quality of institutions that caused the reversal to occur. Possible

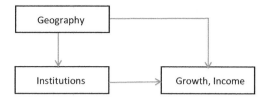

Figure 5.4 Direct and indirect effects of geography on income.

explanations for just why institutions developed so differently in different parts of the world will be discussed in Chapter 6. So if you were wondering above, how come the countries in the Fertile Crescent are not among the richest in the world today, here you have one possible answer.

There is evidence that a variety of factors often synthesized into the single term "geography" do have an impact on economic growth and income levels (Figure 5.4). And very few scholars quarrel with that insight. The main issue that separates people like Jeffrey Sachs and Jared Diamond, on the one hand, from scholars like Daron Acemoglu and James Robinson, on the other, is the channels through which these aspects of geography impact growth.

Fairly early in the debate, Bill Easterly and Ross Levine (2003) were interested in empirically estimating the relative influence of these two channels, i.e., in ascertaining the relative importance of geography compared to the relative importance of institutions. They used a handful of variables to represent geography, and another handful to represent the quality of institutions. They find that latitude, disease environment, and cultivatable crops affect development via institutions. They do not find that latitude, the disease environment, and crops have a direct effect above and beyond the effect already captured via institutions. It thus seems that explanations drawing on geography but omitting geography's effects on institutions are utterly incomplete.

5.2.3 Culture

There is no uniform position within the NIE that deals with the notion of culture. Some scholars consider aspects of culture – just as geography – to be an explanation that competes with explanations based on institutions. In their view, one must choose to focus separately on either institutions or culture. Others take a broader

Competing conjecture 2: Economic growth is determined by culture

view and consider cultural explanations to be part of institutional explanations. In our view, type 2 internal institutions do, in fact, overlap with culture.

Many proposals have been put forward in an effort to define culture. The Italian economists Luigi Guiso, Paola Sapienza, and Luigi Zingales have published many important papers on the relationship between culture and economic outcomes over the last decade. They propose to define culture as: "Those customary beliefs and values that ethnic, religious and social groups transmit fairly unchanged from generation to generation" (Guiso et al., 2006, 23). We agree that beliefs and preferences are key when defining culture but propose to be more specific regarding the way in which they are transmitted. We propose the following definition: *Culture is the sum of rules, beliefs, preferences, and values shared by others that are neither self-enforcing nor enforced by third parties.* According to this proposal, culture does not cover self-enforcing institutions (type 1 institutions), nor rules whose noncompliance is sanctioned by others (type 3 and 4 institutions). But we can think of type 2 institutions as part of culture. This proposal suggests that there is an overlap between institutions and culture. But it also suggests that some institutions are not culture and some aspects of culture do not have the quality of an institution.

Figure 5.5 shows that type 2 internal institutions are special because they can also be thought of as part of culture. Note that our definition of culture is more restrictive than many other definitions. We use this restricted delineation of culture to be able

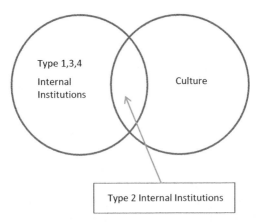

Figure 5.5 The relationship between culture and institutions.

to clearly demonstrate that type 2 internal institutions arise out of culture, while type 1, 3, and 4 internal institutions do not. In this section, only one aspect of culture will be highlighted, namely religion.

Religion is an important part of culture because it is one of the most important ways in which norms are transmitted across generations. There is a well-known theory claiming that religious beliefs have an important effect on economic development. The theory we have in mind was advanced by the German sociologist Max Weber early in the twentieth century. Weber believed that the rise of Protestantism (particularly Calvinism) brought about the internalization by its adherents of a number of secondary virtues that proved very favorable for the development of modern capitalism (Weber, 1993 [1920]). This is frequently summarized as the Protestant Ethic.

The doctrine of predestination holds that God has already chosen those whose souls will be saved. This somewhat fatalistic approach seems an unlikely start for a theory in which personal incentives are to play a major role. But Weber argues that those who are chosen by God are already better off during their lives on this earth. The religious stance goes something like this: To reduce my uncertainty as to whether I have been chosen – and to show my neighbors that I am a chosen one – I do two interrelated things: I will live an ascetic life, wasting neither time nor resources, and I will try to be productive as this is likely to make me well-off. Both of these actions will show my neighbors that I am a chosen one of God. Weber argues that the consequences of these two lifestyle choices not only led to the so-called Protestant work ethic, but also established secondary virtues such as punctuality and honesty, and a continued emphasis on the role of education.

The belief that working hard pleases God is assumed to have made believers work harder. Investing in one's children's education is assumed to increase their productivity. Secondary virtues such as punctuality and honesty imply that fewer transaction costs will arise in exchange. If my employees are on time, I need fewer resources to monitor them. If my contracting partners are honest, there will be fewer conflicts and so on. If time is precious, I will be less inclined to bargain all the time. This is Weber's explanation for fixed – and non-negotiable – prices in most of the Protestant world.

From the very beginning, this theory has polarized scholars. To this day, scholars question the accuracy of Weber's ideas. Martin Luther demanded that all Christians ought to be able to read the Bible. As a result, many Protestant churches put a lot of emphasis on education. Instituting a weekly Sunday school as part of a child's education is just one example. Becker and Woessmann (2009) try to disentangle the effect of the Protestant Ethic from the emphasis on education. They show that most of the differences in economic outcomes can be explained by the latter. According to them, the secondary virtues frequently stressed in discussions regarding Weber's argument can only claim to be of secondary relevance. More recently, Cantoni (2015) used the religious heterogeneity of the German countries between 1300 and 1900 to test Weber's conjecture empirically, and finds no effects of Protestantism on economic growth.

5.3 The Relevance of External Institutions for Economic Growth and Development

In Section 5.2, we briefly laid out the chief conjecture of the NIE, namely that the quality of institutions is the main determinant of economic growth. Over the course of the first four chapters of this book, many arguments that make this conjecture plausible have been presented. These arguments could also be called our theoretical foundation. But to avoid sounding pretentious, we will continue to refer to our key expectation – that institutions are crucial for growth – as a conjecture and not a fact.

We also critically discussed competing conjectures, namely that economic growth is primarily driven by geography or culture. Obviously, the conjecture that institutions are the main determinants of economic growth might be supported by the facts – or refuted by them. To be able to empirically test our conjecture, we need to make institutions measurable. Being able to create a measuring rod allows us to compare institutions across countries and we could then put our conjecture to an empirical test. In this section, we will spend quite a bit of time discussing one of the first indicators developed to make institutional quality comparable across countries. Since the indicator is theory-based, its presentation also enables us to complement our theoretical considerations here and there. At the end of the section, we offer a brief overview of other commonly used indicators.

Measures of institutions a necessity

The following questions are at the core of this section:

1. How can the quality of institutions be measured and compared?
2. Are good institutions closely connected with fast growth and high income levels?
3. Can an improvement in the quality of institutions induce higher economic growth?

5.3.1 How to Measure External Institutions

Surprisingly, the issue of how best to measure institutions played a rather minor role in the NIE for a long time. This is surprising because the claim that "institutions matter" can only be supported or refuted if institutions can be measured. Before attempting to measure institutions, however, a clear and concise conception of the specific institution is necessary. Trying to measure "democracy" or "the rule of law" does not seem to be a promising start. Both are made up of hundreds of different institutions. On the other hand, if we can identify and measure the various single components of, say, the rule of law, it does not seem inconceivable to then add them up and establish an overall measure. But if one is interested in dis-covering "actionable indicators" (i.e., indicators that can be used to improve the situation in a country), then an aggregate indicator that is the sum of single components will be of little use because we would not know where to begin looking for the "actionable indicator."

The presumed effects of institutions arise from both the rule and sanctioning components. This implies that both the rule and the sanctioning component should be explicitly taken into account when measuring institutions. In addition, the effects of institutions will crucially depend on the degree to which noncompliance is actually sanctioned. When we speak of sanctioning, it is critical to determine the probability of noncompliance being detected, and the severity of the ensuing sanction. Rules that exist just "in the books" are unlikely to have important effects on how real people really behave. Two institutions that are formally identical, but are implemented in different ways, are likely to lead to very different behaviors. An obvious implication seems to follow: One must not only analyze and compare institutions as they are written down in some government gazette, but try to take into account the manner in which they are actually implemented.

If one is interested in the effects of a certain institution on specific outcomes, one needs to carefully isolate the institution from the possible effect. Sounds self-evident? Well, it should be – but it is not. Many of the available indicators rely on expert surveys. Suppose the conjecture to be tested is "secure property rights are conducive to economic growth." When answering a question on the security of property rights in a specific country, the experts are likely to make their evaluation knowing the growth rates that that country has achieved over the last couple of years. If that is the case, finding a significant correlation between the two variables is extremely likely – but not very helpful in determining the true relevance of institutions. The general implication from this reflection is that objective data are more suitable than subjective evaluations.

Objectivity in measurement implies that anybody repeating the identical measurement exercise should end up with exactly the same results. This is, however, only possible if the criteria, the coding rules, the various components of a measure, are all disclosed. Unfortunately, some of the most frequently used institutional measures are not that transparent.

Equipped with these simple criteria regarding the measurement of institutions, we now proceed to present a few early attempts to measure external institutions. After that, we present and discuss one indicator in considerable detail.

5.3.2 Early Attempts to Measure External Institutions

Clague et al. (1999) have devised a simple indicator to measure the security of property rights. They measure how much cash – as opposed to bank holdings – an individual holds. They assume that *private actors prefer to hold cash when they fear that banks might renege on their contracts or simply fold.* Simply put, this indicator examines the (subjective) expectations of economic subjects with regard to one relevant aspect of the economy, and objectively measures how those expectations affect behavior. When individuals perceive property rights to be more secure, they are willing to hold more so-called **contract-intensive money** (CIM) (i.e., money that will only be available if contracts are likely to be complied with). This includes money that is used to fulfill contractual obligations to third parties. Clague et al. (1999) operationalize their concept as $(M_2 - C)/M_2$.

Definition

C is currency outside of banks and M_2 is a very broad concept of monetary supply.

The authors show that this indicator *correlates (statistically) significantly and (economically) meaningfully with investment,* even after accounting for inflation, real interest rate, and other common determinants of investment. An important advantage of this indicator is that the underlying data are available for a great number of countries and years. This distinguishes CIM from other, more elaborate indicators that are almost impossible to reconstruct for past years. Further, the indicator is based on objective data.

Henisz (2000) investigates the capability of governments to credibly commit to their own rules. The basic idea for his indicator is simple: *Unanticipated rule changes are less likely, the larger the number of (political) actors required to agree to a rule change.* Even if there is a large number of veto players or chambers, rule change is possible, as long as the members of those chambers are characterized by similar preferences. Henisz accounts for this fact by including the actual distribution of preferences. Thus, this indicator incorporates both institutional and non-institutional (policy) aspects: On the one hand, the formal institutional structure of a separation of power, and on the other hand, the non-institutional political majorities within the respective chambers. The conjectured transmission mechanism is as follows: The higher the number of veto players, the higher the level of legal security, the greater the investment, the faster the economy grows. Henisz finds that his indicator exhibits a positive effect on economic growth that is both statistically significant and economically meaningful.

Number of veto players as indicator

A possible criticism of this indicator is that Henisz has to assume that each political actor that is a *de jure* veto player is also a *de facto* veto player. It goes without saying that many courts and central banks are formally, but not *de facto* independent. Furthermore, this indicator does not tell us anything about the concrete design of institutions. Governmental credibility is probably a necessary but not sufficient condition for economic growth. In a political system with a large number of veto players but with low quality institutions, change for the better is hard to implement precisely because of the large number of veto players.

Implicitly, Henisz has to assume that existing institutions are socially beneficial.

Subjective
indicators Let us move on to studies that utilize **subjective data**. Knack and Keefer (1995) employ information that potential foreign investors use. They are interested in gauging the risk associated with investing in a specific country and comparing this risk across potential investment locations. Such data are collected in the **International Country Risk Guide** (ICRG) and sold by its producer the PRS Group. The ICRG contains several dimensions regarding the security of property rights, such as the strength of the rule of law, the risk of expropriation, the probability of the government disregarding private contracts, the extent of corruption within the government, the quality of the bureaucracy and so on. Knack and Keefer (1995) show that the ICRG index exhibits a *statistically significant correlation with economic growth.*

Brunetti et al. (1998) argue that subjective indicators of uncertainty can be superior to objective indicators. Contrasting with a number of other indicators, they prefer surveying local entrepreneurs rather than foreign investors, because the behavior of local entrepreneurs decisively influences the economic development of a country. The authors interviewed more than 2,500 entrepreneurs in low-income countries and around 200 entrepreneurs in OECD member states. Overall, they collected data from 58 countries. The sub-indicators *security of persons and property* and *predictability of rule making* are most strongly correlated with economic growth, while the sub-indicators *corruption, subjective perception of political instability*, and *predictability of judicial enforcement* are more strongly correlated with investment rates.

Having discussed several studies that seem to support the notion that the content of institutions and/or their credibility must be considered when trying to explain economic growth, we have to admit that a multitude of open questions remains. A central question is concerned with causality: Do good institutions really cause growth? It might be the other way around: Only countries that experience economic growth and have achieved a high standard of living are able to "afford" good institutions. In fact, a debate has been raging around this question ever since the publication of Lipset (1959). Acemoglu et al. (2005b and 2014) are at pains to show that the causal effect is from democracy to income (institutions to growth), and not the other way around.

5.3.3 One Measurement Attempt in Detail

5.3.3.1 Preliminary Remarks

The main concern of this section is to get acquainted with one indicator in more detail. What are its various dimensions, where does the underlying information come from, what drives particular coding choices and so on? The indicator we will look at in more detail is the Economic Freedom Index. The reason we have chosen this indicator is because it was created by relying on the advice of several very clever economists, a few of them Nobel laureates. It is also one of the first very broad indicators and, not least importantly, it has had an important impact in that it has been used in hundreds of studies.

5.3.3.2 The Economic Freedom Index

Beginning in the mid-1980s, the Canadian Fraser Institute gathered together a group of researchers to attempt to operationalize the concept of economic freedom and make it comparable across the world (Walker, 1988; Block, 1991; Easton and Walker, 1992). Their combined efforts resulted in the publication of the Economic Freedom Index (Gwartney et al., 1996; extended and updated in Gwartney et al., 2017). The first Index was published in 1996. Figure 5.6, taken directly from the 2017 edition of the Index, lists the 5 categories and 24 components of the Economic Freedom Index. In the following, we briefly present all 24 components of this Index. We will touch upon the theoretical arguments that led to including each respective component.

Size of Government

This category is concerned with determining whether resources and goods are allocated by the government or by individuals. The first variable used in this group measures **government expenditures as share of total consumption**. The higher the government share of consumption, the less free individuals are in the marketplace with regard to production and consumption decisions.

Another indicator for government influence is the **share of transfer payments and subsidies of the entire GDP**. When the value of this variable is high, representatives of the state will

1. Size of Government

   A. Government consumption

   B. Transfers and subsidies

   C. Government enterprises and investment

   D. Top marginal tax rate

     (i) Top marginal income tax rate

     (ii) Top marginal income and payroll tax rate

2. Legal System and Property Rights

   A. Judicial independence

   B. Impartial courts

   C. Protection of property rights

   D. Military interference in rule of law and politics

   E. Integrity of the legal system

   F. Legal enforcement of contracts

   G. Regulatory costs of the sale of real property

   H. Reliability of police

   I. Business costs of crime

3. Sound Money

   A. Money growth

   B. Standard deviation of inflation

   C. Inflation: most recent year

   D. Freedom to own foreign currency bank accounts

4. Freedom to Trade Internationally

   A. Tariffs

     (i) Revenue from trade taxes (% of trade sector)

     (ii) Mean tariff rate

     (iii) Standard deviation of tariff rates

   B. Regulatory trade barriers

     (i) Non-tariff trade barriers

     (ii) Compliance costs of importing and exporting

   C. Black-market exchange rates

   D. Controls of the movement of capital and people

     (i) Foreign ownership / investment restrictions

     (ii) Capital controls

     (iii) Freedom of foreigners to visit

5. Regulation

   A. Credit market regulations

     (i) Ownership of banks

     (ii) Private sector credit

     (iii) Interest rate controls / negative real interest rates

   B. Labor market regulations

     (i) Hiring regulations and minimum wage

     (ii) Hiring and firing regulations

     (iii) Centralized collective bargaining

     (iv) Hours regulations

     (v) Mandated cost of worker dismissal

     (vi) Conscription

   C. Business regulations

     (i) Administrative requirements

     (ii) Bureaucracy costs

     (iii) Starting a business

     (iv) Extra payments / bribes / favoritism

     (v) Licensing restrictions

     (vi) Cost of tax compliance

Note: Area 2 ratings are adjusted to reflect inequalities in the legal treatment of women. In Chapter 2: Country Data Tables, the adjustment factor is shown in the row labelled *Gender Disparity Index*. See Chapter 3: Adjusting for Gender Disparity in Economic Freedom and Why It Matters (pp. 189–211) for methodological details.

Figure 5.6 Overview of the components of the Economic Freedom Index.

redistribute resources according to their notions rather than paying attention to private property rights and the rules of a decentralized market. If outcomes resulting from decentralized and voluntary market exchange are not accepted, but rather corrected in a discriminatory fashion based on the whim of the state, an imbalance occurs making some better off to the detriment of others.

The third variable is concerned with the **role of state-owned enterprises.** The theoretical argument here is that privately owned firms can only survive in the market if their products correspond to consumer preferences. This is different for state-owned firms. If consumers do not pay a price that covers at least the production costs of their products, these firms are often subsidized, implying that consumers are forced – via taxes – to share in the production costs.

The last variable of this group is based on the premise that the incentives for efficient market production depend in part on the **level of taxation.** The higher the marginal tax rate for productive citizens, the lower their economic freedom.

Notice that none of the four components reflect – or even measure – institutions as such. Instead, all of them are results of policy choices made by government. The Economic Freedom Index is, hence, subject to a critique voiced by Glaeser et al. (2004) that many indicators purporting to measure institutions really only reflect policies. Their critique will be taken up in more detail below.

Legal System and Property Rights

In Chapter 2, we argued that the definition of private property rights, the contract law in place, and the procedural law of a country are crucial determinants of economic activity. The Economic Freedom Index builds on this idea in several ways. This group of variables consists of nine components. The components are named individually in Figure 5.6.

Sound Money

The basic conjecture is that a low rate of inflation (or a stable currency) protects the economic freedom of individuals by enabling them to conserve value and also to enter into predictable long-term transactions. A clear link to institutional economics is already established: the reduction of uncertainty. This group of variables consists of four indicators.

The first indicator measures the average **growth rate of money supply**. The reason for employing this indicator is because when the supply of money grows at a faster rate than GDP, undesirable inflation is the result. Inflation reduces the monetary wealth of individuals and is referred to by the publishers of the index as "wrongful seizure of property" (Gwartney et al., 1996, 3). The second indicator measures the **spread of the annual inflation rates** over the previous five years (in terms of the standard deviation).

Definition

Standard deviation: Statistical measure for the variation of a variable around its mean.

Price instability makes it more difficult for individuals to form stable expectations. Thus, a wider spread of price variations is valued negatively. The third indicator in this group measures the **current inflation rate**. The final indicator is concerned with whether citizens are allowed to **keep bank accounts in foreign currencies** and whether citizens can **legally keep bank accounts in other countries**. The ability to do these two things is valued positively because citizens are then able to substitute the domestic currency for foreign currency in order to compensate (at least partially) for any instabilities (and the associated negative effects) of the domestic currency.

These four measures are neither institutions nor policies but consequences of monetary policy. Of course, they can have substantial impacts on how people behave, but they are certainly not measures of institutions.

Freedom to Trade Internationally

This group has four variables. The basic premise here is that there is no reason to impede citizens from making profits through economic exchange or to disallow international transactions simply because a national border needs to be crossed. The first variable in this group compares the revenue from **taxes levied on international trade** as a share of total trade. The higher the level of such taxes, the more difficult it is to realize gains from trade across borders which thus lowers economic freedom. The second variable consists of two components. The first component measures how strongly **non-tariff barriers** impede cross-border trade. The second component measures the cost of adhering to **import and export regulations**. The third component indicates whether there are **black market exchange rates**. If there are currency regulations, it is usually difficult for domestic agents who are interested in international trade to obtain the required foreign currencies. The higher the black market premium for a unit of foreign currency, the more restrictive currency regulations are, resulting in more restricted economic freedom. The final indicator measures whether the mobility of both capital and people is restricted.

Extent of Regulation in Banking, Labor, and Business

The three components in this group measure the extent individuals are able to pursue their own choices without governmental intervention. This refers to both the production of goods as well as consumption choices. The question boils down to whether individuals, as market participants, decide for themselves or whether state representatives dictate these decisions.

With regard to the **regulation of banking**, three aspects are measured: Who owns banks, is credit supplied to the private sector and if so, to what extent is there governmental regulation of interest rates? With regard to the **regulation of labor**, potential restrictions of economic freedom are seen in the existence of minimum wages, regulation of hiring and firing, and whether there is mandatory military service.

The last component assesses the strength of **governmental influence towards the management of businesses**. This includes variables that indicate how expensive it is to establish a new firm and whether businesses can freely set their prices. Furthermore, this component uses variables that indicate whether bribe payments are necessary to operate businesses and how complicated it is to fulfill tax regulations.

Method of Evaluation

The Economic Freedom Index includes data from more than 150 countries for the 24 indicators. The highest possible rating of an aspect is 10, the worst is 0. The authors of the study emphasize that it is important to rely on as few value judgments as possible.

Thus, they use (when available) variables that can be operational-ized and are objectively measurable. Whenever that is not possible, they use ratings of other studies (such as the *Global Competitive-ness Report* or the *International Country Risk Guide*).

Figure 5.7 is taken from the 2017 edition of the Index. It shows the 2015 country ratings for economic freedom. The subsequent figures show correlations between the Index and various measures of wealth, such as income or income growth, but also the income share of the poorest. The results are surprisingly clear: More eco-nomic freedom is strongly correlated with better economic outcomes.

> **Note**
>
> Breaking down a distribution into equally sized groups results in quantiles. Four equal groups are called quartiles, five are called quintiles, ten are called deciles, and one hundred equal groups are called percentiles.

In Figure 5.8, the distribution of countries was grouped into four quartiles. We can see that there is a clear correlation between the extent of economic freedom and **per capita income**. Figure 5.9 shows that the relationship between economic freedom and **growth** of per capita income is not as clear.

Non-economists might interject that the importance of income and income growth is exaggerated and that other indicators such as the income share of the poorest 10 percent of the population are much more important. Figures 5.10 and 5.11 show that more economic freedom is not correlated with a lower income share of the poor. Formulated differently, extensive economic freedom and fast growth are essentially uncorrelated with income inequality.

The authors of this study assume that the results depict not mere correlations, but rather unambiguous causality.[1] Countries that increased their level of economic freedom exhibited increased growth rates only several years afterward. It is, therefore, assumed that the improvement of economic freedom caused the higher growth rates. Academics are much more critical and skeptical about buying into these conclusions. Economic freedom is, as repeatedly

---

[1] The distinction between correlation and causality is discussed in more detail in the econometrics primer in the appendix to this chapter.

Rank	Country	Score		Rank	Country	Score
1	Hong Kong	8.97		42	Czech Republic	7.46
2	Singapore	8.81		43	Belgium	7.44
3	New Zealand	8.48		43	Peru	7.44
4	Switzerland	8.44		45	Mongolia	7.43
5	Ireland	8.19		45	Qatar	7.43
6	United Kingdom	8.05		47	Seychelles	7.42
7	Mauritius	8.04		48	Bulgaria	7.39
8	Georgia	8.01		49	Bahrain	7.38
9	Australia	7.99		50	Botswana	7.37
10	Estonia	7.95		51	Poland	7.34
11	Canada	7.94		52	France	7.33
11	United States	7.94		53	Slovak Republic	7.31
13	Lithuania	7.92		54	Bahamas	7.30
14	Cyprus	7.79		54	Honduras	7.30
15	Chile	7.77		54	Hungary	7.30
15	Denmark	7.77		54	Italy	7.30
17	Finland	7.75		54	Jamaica	7.30
17	Latvia	7.75		59	Nicaragua	7.28
9	Netherlands	7.74		60	Uganda	7.25
20	Romania	7.72		61	Gambia, The	7.24
21	Malta	7.70		62	Iceland	7.23
21	Taiwan	7.70		63	Cambodia	7.21
23	Germany	7.69		63	Dominican Republic	7.21
23	Guatemala	7.69		65	Malaysia	7.19
25	Norway	7.67		66	Kazakhstan	7.18
26	Austria	7.66		67	Macedonia	7.17
27	Sweden	7.65		68	Uruguay	7.16
28	Luxembourg	7.63		69	El Salvador	7.13
29	Armenia	7.60		70	Bhutan	7.11
30	Panama	7.59		70	Kenya	7.11
31	Rwanda	7.57		72	Croatia	7.02
32	Albania	7.54		73	Indonesia	7.00
32	Korea, South	7.54		73	Slovenia	7.00
34	Portugal	7.53		75	Laos	6.98
35	Costa Rica	7.52		76	Mexico	6.95
36	Spain	7.51		77	Tanzania	6.92
37	United Arab Emirates	7.50		78	Lebanon	6.91
38	Israel	7.49		78	Paraguay	6.91
39	Japan	7.47				
39	Jordan	7.47				
39	Philippines	7.47				

Figure 5.7 The country ranking of the Index for 2015.

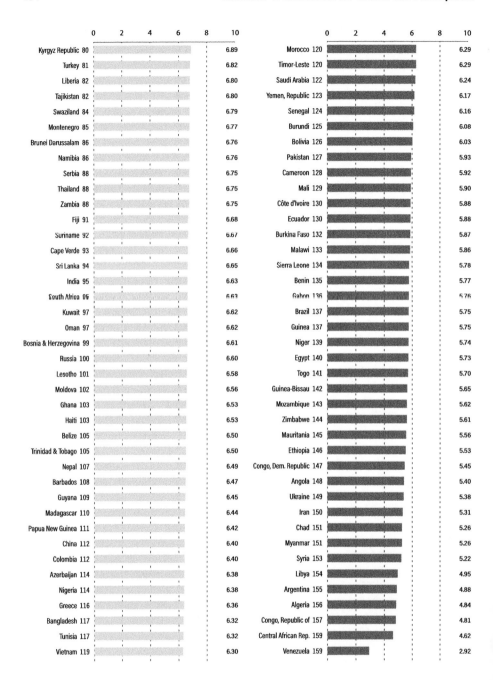

		0	2	4	6	8	10
Kyrgyz Republic	80						6.89
Turkey	81						6.82
Liberia	82						6.80
Tajikistan	82						6.80
Swaziland	84						6.79
Montenegro	85						6.77
Brunei Darussalam	86						6.76
Namibia	86						6.76
Serbia	88						6.75
Thailand	88						6.75
Zambia	88						6.75
Fiji	91						6.68
Suriname	92						6.67
Cape Verde	93						6.66
Sri Lanka	94						6.65
India	95						6.63
South Africa	95						6.63
Kuwait	97						6.62
Oman	97						6.62
Bosnia & Herzegovina	99						6.61
Russia	100						6.60
Lesotho	101						6.58
Moldova	102						6.56
Ghana	103						6.53
Haiti	103						6.53
Belize	105						6.50
Trinidad & Tobago	105						6.50
Nepal	107						6.49
Barbados	108						6.47
Guyana	109						6.45
Madagascar	110						6.44
Papua New Guinea	111						6.42
China	112						6.40
Colombia	112						6.40
Azerbaijan	114						6.38
Nigeria	114						6.38
Greece	116						6.36
Bangladesh	117						6.32
Tunisia	117						6.32
Vietnam	119						6.30

		0	2	4	6	8	10
Morocco	120						6.29
Timor-Leste	120						6.29
Saudi Arabia	122						6.24
Yemen, Republic	123						6.17
Senegal	124						6.16
Burundi	125						6.08
Bolivia	126						6.03
Pakistan	127						5.93
Cameroon	128						5.92
Mali	129						5.90
Côte d'Ivoire	130						5.88
Ecuador	130						5.88
Burkina Faso	132						5.87
Malawi	133						5.86
Sierra Leone	134						5.78
Benin	135						5.77
Gabon	136						5.76
Brazil	137						5.75
Guinea	137						5.75
Niger	139						5.74
Egypt	140						5.73
Togo	141						5.70
Guinea-Bissau	142						5.65
Mozambique	143						5.62
Zimbabwe	144						5.61
Mauritania	145						5.56
Ethiopia	146						5.53
Congo, Dem. Republic	147						5.45
Angola	148						5.40
Ukraine	149						5.38
Iran	150						5.31
Chad	151						5.26
Myanmar	151						5.26
Syria	153						5.22
Libya	154						4.95
Argentina	155						4.88
Algeria	156						4.84
Congo, Republic of	157						4.81
Central African Rep.	159						4.62
Venezuela	159						2.92

Figure 5.7 (*cont.*)

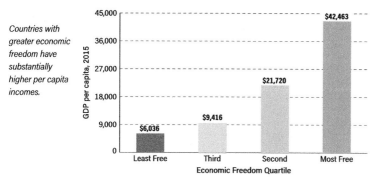

Countries with greater economic freedom have substantially higher per capita incomes.

Note: Income = GDP per capita, (PPP constant 2011 US$), 2015.
Sources: *Economic Freedom of the World: 2017 Annual Report;* World Bank, 2017, *World Development Indicators*

Figure 5.8 Economic freedom and per capita income.

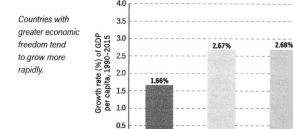

Countries with greater economic freedom tend to grow more rapidly.

Note: The growth data were adjusted to control for the initial level of income.
Sources: *Economic Freedom of the World: 2017 Annual Report;* World Bank, 2017, *World Development Indicators*

Figure 5.9 Economic freedom and per capita income growth.

pointed out above, a policy choice and, hence, endogenous. It could be that only rich countries are able to afford good institutions. If this is the case, the causality would run from income to economic freedom and not the other way round.

5.3.3.3 Criticisms of the Economic Freedom Index

Let us now consider some critical issues regarding the design of the Economic Freedom Index. These issues are, in fact, important for the construction of all indices.

*The share of
income earned
by the poorest
10% of the
population
is unrelated
to economic
freedom.*

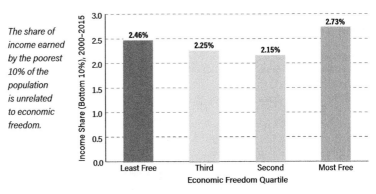

Sources: *Economic Freedom of the World: 2017 Annual Report*; World Bank, 2017,
World Development Indicators

Figure 5.10 Economic freedom and the income share of the poorest 10%.

*The amount
of income, as
opposed to the
share, earned by
the poorest 10%
of the population
is much higher
in countries with
higher economic
freedom.*

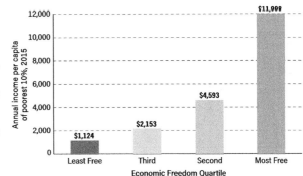

Note: Annual income per capita of poorest 10% (PPP constant 2011 US$), 2015
Sources: *Economic Freedom of the World: 2017 Annual Report*; World Bank, 2017,
World Development Indicators

Figure 5.11 Economic freedom and the income earned by the poorest 10%.

1. The weighting issue: As mentioned above, the Economic Freedom Index consists of 24 different indicators. The underlying
   idea is to aggregate various important aspects into a single
   number. But according to what aggregation rule? Are all
   24 indicators equally important? As just described, the authors
   of the Economic Freedom Index group their 24 indicators into
   five different areas. Should all five areas be attributed equal
   weight? And if not, how should the weights be determined?
   Are there convincing arguments that all areas are necessary for
   citizens to enjoy economic freedom? If that is the case, it might

make sense to multiply the values of the areas with each other. If, however, low scores in one area can be compensated by high ones in another area, adding up the various scores makes more sense.

2. Institutions have been defined as rules endowed with a sanctioning mechanism. Policies can be thought of as choices made by politicians under given institutions. And outcomes are the consequences of policy choices. The Economic Freedom Index consists of all three types of indicators. As an index for the quality of institutions, it is, therefore, not entirely adequate.

3. Above, it was argued that objective indicators enjoy the advantage of being replicable by any scholar interested in replicating them over subjective indicators that measure the perceptions and evaluations of individuals. Some of the indicators used here rely, however, on subjective measures.

The Economic Freedom Index is only one among quite a few measures that have been produced over the last ten or fifteen years. We cannot give all of them the same detailed discussion we gave to the Economic Freedom Index, but the following box summarizes the basic purposes of many of them.

A short summary of several indicators

1. The non-governmental organization *Freedom House* annually publishes the report **Freedom in the World,** which includes two indicators: one concerning **political rights** and one concerning **civil liberties**. The 195 countries included in the study are rated on a scale of 1 (free) to 7 (not free). Freedom House has made these indicators available since 1973. Freedom House also publishes an indicator on press freedom.

2. A group of researchers are responsible for the **Polity IV** indicators, which aim to capture the **extent of democracy** as actually realized across countries and years. Countries that are completely autocratic are coded −10, while perfect democracies are coded +10. The indicator codes countries all the way back to 1800. This makes it a very valuable source of data for studies interested in the long run.

3. Polity IV does have its critics. One frequently raised point claims that democracy and dictatorship are categorical

concepts where you either are democratic or not. A continuous scale would, hence, not make much sense. On the basis of this idea, Cheibub et al. (2010) propose a **Democracy–Dictator** indicator which is available for 199 countries on an annual basis between 1946 and 2009.

4. The first couple of indicators deal with broadly conceived civil and political rights; we now turn to indicators interested in reflecting economic institutions. The indicator that is conceptually very similar to the **Economic Freedom Index** is the **Index of Economic Freedom** which is published by the conservative *Heritage Foundation* jointly with the *Wall Street Journal*. It is published annually and covers up to 186 countries for the period from 1995 until today.

5. The *World Economic Forum*, which is best known for its annual convention in Davos, publishes the annual **Global Competitiveness Report**, which tries to quantify a nation's competitiveness based on twelve dimensions. To a large degree the indicator relies on the evaluations of experts, mostly business people. In its current construction, it has been available since 2004. It is produced on a yearly basis for 137 countries.

6. A similar report, the **World Competitiveness Yearbook**, is published by the *Business School IMD* in Lausanne. It also relies on a mixture of survey and expert data and also has its primary focus on competitiveness. Its advantage over the Global Competitiveness Report is that its data go back to 1989; its disadvantage is that it only covers 60 countries.

7. The last three indicators briefly portrayed cover a country's environment for private business in a fairly general manner. This is different for the next two indicators to be presented. They are for profit indicators that cater to (potential) foreign investors who are interested in the particular risks they might be subject to in their destination country. The *Political Risk Services Group* (located in Syracuse, New York) publishes the **International Country Risk Guide**, which is used by potential foreign investors to gauge the security of investing in countries all over the world. It has been published since 1980 on a monthly basis.

8. A very similar analysis called **Business Risk Service** is published by *Business Environment Risk Intelligence*. The

company has been around since the 1960s and it produces risk assessments for 50 countries three times a year. Almost needless to say, the indicator is based on expert evaluations.

9. *Transparency International* is a globally active non-governmental organization whose main goal is to fight corruption. Since 1995, it annually publishes the **Corruption Perceptions Index** (CPI), which assesses the perceived level of corruption in up to 176 countries. Objective data are very hard to get regarding corruption. The CPI is based on a variety of different surveys. This is why it has also been called a survey of surveys.

10. Since 2003, the *Bertelsmann Foundation* has been publishing the **Bertelsmann Transformation Index** (BTI), which tries to document the institutional development of up to 129 less developed countries. Its premise is that sustainable development will only be achieved with an adequate change in both political and economic institutions and is divided into political transformation, economic transformation, and an index of "transformation management" which tries to evaluate the quality of transformation management by the respective governments. The BTI is produced on the basis of expert evaluations.

11. Since 2008, the *World Justice Project* has published its **Rule of Law Index**. It measures the rule of law according to 47 indicators grouped around 8 themes. It is composed of two surveys, namely a general population survey as well as an expert survey and has been carried out in 113 countries.

12. The **Worldwide Governance Indicators**, published by the *World Bank* since 1996, consist of six composite indicators that are compiled on the basis of a multitude of available data from other organizations. It has been heavily criticized for various reasons, the most basic one that it lacks a clear theoretical foundation.

5.3.4 Results of Empirical Studies

Figures 5.8–5.11 are a graphic representation of the bivariate relationship between the Economic Freedom Index and one other variable (namely per capita income, income growth, and income share of the poorest 10 percent). Bivariate (based on two variables) relationships are easy to depict graphically. However, we should not draw any premature conclusions based on bivariate relationships. For instance, it could well be that economic growth is influenced by a number of other factors, including the rate of investment, population growth, the rate of inflation, and global market integration, just to name a few. Further, the direction of causality is unclear. And further still, the two variables might only be correlated, and determined by yet another variable. In order to arrive at reliable results, we need to employ **multivariate** methods that account for this multitude of influences. Over the last 15 years, quite a few studies have tried to determine the effects that institutions have on economic growth. Rather than a systematic survey, we will only highlight the main findings of several studies that set the path for many subsequent papers.

We now know that the Economic Freedom Index contains 24 indicators. Let us assume the objective of a politician is to increase the rate of economic growth. Turning to the Economic Freedom Index as a source of information that might help in achieving this objective will probably not be very useful. In all likelihood, not all indicators have a significant effect on growth. Starting from this possibility, several authors have attempted to discover which areas covered by the Index are significantly correlated with growth – and which are not. According to one study (Carlsson and Lundström, 2002), the only variables that survive all robustness tests relate to legal structure and the security of private property rights. The variable concerning the freedom to use foreign currency comes close, while all other indicators failed robustness checks.

Estimations are considered to be robust if moderate modifications of the model do not significantly change their qualitative results

Now, empirical confirmation that the security of private property is key accords well with theoretical priors. In fact, quite a few studies interested in a simple measure for the quality of institutions rely on the security of private property rights.

Earlier in this chapter, we mentioned that some economists believe geography is the single most important determinant of economic growth and income. We presented the results of a study by Easterly and Levine (2003). They show that if one explicitly controls for the effects of geography mediated via institutions, the direct effects of geography are of secondary importance. The outcome of a study by Rodrik et al. (2004) is unambiguously summarized in its title, namely *Institutions Rule*. The authors of this study run a "horse race" between three competing explanations, namely geography, institutions, and international trade. By now, you are very familiar with the first two approaches. The third one argues that growth will pick up considerably when a country is closely connected with the rest of the world via international trade. The Rodrik et al. study is broader than that by Easterly and Levine because it takes international trade explicitly into account. But the main results are very similar as Rodrik et al. also find that institutions are crucial for economic development. Geography is important in the sense that it has an effect on institutions. The direct channel from geography to growth again appears to be rather negligible.

A significant paper by Acemoglu and Johnson (2005) adds another aspect to the discussion. They propose to separate ("unbundle") property rights institutions from contracting institutions. The idea is that secure private property rights primarily imply protection from government intervention. The government cannot simply take property away from you without adequate compensation. Contracting institutions basically enable people to enter into contracts voluntarily. If private firms want to enter into contractual relations with each other, they can often also do so without relying on the state. If private firms are not comfortable with contracting institutions provided by the state, they might turn to privately provided ones (e.g., those offered by private arbitration organizations). Sidestepping the government with regard to property rights institutions is, however, impossible. Based on this argument, Acemoglu and Johnson expect the security of private property rights to be relatively more important for economic growth than contracting institutions. Their hypothesis is supported by their empirical analysis.

In sum, there is strong evidence that institutions affect economic outcomes significantly. This not only holds for bivariate correlations (on which we spent some time because they can easily be depicted in figures) but also for analyses based on multivariate models.[2]

5.3.5 Institutions or Policies?

The first attempts to empirically estimate the relevance of institutions for the growth of economies are relatively recent. Comparable data for the quality of institutions across countries have

---

[2] In addition, the papers described in this section also take some other econometric worries – such as endogeneity – explicitly into account. A little more on these issues can be found in the appendix at the end of this chapter.

become widely available only since the mid-1990s. In these early investigations, the question of whether or not such data are suitable to measure the quality of institutions was not widely considered.

Don't mistake policies for institutions

Glaeser et al. (2004) are an exception. They put forward a general critique of these estimations, arguing that many studies did not measure the effects of institutions, but rather the effects of policies. They further suggest that institutions have to be relatively stable over time in order to constrain political behavior. This is not compatible with the observation that many institutional indicators vary significantly over short time periods. Glaeser et al. (2004) conclude that such studies measure – at least partially – the effects of short-term policies instead of long-term institutions. Although this critique is overstated in many regards, the conclusion that empirical indicators for institutions should be assessed for their quality is surely justified.

The studies we have discussed so far are concerned with the analysis of external institutions and their enforcement. In the following, we will consider the potential relevance of internal institutions for economic growth and societal development.

5.4 The Relevance of Internal Institutions for Economic Growth and Development

Only recently did the relationship between internal institutions and economic development attract the interest of economists. Before 2000, there were almost no empirical studies analyzing this relationship. Since then, quite a few studies have inquired into the effects of different concepts such as trust and culture on economic

Individual beliefs and economic growth

development. Before turning to some empirical results, we present a few theoretical arguments connecting both beliefs and internal institutions with economic development. Remember that institutions come with a sanctioning mechanism whereas beliefs do not. Putting aside the interrelationship between internal and external institutions, the primary question is which internal institutions are conducive for economic growth and development.

The following individual beliefs and internal institutions have been argued to be conducive to economic growth (Voigt, 1993):

1. *The individual is responsible for setting his/her own objectives, for the choice of means to reach them, and the degree to which they are actually reached.* If a large proportion of actors are

convinced that individual effort is irrelevant for their achievements and that fate or God or some other external factor
determines their success, it is hard to picture a prosperous
economy with many entrepreneurs and high rates of economic
growth. It is equally difficult to imagine a functioning system of
private property rights, given that property rights represent a
link between individual efforts and the fruits of those efforts.
Private property rights not only give the rights holders the right
to use and sell a good, but also imply a certain responsibility
for their property (such as a cattle herd trampling a
neighbor's crops).

2. *Economically successful individuals are considered to be role
   models rather being frowned upon.* This implies that perceived
   inequality resulting from differences in (legitimately attained)
   economic success is accepted to some degree. Furthermore, envy
   can be associated with positive effects if it induces incentives to
   imitate the envied.

3. *Actors are socially and geographically mobile.* Geographical
   mobility is advantageous as it enables the efficient combination
   of mobile input factors with immobile input factors. This atti-
   tude should be shared even by immobile societal members. If
   immobile actors share an aversion for the unknown – for
   instance, because they fear increased competition and resulting
   wage decreases – an inefficiently low factor mobility might
   result, leaving unrealized growth potential on the sidewalk.
   Social mobility implies that individuals can climb as well as
   descend the social ladder. If individuals that have climbed the
   social ladder are thought of as role models, higher growth could
   result through imitation. Optimally, individuals that have des-
   cended in their social status should not be stigmatized to prevent
   higher risk aversion and decreased entrepreneurship.[3]

4. *A certain portion of society behaves innovatively.* Innovative
   behavior is not only limited to production decisions, but can

---

[3] Tocqueville (2003 [1840], 274) describes a society in which social descent is not
associated with stigmatization: "In the United States hardly anybody talks of
the beauty of virtue, but they maintain that virtue is useful and prove it every
day. The American moralists do not profess that men ought to sacrifice themselves for their fellow creatures because it is noble to make such sacrifices, but
they boldly aver that such sacrifices are as necessary to him who imposes them
upon himself as to him for whose sake they are made."

also refer to consumption choices. The latter, the so-called *consumption pioneers*, are crucial with regard to the diffusion of new products.

5. *Large parts of society share a certain level of tolerance.* There is a broad acceptance that other people are different and that this difference is a good thing. It is important that a society does *not exhibit a militant aversion against the unknown*. This relates to foreign investors and foreign workers, but also to foreign products.

6. Large sections of society are willing to accept that some individuals will attain *great prosperity with seemingly unproductive activities*, such as financial services.

7. Large parts of society share certain *secondary virtues*, such as honesty, punctuality, and so on. If, for a simple transaction, one can reasonably expect not to be cheated, the resulting transaction costs will be lower.

Naturally, many individuals who do not share the above listed beliefs reside in countries with a high per capita income or high growth rates. Thus, the mere pervasiveness of such individual beliefs and internal institutions cannot be a necessary condition for high economic growth. At the same time, individuals who exhibit the beliefs listed above should not be impeded in behaving according to these beliefs. Put differently, although it might not be necessary that appropriate institutions support the beliefs listed above, existing institutions should not punish individuals who base their behavior on these beliefs. These are just tentative arguments on this topic which need to be expanded. For instance, one could ask whether there is a threshold share of the population that should hold the listed attitudes in order to ensure sustainable economic growth.

To be able to test these conjectures empirically, measures for beliefs and trust are needed. The following box briefly summarizes some of the sources that economists have used to make beliefs and trust comparable across countries or regions.

How to measure beliefs and trust?

A number of indicators have been presented that are often used as proxies for external institutions. Here is a short overview of sources often used to generate indicators for trust and beliefs. Unfortunately, a list of indicators measuring internal institutions proper cannot be offered as measurement of internal institutions clearly lags behind the measurement of external institutions. Measurement of internal institutions is a serious challenge for scholars within the NIE.

1. Geert Hofstede is a social psychologist and former IBM manager who proposed four basic dimensions to identify the effects of culture on values. These are power distance, individualism, uncertainty avoidance, and masculinity. Hofstede conducted several IBM employee surveys; the largest survey polled 117,000 employees. This was the first broad survey-based cross-country study. Since these employees share many characteristics and attitudes, the differences in their beliefs can be more easily ascribed to the different national cultures to which they belong.

2. The **World Values Survey** was first conducted in 1981, with six subsequent waves. With some 250 items, the survey delves into many details of a person's values and beliefs. The current survey includes a representative sample of the entire population of almost 100 countries. One item of the survey directly asks about trust: "Generally speaking, would you say that most people can be trusted or that you need to be very careful in dealing with people?" In a host of studies, the percentage of the population that answers "most people can be trusted" has been used as a measure for the societal level of trust in the respective country. But the survey also asks a number of questions that have been used as measures for culture. They include questions about:
   • beliefs in the importance of individual effort;
   • generalized morality;
   • obedience.

3. *Gallup* is a US based management consultancy firm that has become famous for its polls. The **Gallup World Poll** is an opinion survey that includes questions on confidence in institutions and personal well-being. It is conducted in more than 160 countries worldwide and has been used mainly by international organizations but also by some scholars.

> 4. Similar to Gallup, the *Pew Research Center* is also known for its surveys. The survey most relevant for the measurement of internal institutions across the globe is its **Global Attitudes Project** that covers topics such as a personal assessment of one's own life, religion, crime and corruption, and political participation.
> 5. The GLOBE study on culture, leadership, and organization is interested in the impact of different values and norms on firm behavior, in particular different leadership models. GLOBE is an acronym derived from "Global Leadership and Organizational Behavior Effectiveness Research Program." Some of their nine dimensions extend beyond firm behavior and have also been used as proxies for preferences and beliefs more generally. The GLOBE data are compiled from questionnaire responses of 17,300 middle managers in 951 corporations and 62 societies.

Trust is conducive to economic growth … In Chapter 2, you were introduced to Putnam's (1993) analysis on the effects of trust on the quality of local governments. His argument is that the *de facto* quality of Italy's institutions can be explained by the extent of civil society. La Porta et al. (1997) ask whether these results might be generalizable beyond the case of Italy. The authors use data from the World Values Survey and attempt to measure the propensity to trust by examining the extent to which actors exhibit trust towards others. La Porta et al. (1997) find that trust has a statistically significant and quantitatively meaningful effect on the economy.

La Porta and his co-authors are not the only ones who find that trust has important economic effects. Guiso et al. (2006) find that trust is associated with a higher likelihood of becoming a successful entrepreneur. In settings where contracts are incomplete (in other words, everywhere), contracts always involve a certain amount of trust. Being perceived as trustworthy has an advantage as it will facilitate the conclusion of contracts. People believed to be trustworthy, therefore, enjoy a comparative advantage as entrepreneurs. Higher levels of trust are also associated with lower levels of corruption (Uslaner, 2002; Bjørnskov, 2010) and stronger economic performance (Knack and Keefer, 1997; Zak and Knack, 2001).

The relevance of beliefs regarding others' trustworthiness

Trustworthiness is not only likely to make you a more successful entrepreneur, it also affects international trade. The trustworthiness of people in other countries is often not determined by our experience but by our beliefs. Assume, for instance, that Swedes do not believe Spaniards to be trustworthy but believe Austrians to be so. If that is the case, then Swedes are unlikely to trade many goods with Spaniards which gives them few reasons to ever correct their beliefs. In other words, beliefs can be an important determinant of trade patterns, even if they are not substantiated by any real-life experience. These conjectures are empirically supported by the work of Guiso et al. (2004a, 2004b). This holds for trade in goods, as well as investment across borders.

There is, however, an institutionalist school that makes the argument that trust might also be determined by the institutional environment. In other words, trust might not be exogenous. On the other hand, the culturalist school argues that people learn a basic sense of trust early in life. As a consequence, at least the core of trust is assumed to be stable over time. And there is substantial evidence that this is really the case. For example, emigrants from low-trust regions in southern Italy carry their mistrust with them to their new locations (Guiso et al., 2004a). Similarly but more generally, Berggren and Bjørnskov (2011) find that differences in trust levels between US states today are directly related to the country of origin of the families who immigrated to a particular state. To recap, trust levels are often remarkably stable. This makes it possible to treat them as "quasi exogenous" and to use them as explanatory variables as has been done many times as just reported.

… but what determines trust?

If you recall our earlier discussion, the north of Italy performed significantly differently from the south. This is astonishing considering the entire country has been subject to the same external institutions for more than 150 years. As described in Chapter 2, Putnam (1993) argued that these differences could best be explained by historical factors. But there were at least two issues that shed doubt on the reliability of his results: (1) the number of

Italian regions is fairly small and reliable econometric tests were not possible on the limited dataset; (2) the study was confined to a single country, namely Italy.

Being inspired by Putnam's analysis, and taking the possible weaknesses of that analysis explicitly into account, Italian economist Guido Tabellini (2010) puts forth the observation that formally identical institutions can have very different consequences. He goes on to conjecture that internal institutions might actually be more important than external ones. He asks whether stable components of culture can explain differences in the economic development of regions that share formally identical external institutions. This implies that he assumes culture is an important determinant in the way external institutions are actually implemented.

Guido Tabellini expands on Putnam's study by analyzing a larger number of regions – namely 69 – in eight different countries (the UK, the Netherlands, Belgium, France, Spain, Portugal, Italy, and Germany). He relies on survey answers taken from the World Values Survey to capture four different aspects of culture: trust, respect for others, individual self-determination, and obedience. The first three aspects are assumed to have positive effects, the fourth one negative effects. The first two traits are assumed to increase the number of welfare-enhancing social interactions, including anonymous exchange, but also the voluntary participation in the provision of public goods. The latter traits are assumed to make entrepreneurial behavior more likely. In a sense, the first two traits capture what has been called "social capital" and the latter ones something akin to "confidence in the individual."

There is a strong correlation between culture and economic development. Unfortunately, that is insufficient to prove that it is culture that determines economic development. Remember that the causation could also run from economic development to culture. How do we resolve this ubiquitous problem? By relying on instrumental variables. Tabellini does not assume culture to be completely invariant over time. He believes that historical institutions shaped culture as defined by him. He proposes two instruments, namely the literacy rate in the second half of the nineteenth century and the quality of political institutions between 1600 and 1850. The quality of political institutions is measured by determining the degree to which the executive was constrained in its actions. The more constrained, the more predictable its behavior. The idea is schematically depicted in Figure 5.12.

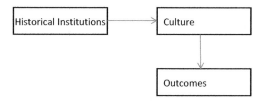

Figure 5.12 Instrumenting culture with historical institutions.

To exclude the possibility that it was economic development in 1850 that determined culture, Tabellini includes a variable that controls for economic development at that time. Since no reliable income data are available, he uses the degree of urbanization in 1850 based on the assumption that city inhabitants relied on more modern technology and were more productive. Tabellini finds that his culture variable is significant for explaining both differences in productivity levels and growth across the 69 regions analyzed.

5.5 On the Interplay between External and Internal Institutions and its Relevance for Economic Growth and Development

In Section 5.3, we showed that adequate external institutions are associated with high rates of economic growth. In Section 5.4, we showed that there are plausible theoretical arguments and some empirical evidence for a positive relationship between adequate internal institutions and economic growth. There are, however, hardly any empirical studies that examine the interplay between external and internal institutions and its relevance for economic growth.

In Chapter 1, we suggested that it is possible to distinguish four relationships between external and internal institutions. They can be (1) complementary, (2) substitutive, (3) conflicting, and (4) neutral. Williamson and Mathers (2011) inquire whether good external and good internal institutions independently of each other have a positive effect on growth or whether it is sufficient to have either good external or good internal institutions. Coined differently, they are interested in determining whether good external and good internal institutions act as complements or as substitutes. Their approach is straightforward. They use the Economic Freedom Index (described earlier) as a proxy for good external institutions and follow the approach taken by Tabellini (described in Section 5.4) as a proxy for favorable internal institutions (culture). They find good external institutions to be vastly more important than good internal ones, lending support to the view that the relationship between external and internal institutions is substitutive, rather than complementary. Their study is definitely only a very first take on this important question.

5.6 Open Questions

Traditional growth economics assumes that economic growth can be explained solely by the factors of labor and capital. New growth economics brings the role of human capital into the equation by indirectly measuring the quality of the educational system in a country. But fundamentally, neither branch of growth economics considers the quality of institutions, such as economic freedom rights, to affect the growth rate of an economy. In the language of growth economics: The effect of institutions on growth is primarily mediated via the so-called total factor productivity. Institutional economists conjecture that neither physical nor human capital actually causes growth on its own. It is the interaction of these factors with institutions that determines the degree of economic growth.

Over the last two decades, many scholars have devoted lots of time to dealing with these issues and there are many contributions that we cannot describe in detail here. For instance, whether the legal origins of a country – operationalized by the distinction between *common law* and *civil law* countries – are relevant for the current quality of financial markets (see e.g., La Porta et al., 1998, 1999). Another strand of literature considers the conditions that must be met for "implanted legal orders" to be actually implemented in the importing country and exhibit positive effects (see Pistor, 2002).

QUESTIONS

1. Discuss advantages and disadvantages of subjective data vs. objective data.
2. Think of other criteria you could use to categorize datasets for comparing institutional quality in different countries.
3. Discuss mechanisms through which a democratic form of government might impact the growth prospects of an economy.

4. Discuss why a "maximization" of economic freedom is probably not socially beneficial. Begin by defining what a maximization of economic freedom means.

5. Section 5.4 contains a list of seven factors supposedly conducive to economic growth without explicitly separating beliefs from internal institutions. Go through the list and separate them from each other.

6. Show that the widespread acceptance of secondary virtues such as honesty and punctuality can be associated with reduced transaction costs.

FURTHER READING

Daron Acemoglu and James Robinson are probably the staunchest representatives of the view that it is only institutions, not geography or culture, that determine economic development. An accessible yet precise and detailed summary of their main contributions is Acemoglu and Robinson (2005).

Jeffrey Sachs is probably their most popular counterpart arguing that it is geography, particularly the disease environment, that determines the growth prospects of a country. One concise statement of his position can be found in Sachs and Malaney (2002). Both Acemoglu and Robinson as well as Sachs have their own blogs. If you are interested in discovering why each side believes it has the better arguments, you might want to turn there (whynationsfail.com and jeffsachs.org, respectively).

Scholars affiliating themselves with the NIE are united in their conviction that institutions are important. For a long time, however, the question of how to measure institutions only received scant attention. Voigt (2013) takes up the question and makes a number of proposals. Some attempts to make institutions measurable have been met with fierce criticism. The indicators produced by the World Bank are particularly prone to critique. This holds true both for the *Worldwide Governance Indicators* as well as for *Doing Business*. The latter purports to measure the difficulty of setting up shop and compares it over many countries. The underlying assumption seems to be "the cheaper the better." This view has been criticized by many. A number of formal requirements to register a business might be costly now, but might still have overall positive returns. Arruñada (e.g., 2007) points out that the existence of up-to-date registries can save lots of costs later on (like finding out who owns what parcel of land, who are the owners of a particular firm, how creditworthy a firm is, and so on).

The Nobel Prize in 1993 was awarded to Douglass North. As an economic historian, he put a lot of emphasis on the role of institutions for development over time (see North, 1994).

Virtually all indicators briefly presented above are available online. The Economic Freedom Index has an appendix which lists a selection of publications that utilize the Index. Haan and Sturm (2000) is just one example of a study which critically discusses the Economic Freedom Index.

The debate as to whether democracy causally induces higher economic growth or higher economic growth leads to a demand for democracy, originates from Lipset (1959). Przeworski and Limongi (1993) is a survey of empirical studies. Acemoglu et al. (2014) is an attempt to prove that democracy does cause growth, relying on up-to-date econometric tools as well as recently published datasets. The modern classic arguing that extending the franchise leads to more redistributive policies is Meltzer and Richard (1981).

Using settler mortality as an instrument for the quality of institutions has been very successful, but has not remained without critics. For instance, Albouy (2012) heavily criticizes the way in which Acemoglu et al. (2001) produced their numbers; Acemoglu et al. (2012) is the response to these criticisms.

The most comprehensive study regarding the function and effects of envy is by Helmut Schoeck (1987).

The appendix tries to give you an impression of what econometrics is all about. There are a host of very serious introductions to econometrics available. If you want to read a funny one, I suggest you turn to Studenmund (2010). Angrist and Pischke (2009) is a wonderful companion for people who want to use econometrics and reassure themselves of the implied underlying assumptions. How the science of statistics evolved is described amusingly in Salsburg (2001).

Appendix

A Ten-Minute Primer in Econometrics

Econometrics is the subdiscipline of economics that is concerned with the measurement and statistical analysis of economically relevant variables. Naturally, ten minutes are not enough to teach you everything that is taught over several semesters in econometrics courses. Here, we will make you familiar with some core ideas of econometrics.

Econometric techniques are used to empirically assess questions regarding causal relationships. An example of a question highly relevant in the NIE could be: "Does democracy cause growth?" To answer this question (or other questions on causal relationships) a so-called randomized experiment would be ideal. With regard to our question, this could mean making half of the world's countries democracies and the other half autocracies in a random fashion. Because countries are chosen randomly, other factors – like their geographical location, their resource endowment, and so on – are unlikely to distort the findings. Econometricians would argue that under randomization, selection bias is negligible or even non-existent. In other words, the findings would be undistorted. Unfortunately, most real-world institutions do not allow for randomized experiments. To answer the question whether democracy causes growth convincingly, we would like to make half of the world democracies not today, but 100 or 200 years ago to be able to ascertain possible long-term effects. As time-machines have not been invented, such experiments are impossible even with loads of research grants.

So choosing a convincing research strategy boils down to the question of how closely one can mimic randomized experiments when drawing on natural experiments or on existing observational data. Natural experiments are instances in which institutional change was implemented thanks to "mother nature." Some exogenous event might take place that can be used to make causal inferences. Earlier in this chapter, we argued that the way Germany was divided after World War II, and the way their institutions were implemented in the two newly established countries, was something like a natural experiment.

Even when we think hard about natural experiments that might be used to establish a causal relationship, sometimes none will come to mind. In such cases, most researchers proceed by relying on observational data. These come with many problems, but econometricians have developed lots of useful tools to mitigate these problems. Selection bias was already mentioned. The influence of variables not taken explicitly into account ("omitted variable bias"), or the possibility that growth causes democracy and not the other way round ("reversed causality"), are other examples of such problems. The ways in which researchers handle these problems are often called their **identification strategy**. The term describes the ways in which observational data are used to mimic a real experiment.

The final issue is concerned with the most adequate estimators given certain properties of the conjectured underlying relationship (for instance, if it is linear or not) and the data (whether the dependent variable is binary or not, for example). In what follows, our intention is to give you a feel for the most frequently used estimator in econometrics: ordinary least squares.

Assume we are concerned with the question whether body height is correlated with body weight. Note that we do not speak of causation here but simply of correlation. Further assume that we obtained information for some 100 students concerning their body weight as well as their height. In two-dimensional space, we are then able to depict each student as a point which reflects the respective combination of body weight and height. We conjecture that body height and weight might be positively correlated, i.e., taller students tend to be heavier. Looking at the scatter plot here, we find evidence in favor of that conjecture. Say we are interested in knowing the expected weight difference between two students of height 170 cm and 180 cm. In order to find that out, we draw a straight line through the scatter plot. One common way of determining the gradient of this line is the following rule: Draw the line such that the sum of the squared differences between the respective data points and the line is minimized. This method is called *Ordinary Least Squares*, often abbreviated OLS.

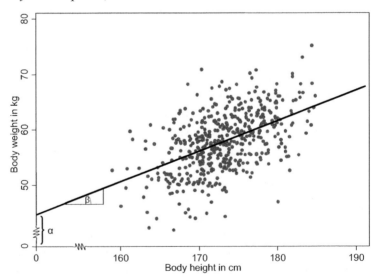

In terms of a mathematical equation, what we just described can be formulated as:

$$y = \alpha + \beta x + \epsilon$$

where y is the dependent (or explained) variable, in our example body weight. In another context, the dependent variable could just as well be per capita income or the rate of economic growth. x is the independent (or explanatory) variable, here body height. In another context, this might be the quality of institutions or democracy. The value of β, which tells us about the slope of the fitted line, is of primary interest. It tells us how strongly a change in x translates into a change in y. However, it makes sense to assume that body weight is not solely determined by height (in the same manner that economic growth is not solely determined by democracy). For instance, bone structure (or the rate of investment) might be another relevant factor. We can account for this additional factor by expanding the above equation to:

$$y = \alpha + \beta x + \gamma b + \epsilon$$

Although we can no longer depict this relationship in two-dimensional space, the estimation should be more precise. "Estimate" here means that we assume that there is some "true" relationship between the independent and the dependent variable in the real world and by drawing on the data at our disposal we try to "estimate" this relationship as accurately as possible. What is the meaning of the remaining Greek letters? α describes the intercept. For instance, a positive α shows that even for a value of zero for x (and β), the value of y is still positive. ϵ is the so-called error term and contains all that cannot be explained by the explanatory variables.

To be able to "explain" the dependent variable, the independent or explanatory variable needs to be "exogenous" from the model, meaning that its value is not influenced by any other component of the model but comes from outside the model. Until now, we have assumed that this is the case. But in reality, it is often not the case. For example, to this point we have implicitly assumed that good institutions (such as secure property rights) will cause faster growth and higher income. But the reverse relationship might also be true, namely, that only more affluent societies can "afford" to implement good institutions. This is also called "reverse causality" which is a particularly severe form of the absence of exogeneity (the "absence of exogeneity" is also referred to as **endogeneity**). This problem is particularly severe with regard to institutions. Institutions are never truly exogenous, as they are always man-made. How do we resolve this quandary?

Econometricians have come up with a number of proposals as to how endogeneity can be dealt with. Here, we focus on a particularly intuitive and popular approach, called **instrumental variables**. The basic idea is straightforward: If we are not sure whether the explanatory variable is truly exogenous, we ask whether this variable is, in turn, determined by another variable that could not possibly have been influenced by the dependent variable. To illustrate, let us continue with the example from above. An adequate instrument for "good institutions" would determine their quality but would be completely independent from the assumed outcome, namely income. Acemoglu et al. (2001) made an ingenious proposal for such an instrument. They assert that European colonizers had very different incentives to set up good institutions depending on the local mortality rate in the respective colonies. Their rationale is that in areas with high settler mortality, colonizers were interested in becoming rich quickly and then leaving the area. Thus, they had incentives to set up what Acemoglu and his co-authors call "extractive institutions." In contrast, in areas where settler mortality was low, colonizers might really settle and develop a long-term horizon, perhaps even thinking that their children and grandchildren could also live there. They had, therefore, incentives to set up good institutions, including secure property rights. It is easy to see that per capita income today has no effect on settler mortality rates hundreds of years ago. Endogeneity can, hence, be excluded, which is exactly the purpose of the instrumental variable.

Finally, a few hints on how to read econometric results tables. After considering the number of observations (having more of them is better), it is worth taking the time to look at the so-called coefficient of determination (R^2). Put simply, it tells us the percentage of the total variation in y that can be explained by the variation in the explanatory variables (here: x and β). What is central, however, is whether the estimated coefficient (β in the example above) is "significant." Economists distinguish between two kinds of significance, namely statistical and substantive significance. The coefficient is said to be statistically significant at the 5 percent level if the likelihood that it was caused by a chance event is lower than 5 percent. Substantive significance asks what the size of the coefficient means for the dependent variable. What the coefficient means in a particular model depends on the coding of both the independent and the dependent variable. Ultimately, economists are, of course, interested in substantive significance. But they will only turn to it given that the variable is statistically significant.

6 Explaining Differences in External Institutions across Societies

6.1 Introductory Remarks

Chapters 6 and 7 comprise the third part of this book. In Chapters 2 to 4, we assumed institutions – both external and internal – to be exogenously given and inquired into the consequences for individual choices. In Chapter 5, we looked at the consequences of different sets of institutions for economic growth and other economically relevant indicators at the aggregate level. We attempted to explain certain phenomena by differences in institutions. Hence, in Chapters 2 through 5, institutions served as *explanans*.

Explanans: Explanatory variables

In Chapters 6 and 7, we shift our focus and investigate whether we can use economic theory to explain the origins and changes in institutions. Institutions are thus no longer exogenously given; instead, we now ask which incentives and mechanisms might lead to the choice and change of institutions. Hence, institutions now serve as *explanandum*. For purely practical reasons, we first deal with external institutions, then with internal institutions. Simply put, there has been more research into the origins of external institutions than into the origins of internal institutions. If we were to proceed purely chronologically, it would make sense to first deal with the origins of internal institutions. A great number of institutions were internal institutions before evolving into external institutions by collective action. Chapters 6 and 7 each cover "hot" topics in the sense that over the last couple of years, much original research has been published on the questions introduced here.

Explanandum: Explained variables

Explaining the origins and the change of institutions also involves questions regarding groups of institutions that are closely connected to each other and that as a group constitute a regime type. Democracies, for example, are made up of dozens of different institutions, many of which deal with the ways in which elections are to be held, popular votes are to be transferred into parliamentary seats, the government is to be elected and so on. The rule of law as the attempt to make everybody subject to rules that share certain qualities and are produced according to a

transparent and highly regulated procedure is another example.
Possible questions regarding these groups of institutions are: Under
what conditions are people likely to establish those institutions that
make up democracy? What are likely paths in the development of
these institutions over time? When will institutions be implemented
that foster the rule of law? For a long time, these questions were
almost completely ignored by economists, but this has changed in
the last decades. From the point of view of traditional economists,
these questions seemed a bit aloof. At second glance, however, they
seem almost obviously relevant. After all, the democratic form of
government has been the exception throughout human history; still
today, the overwhelming majority of humans live in autocratic
states. In Chapter 5, we saw that economic freedom is directly
related to income and economic growth. Thus, the questions just
posed are also economically relevant. Since the 1990s, there has
been a fundamental transformation in Central and Eastern Europe,
and also elsewhere in the world. Consider, for instance, the processes of democratization in East Asia and Latin America. To make
well-grounded policy recommendations to policymakers in such
states, we first require knowledge about the different sets of institutions – or regime types – as well as about the difficulties inherent
in transitioning from one form to another. More generally, if we are
interested in successfully implementing a specific set of institutions, we need to be clear about the factors that determine the
presence – or absence – of those institutions. Suppose some institutions were completely determined by factors beyond our control,
such as the climate or resource endowment. In such a case, trying to
create these institutions in inhospitable climates or in the absence
of necessary resources would be futile.

Under what conditions does democracy manifest?

Chapter Highlights

- Critically discuss various theories on the emergence of private property rights.
- Understand how governments use the delineation of property rights to further their own interests.
- Familiarize yourself with some "grand theories" purporting to explain institutional change.
- Get acquainted with the concept of institutional competition.
- Have a look at the components that a "general theory of institutional change" is likely to comprise.

This chapter is structured as follows. In Section 6.2, we discuss the traditional theory of the development of property rights which has also been coined the "naïve" theory. In Section 6.3, we present a theory that is less naïve, as it explicitly accounts for political economy aspects, i.e., it takes the interests of the relevant actors explicitly into account. In Section 6.4, we move from discussing a specific group of institutions – property rights – to institutional aspects of whole governments, that is, autocracies and rule-of-law states. The concept of institutional competition is briefly discussed in Section 6.5. In Section 6.6, we attempt to name the elements for which a general theory of institutional change needs to account. Section 6.7 formulates open questions.

6.2 Origins and Change of Property Rights: A Traditional View

In this section, we focus on the development of and change in a specific type of institution that is crucial for economic development – property rights. When economists think "high quality institutions" – they often think "secure property rights." This is why we begin this chapter by looking into how property rights might have first emerged and then changed over time.

Assume that a state exists and that, on a fundamental level, a decision has been made to grant private property rights. All well and good. After such a basic decision, a great number of details remain to be resolved such as goods possibly exempted from being held as private property, the terms under which private property rights can be exchanged, the responsibilities attached to property, and so on. To begin with, it seems plausible (and innocent) to assume that the state is interested in designing private property rights such that private actors are able to conduct as many mutually beneficial transactions as possible. The better off private actors are, the higher the national income, and, perhaps more important to the state, the higher the tax revenues.

Since the 1960s, economists have been devising theories to explain the origins of property rights, for example, the one by Harold Demsetz (1967), which Eggertsson (1990, 249ff.) sees as part of a "naïve theory of property rights." Models found in this branch of theory refrain from explicitly modeling the political process or the conflicting interests of the actors involved.

Demsetz's (1967) central idea can be summarized in one sentence: (Private) *property rights develop if an internalization of externalities is associated with social net benefits.* Hence, the development of and change in property rights can be due to at least two causes:

Property rights as result of a process of internalization

1. A change over time in externalities associated with some activity.
2. Due to technical change, internalization is possible at lower cost than before.

Demsetz draws on the case of the Inuit in Labrador, Canada to illustrate his theory. Originally, the Inuit hunted beavers only for subsistence. In the early 1800s, however, due to a sharply increased demand for beaver fur by the Hudson Bay Company, the Inuit had an incentive to hunt more and more beavers. You already know the resulting **common pool problem**. It is individually rational to hunt beavers to the extent that the marginal revenue for fur just covers the cost of hunting. Collectively, this result is not necessarily optimal, as the beaver population might shrink over time, possibly even become extinct. Thus, it can be socially optimal ("collectively rational") to restrict beaver hunting in the present in order to prevent beavers from dying out in the future and ensure that there still will be beavers to hunt in the future.

As long as there are no exclusive rights to parts of the beaver population, hunters have an incentive to "produce" a negative externality, that is, to hunt more beavers than socially optimal. Internalization was possible in this case as the cost of implementing private property rights, for instance, in the form of fences, was lower than the expected benefits associated with it. "Putting up fences" created private property rights to beavers – as well as the land on which they lived – and excluded all non-owners from hunting beavers on grounds that they did not own. Private property rights could also have developed if – independent of beaver fur prices – the cost of erecting fences had decreased through technological progress. Demsetz compares the development of private property rights in Labrador with that of Native Americans in the southwest of the USA. There, hunting animals was not associated with any commercial activity. Instead, livestock that required a great deal of pasture space were important. As there was no benefit to erecting fences in this environment, fences were not built and no private property rights that would have enabled the owners to exclude non-owners were created.

You might have noticed that Demsetz *does not explicitly model the political process*. There is no discussion of how the Inuit managed to overcome the problem of collective action, or of what incentives the local government had to support the creation of private property rights. Implicitly, this theory is based on (at least) two problematic assumptions:

1. Governments are benevolent, that is, they have an incentive to design property rights optimally.
2. Political transaction costs are zero.

In a paper that appeared eleven years later, Gary Libecap (1978) asks the same question as Demsetz, but with regard to the emergence of property rights in mining in the western part of the USA. He finds that changes in mining rights occur as a response to increases in the value of mining resources, so his findings are completely in line with those of Demsetz. His research deserves mention not only because he relied on statistical analysis to arrive at his conclusions, but also because the demand for more precisely defined rights is seen as a function of how much the resource is valued. The explanations regarding the emergence of private property rights and their change over time offered by both Demsetz and Libecap can be interpreted as the view that institutions will adjust to changed circumstances and that this adjustment will be towards the highest possible degree of efficiency. Now, institutions do not adjust themselves but as a consequence of relevant actors bringing change about. Before we proceed to explanations taking the interests of the relevant actors explicitly into account in Section 6.3, we turn to a contribution that puts measurement costs at center stage. Here, change towards more efficient institutions was driven by technological progress which made the precise measurement of both inputs and outputs possible.

Douglas Allen (2011) posits that the Industrial Revolution enabled an "institutional revolution" that unfolded between 1780 and 1850. "Measurement" costs play a central role in this theory. Allen argues that before the Industrial Revolution, reliably measuring time – not to mention the weight of output – was close to impossible. This makes any kind of cooperation in which time plays a role costly: for example, meetings at a specific time are difficult to have if those who want to meet do not have identical information about what time it is. Any inputs based on time – such as the hourly wage rates covered in most modern labor contracts – are impossible without being able to reliably measure time. More generally, monitoring agents is extremely costly in such an environment and other ways to constrain "cheating, fraud, embezzlement, theft, shirking" (Allen, 2011, 11) are necessary. One result of the Industrial Revolution was a significant decrease in measurement costs, thus making certain institutions possible. Allen is particularly interested in public governance – the ways in which the state supplies public goods – and argues that the modern public bureaucracy, which is bound by general rules and largely based on merit, would have been impossible prior to the Industrial Revolution.

Making sense of the strange mores of British aristocrats

The most fascinating part of Allen's *The Institutional Revolution* is his attempt to make sense of seemingly strange institutions that were in place before the institutional revolution occurred. Seen from today, the traditional mores and conventions of British aristocrats are anywhere between appalling and outright strange or even comic. They used to live in countryside mansions that were usually much too large for them and more or less isolated from modern urban life. They socialized only with each other, making the aristocracy a very homogeneous group. They did not engage in any kind of traditional business such as buying and selling goods. Instead, they spent a great deal of time on leisure activities. From the outside, it might appear that they were just rather lazy parasites. Allen explains that such an evaluation would be utterly wrong.

In a monarchy, the monarch needs agents that supply public goods, for example, defense of the country or management of the law courts. The monarch also, perhaps especially, needs tax collectors, which is, essentially, the function of an aristocracy. If a public bureaucracy in the modern sense is impossible (e.g., because of measurement costs, as discussed above), there are two alternatives: either sell a public office to the highest bidder or grant patronage to trustworthy aristocrats. Both mechanisms have their pros and cons and which one is better is case-specific.

Let us focus on patronage. Patronage essentially means that in the event an aristocrat was caught cheating, the monarch had the power to throw him out of the aristocracy. This, of course,

> could be a serious threat only if such ostracism was really costly to those caught cheating. And that is where the strange mores come in. First, to enter into aristocracy, "fungible" assets had to be converted into assets that were difficult to liquidate, hence the mansions that were usually much too large. In the event an aristocrat was banished from the aristocracy, he could not simply move to the city and start over as an ordinary person because getting rid of these large mansions was extremely costly. Making sure that aristocrats got rid of all their business interests ensured that no attractive option outside of aristocratic life existed for them. Making sure that aristocrats socialized only with each other ensured that once removed from the group, a former member would no longer have any friends, with all that that implies. And so forth. In economic terms: *By incurring sunk costs and deliberately creating hostage capital, aristocrats were able to credibly signal their loyalty to the monarch.* The price of being caught stealing or shirking was so high, it virtually guaranteed that they would not engage in such behavior.

Critique Allen's "institutional revolution" is fascinating, but not entirely convincing. The technological advances that accompanied the Industrial Revolution were not confined solely to the West, and yet the institutional revolution only took place there. There does not seem to be any plausible reason why the general trend towards ever more efficient institutions would occur only in the West. And, of course, we have presented his approach in this section because political economy considerations are largely absent from his account.

As mentioned before, this view of institutional development has been called "naïve" (by Eggertsson, 1990, 249ff.); I prefer to call it the "efficiency view" of institutions. It is based on the assumption that if the value of a resource increases and it makes sense ("is efficient") to clarify ownership by creating property rights, this will happen. However, there is no attempt to explain the mechanism through which this occurs. At the extreme, such a view implies that we are living in the best of all possible worlds, a doubtful proposition at best, given the poverty and hunger so prevalent across the globe. And yet, such efficiency arguments continue to be made, most forcefully by Donald Wittman (1995) who claims that political institutions are efficient in democracies. In Section 6.5, we present and discuss a mechanism that is said to lead to more efficient institutions everywhere and that has been discussed extensively over the last 20 years or so, namely, institutional competition.

6.3 Origins of and Change in Property Rights and the State: Accounting for Political Economy Factors

In his 1981 book *Structure and Change in Economic History*, Douglass North develops a theory of the state that focuses on the exchange relations between representatives of the state and the populace. He begins with a paradoxical observation: *On the one hand, the existence of the state is a necessary condition for economic growth, but on the other, the existence of the state is also a source of economic decline* (North, 1981, 20). North's theory goes beyond the naïve theory of property rights, because, according to North, the state is often responsible for **inefficient property rights** that do not fully exploit a society's growth potential. North uses his theory to explain the **origins of inefficient property rights** regimes, i.e., a delineation of property rights that does not lead to maximizing national income. By accounting for political economy factors, North explicitly takes the interests of those running the state into account. This is why this section is broader than the previous one and includes the state as a subject of analysis.

Why are property rights often designed suboptimally?

North defines the **state** as an "organization with a comparative advantage in violence, extending over a geographic area whose boundaries are determined by its power to tax constituents" (North, 1981, 21). Although property rights are not explicitly mentioned in this definition, a connection between the state and property rights is easy to establish. Property rights entail the right to exclude others from use. An organization with a comparative advantage in the use of force is capable of delineating and enforcing private property rights. One central condition for productive domestic exchange of goods is to keep invaders away from the state's territory, which has long been recognized as one of the state's fundamental functions. North (1981, 21) even claims that it is impossible to develop a useful theory of the state divorced from property rights.

According to North, all theories on the existence of the state can be assigned to either of two groups: **contract theories** (à la Hobbes) or **predatory** or **exploitation theories** (à la Marx). As we just saw, theories regarding the development of property rights are closely linked to theories of the state.

Contract theories vs. predatory exploitation theories

Note
Contract theories are based on the notion that societies collectively agree on a social contract that specifies how they will live together. Predatory exploitation theories are based on the notion that some parts of a society are able to increase their wealth at the expense of other parts of society (thus "exploitation").

The central idea of contract theory à la Hobbes is compatible with economic arguments: All members of society will be better off by avoiding a state of anarchy in which life is "solitary, poor, nasty, brutish and short" (Hobbes, 1982 [1651]). They can do so by subordinating to a ruler whose authority is limited by a social contract. Hobbes assumes that the physical capabilities of individuals are not so unevenly distributed that one member of society – or a very small group – is able to impose his ideas on the rest of society. The normative branch of constitutional economics builds its central idea on the notion of a social contract. All members of society can be made better off if they voluntarily give up their (implicit) right to fight, since fewer resources need to be spent on stealing others' goods and protecting one's own goods. James Buchanan is the best-known advocate of this approach in economics.

In contrast to Hobbes, Marx assumes, first, that common interest within different social groups ("classes") leads to collective action and, second, that in every historical era, one class has been able to enrich itself at the expense of other classes. For instance, in capitalism, the capitalists exploit the working class. Predatory theories are quite popular among institutional economists: Daron Acemoglu and his various co-authors, for example, always start from the assumption that a small elite runs the state attempting to maximize its rents from doing so. But North and his various co-authors also rely heavily on predatory theories of the state. For them, changes of property rights are a consequence of changes in the bargaining power of the ruling elites vis-à-vis the non-ruling masses. Technological progress – and in particular technological progress regarding military technology – is an important determinant of bargaining power.

According to North, *both groups of theories have their benefits and drawbacks.* Contract theories emphasize the advantages resulting from the initial social contract, but tend to ignore later interactions. Predatory exploitation theories emphasize the potential for exploitation by those who control the state, but ignore the advantages that can result from the existence of the state.

The model proposed by North is based on the assumption that all individuals maximize their utility and is characterized by the following three properties:

1. The state exchanges several services (protection, justice) for revenues. Because the production of protection and justice exhibits **economies of scale**, the state is able to provide these services at lower costs than the citizens. This implies that the overall income of society is higher if a state exists.

Note
Economies of scale exist if production output can be doubled without having to double production *inputs*.

---

2. The state and its representatives attempt to behave like a **discriminating monopolist**, and thus try to tax different social groups according to their inability to avoid taxes in order to maximize government revenues.
3. Maximization of state revenues is subject to a **restriction**: There are other states, but also individuals within state territory, that are willing to provide the same services as the state. The easier it is to substitute these suppliers for each other, the narrower the scope of actions available to state representatives.

The services offered by the state include, among other things, the design of property rights and their enforcement. The governing actors are interested in *maximizing* their *revenues* and thus design property rights accordingly. If national income can be maximized by reducing transaction costs, rulers will go for it because this leads to an increase in their tax revenues. According to North, this implies that the state will provide several public goods. However, the nexus between lower transaction costs and higher tax revenues frequently does not hold. From the state's just mentioned objectives, North derives **three implications** (1981, 24f.). Only two of them are relevant here:

1. Maximizing tax revenues is frequently incompatible with maximizing national income. If such friction exists, rulers will opt in

favor of maximizing their rents – and inefficient property rights will result.

> ## Example
>
> Here is an example for a conflict between maximizing the rents of the ruler and maximizing societal welfare. Granting a corporation a monopoly in the production of certain goods – examples range from lighters to high-tech weapons – is likely to be suboptimal from the point of view of national income: there will be little competition. High prices and little innovation are the likely outcomes. A ruler might nevertheless be interested in granting such monopolies because taxing a very small number of monopoly firms is a lot easier than taxing many small competing firms.

For many rulers, granting monopoly rights is attractive

Also, if powerful constituents can threaten to move to another state or to stay and throw out the current ruler, the ruler has incentives to discriminate between subjects and to offer more favorable property rights to the relatively more powerful. According to North, these are the two main reasons why states so often provide inefficient property rights.

2. Specification and enforcement of property rights require that state representatives delegate part of their power to agents. This implies that the *principal–agent problem* you encountered in Chapter 3 comes into play. You can also think of the strange mores of the British aristocracy that were described earlier as the means by which the British king tried to mitigate some of the principal-agent problems that North has in mind.

Based on the observation that collective action often occurs even in the presence of widespread free-riding, North derives several conclusions and open questions for his model. He summarizes his conclusions thus:

1. The stability of states can, *inter alia*, be explained by the difficulties associated with overcoming the problem of collective action.
2. Institutional change is primarily initiated by the rulers, not the ruled, as the latter are not able to overcome free-riding problems.
3. Revolution will originate within the ruling class, not on the streets. In such revolutions, the existing ruler is exchanged for a different ruler from the elites.

4. If the ruler is the agent of a social group or class, succession rules will be in place so as reduce the probability of violent regime change after the ruler's death.

Finally, North suggests that a theory of ideology is necessary to explain under what conditions the problem of collective action can be solved and under what conditions there is no solution.

Ideology

Merriam-Webster defines ideology, *inter alia*, as "a manner or the content of thinking characteristic of an individual, group, or culture." For North, ideologies are key to understanding human behavior. In *Structure and Change in Economic History* (1981, 48), he describes ideologies as "intellectual efforts to rationalize the behavioral pattern of individuals and groups." He emphasizes three functions of ideologies:

1. They are an instrument of economization with which individuals can reduce decision costs.
2. They are indissolubly linked to moral and ethical judgments about fairness.
3. They are changed when they are not consistent with individual experiences.

North stresses, in multiple publications, the crucial importance of ideologies in explaining human behavior (e.g., North, 2005). Some of his insights regarding the relevance of ideas are taken up in Chapter 7.

There is a clear difference between the naïve theory of property rights presented in Section 6.2 and the theory presented here: North offers convincing *arguments why rulers might have an incentive to design property rights suboptimally*, implying that with a different delineation of property rights, national income could be higher.

6.4 Explaining Differences in Institutions

6.4.1 Preliminary Remarks

For a long time, economists assumed that their results were valid irrespective of the type of regime in place. They assumed, in other words, that it did not matter whether the country was ruled by an autocrat or democratically. In the 1950s, several economists began to ask whether one might be able to explain political processes using the economic approach. This was the birth of public choice theory, a research program that began in the USA and spread from there to Western Europe. Given the history of the economic theory of politics, it is understandable that most scholars in this field initially analyzed different institutional arrangements within democratic systems. Thus, the fundamental assumptions of early public choice theory included (a) that regimes were given and (b) that they were democratic.

There are many explanations for why institutions vary so widely across countries. Consequently, there are also many explanations of regime change. I distinguish between three approaches used to explain these differences here: approaches based on geography (Section 6.4.2), approaches based on culture or history (Section 6.4.3), and approaches based on the social conflict view (Section 6.4.4). The explanations do, of course, overlap sometimes, but they are distinct enough that sorting them this way has some value. The following sections can be brief because we touched upon these issues already in Chapter 5.

6.4.2 Explaining External Institutions Based on Geography

Geographic conditions can impact the likelihood of state formation

In Chapter 5, we saw that the quality of some institutions can be explained by a country's resource endowment. There, climate and soil, the disease environment, whether a society had access to the sea or was landlocked, and even the orientation of continents were mentioned. Here, we go one step further and ask whether differences in geography can explain even the emergence of states as we know them. Moselle and Polak (2001) ask how the development of states can be explained at all. After all, it is by no means self-evident that historical processes would always lead to the emergence of a single actor or organization enjoying a *de facto* monopoly in the use of violence. In countries such as Afghanistan, Rwanda, or Somalia, the use of violence is not a government monopoly. Indeed, the phenomenon of **failed states** is evidence that development towards a state in the modern sense is by no means certain or guaranteed. Moselle and Polak argue that the probability of state development varies across different regions of the world and that statelessness is more likely in lowlands and steppes than in hilly and fertile regions, as the former are harder to protect. Moselle and Polak use this idea to explain why there were so few states in pre-colonial Africa. This approach is thus more interested in explaining the *absence* of a set of institutions that make for what we call a state, rather than the existence of a particular set of them.

6.4.3 Explaining External Institutions Based on Culture or History

It is possible that some of the large differences in external institutions across countries are due to the history of those countries. Certain historical events might have very long-lasting effects. This would imply that the external institutions prevalent in a country today are a consequence of external institutions possibly implemented hundreds of years ago. Today's external institutions might also be determined by the internal institutions that were valid in a country a long time ago. As a sort of shorthand, one can refer to this as the effect of culture on external institutions. Let us first look at (historical) external institutions that have an influence on today's external institutions.

Historic external institutions can impact today's external institutions

Being invaded or even colonized by another power is likely to have important effects on a country's institutions. One important example in which the identity of the colonizer still matters today – often decades or even centuries after colonization occurred – is the country's legal system, or, in other words, the external institutions of a country in their entirety. Legal scholars divide the world's legal systems into a very limited number of **legal families**. Aside from legal systems based on religion (such as Islamic or Hindu law), the first important distinction is between the civil law and the common law family. Under **civil law**, law is almost exclusively produced by legislators and the role of judges is limited to "*la bouche de la loi*" (the mouth of the law). Under **common law**, the role of the judge is much more important. Should there be gaps in legislation, it is the judges who fill them with their decisions. Therefore, this kind of law is often referred to as case law. Rules regarding court procedure differ widely under the two families. Under common law, the adversaries themselves accuse or defend. As a consequence, lawyers and their strategies play an important role. Under civil law, it is the judge who questions the parties.

The common law emerged in England. Today, England and most of its former colonies are coded as belonging to the common law family. This includes countries such as Australia, Canada, and the USA, as well as Bangladesh, India, and Pakistan, among others. Regarding civil law, many scholars propose a tripartite division into French, German, and Scandinavian, of which the French has been most influential. In Europe, countries such as Italy, Spain, and Portugal, as well as the Netherlands, are coded as belonging to this group. Since Spain and Portugal exported their laws into their colonies, virtually all of Latin America is said to belong to the "French civil law" family. There is also socialist law, which is based on the idea that productive resources should not be the property of individuals but the state.

In a series of articles, Rafael La Porta and his co-authors show that being part of a particular family of law has important consequences for a wide variety of institutions, including how difficult it is to set up a new firm (more difficult in French civil law countries), the degree to which the media is owned by the state (higher in French civil law countries), the regulation of labor (more difficult to fire people under French civil law), and so on. The authors find that countries belonging to the French civil law family come out worst, a view well summarized by former US President George W. Bush when he said: "The problem with the French is that they do not even have an own word for entrepreneur." Given that the French civil law countries usually come out worst, one might expect them to be the slowest growing. However, although there seems to be a strong link between a country's colonization experience and many of its currently valid institutions, there is no strong link between these institutions and the speed at which the economies in the various countries grow. The papers on legal origins are among the most cited of all papers in economics, but they are also among the most criticized. For example, Daniel Berkowitz and his co-authors (2003) argue that the way the law was initially transplanted and received is a more important determinant than affiliation with a particular legal family. They claim that the origin of a legal system is not a good predictor for the actual implementation of the law. The authors consider as far more important whether the law was transformed according to the specific situation of a society, whether it was imported voluntarily or enforced by a colonial power, and so forth. According to their findings, countries that have developed legal orders internally or adapted transplanted legal orders to local conditions and/or had a population that was already familiar with the basic legal principles of the transplanted law have more effective legal rules than countries that received foreign law without similar predispositions.

When in 1972 Chinese Prime Minister Chou en Lai was asked about the impact of the French Revolution, he is said to have answered: "It is too soon to tell." Now, Daron Acemoglu and his co-authors (2011) believe that the time for definitive answers has come. They ask whether countries that were invaded by the French were observed to grow faster because the French implemented radical institutional reform that enabled the Industrial Revolution to take off. Examples of such reforms include drastically reducing the power of the landed aristocracy and breaking up cartels, such as merchant guilds, that made it very difficult or even outright impossible for outsiders to enter a market.

Around the turn of the nineteenth century, Germany was made up of dozens of rather small states. Some of these were not only invaded by French armies but the French also implemented far-reaching institutional reforms in them. These are the states that were "treated" by the French. There were also numerous German states – primarily in the east and south of the country – that were not invaded by the French and can be thought of as "untreated." Acemoglu and his co-authors compare the development of the treated with that of the non-treated German states. As a proxy for income and wealth, they use urbanization rates (defined as that part of the entire population that lives in cities with 5,000 or more inhabitants). They find that urbanization rates in treated areas start to diverge significantly from those in untreated areas only after 1850.

In Chapter 5, we learned that Acemoglu and his co-authors believe that the colonization history of a country can have persistent negative effects on its long-term development. If the disease environment made survival difficult, colonizers were likely to establish extractive institutions that enabled them to take a great deal of wealth out of the country in little time. Countries that were so "treated" still have problems developing. With regard to the French Revolution, the authors show that development-enhancing treatments are also possible. Their message is clear: powerful players are free to set and implement external institutions at their discretion. These institutions are the most important single determinant of future economic growth.

This approach is not without its critics. There are many scholars who believe that external institutions, at least to some degree, need to rely on internal institutions. If this is true, then the power to improve people's lot in a short time by importing external institutions that function well elsewhere might be severely constrained. There are many historical examples of not only foreign powers, but also domestic revolutionaries, attempting an extreme overhaul of institutions that failed miserably. Gregory Massell (1968) recounts the story of how the Soviets tried to make the populations in their central Asian republics give up the *Sharia* – and how their efforts ended in almost complete failure. Berkowitz et al.'s (2003) observation that legal transplants are more likely to be successful if they are adapted to local conditions was mentioned previously. A more recent example, and a cautionary tale, is that of the USA – and other Western powers – spending billions and billions of dollars and sacrificing the lives of hundreds of soldiers to implement external institutional institutions conducive to growth and development in Afghanistan and Iraq. As of now, it seems that these efforts have had very limited success.

6.4.4 Explaining External Institutions Based on Social Conflict View

All of the "social conflict" explanations assume that different actors have different interests and that their interests would be best served by different institutions. In that sense, these different actors, or groups of different actors, are thus in conflict with each other. However, this conflict is only partial because they would all be worse off if no cooperation between them took place. In game theory terminology, the game they are playing is, hence, a mixed-motive game. On the one hand, there are advantages of cooperation, in that everyone will obtain at least some benefit. On the other hand, there are disadvantages to cooperation, the chief of these being that no one is going to get exactly what he or she wants.

Institutions have distributive consequences. In all likelihood, different institutions will make some people worse off – and others better off. Those who are satisfied with the currently valid institutions are unlikely to demand major change, whereas those who believe that the currently valid institutions are unfavorable to their interests are likely to favor change. The chances of getting one's most preferred institutions are assumed to be a function of one's **bargaining power** vis-à-vis the rest of society.

	Note

Bargaining power can be defined as the ability and willingness to inflict costs on others and thereby reduce the total social surplus.

The currently valid institutions can be thought of as reflecting the relative bargaining power of the relevant groups. As long as their relative power remains unchanged, the institutional status quo can be considered an equilibrium. Institutional change becomes more likely when the bargaining power of a particular group improves relative to the bargaining power of other groups, which could occur, for example, as the consequence of technological change.

It is important to realize that not all individuals who share the same interests manage to become groups. The difference between latent and actual or manifest interest groups is pointed out by Mancur Olson (1965) in a rightly famous book. We have already relied on some of Olson's arguments in Chapter 4; here, we present the core of his book in a little more detail.

On the organization of consumer and producer interests: the collective action problem

In Chapter 4, using the example of the dam, we saw that the voluntary provision of a public good by those who benefit from it is rather unlikely. The individual hopes that the sum of voluntary contributions by everyone else is sufficiently high to ensure provision of the public good. But because all individuals share this expectation, no public good will be privately provided. In reality, however, certain groups are able to overcome the collective action problem. Olson (1965) describes in which situations this is more likely to occur.

1. When public good provision is **coupled with the provision of a private good** that can be consumed only by those who contribute to the public good. For instance, the public goods bundle provided by labor unions – improved wages and working conditions – can also be consumed by non-members. However, labor unions often additionally provide private goods such as insurance and consulting services that are limited to their members. If access to these private goods is

attractive, there can be sufficient private incentive to join and thus contribute to the costs of providing the public good.

2. When there is **compulsory membership**. For example, perhaps you can work for a firm only if you are a union member (a *closed shop*). This is not necessarily a convincing condition for (initially) overcoming the collective action problem, but a mechanism with which the continuity of an already existing organization can be ensured. Compulsory membership presupposes legislative action or a general agreement with the employer. Both require that the labor union has already overcome the collective action problem and, furthermore, that it possesses significant strength. Otherwise, legislators or employers would not have consented to the institution of compulsory membership.

3. **Low number of involved individuals**. It is immediately clear that the provision of the dam is more likely if five farmers attempt to set it up than if 500 farmers try to do so. As soon as one of the five is not cooperative, the other four can (informally) sanction him much more easily than 400 farmers could sanction 100 farmers because it will be more difficult for 400 than for four farmers to coordinate their behavior.

The latter argument implies that there is an asymmetry in the **organizability of interests**. Since in general, the number of producers is lower than the number of consumers, **producer interests** are **easier to organize than consumer interests**. Beside the number of involved individuals, the importance of producing a particular collective good for the utility level of the potential providers might play a role: For farmers, subsidies to milk production can be existentially important so they seem to be more likely to overcome the problem of collective action. On the other hand, consumers usually spend only a very small part of their entire budget on agricultural products. Trying to set up the "organization of milk drinkers" to give weight to consumer interests appears, therefore, rather unlikely.

Olson's theory thus predicts that only a few groups are likely to overcome the problem of collective action. The number of manifest interest groups is likely to be limited, and the number of those groups commanding veto power will be even smaller. This view of institutional change is elaborated on in Voigt (1999a).

Daron Acemoglu and James Robinson (2005) proffer a similar explanation of regime change. They distinguish between two groups: the powerful elites and the less powerful non-elites. The non-elites demand a distribution of the collective surplus that is more favorable to them. If their threat to stage a revolution appears credible, the elites have an incentive to start negotiations and make at least some political concessions to the non-elites. The credibility of threats can change over time, for example, because the non-elites overcome the dilemma of collective action, because of technological progress that makes their input more valuable, and the like. Acemoglu and Robinson assume that negotiations take place and the two groups agree on a modified constitution that entails a larger share of the collective surplus for the non-elites. At this point, the elites face the problem of being unable to credibly commit to their own promises. If the non-elites are demonstrating in front of the palace, the elites have an incentive to promise improvement. But why would they keep their promise once the heat of the moment has passed and demonstrators are back at home?

External institutions reflect the relative bargaining power of competing groups of society

According to Acemoglu and Robinson (2005), democracy can serve as a tool that helps the elites turn their promises into credible commitments. If most voters are poor, they are likely to vote in favor of (re-)distribution, for example, in the form of social and welfare policies. Extending the right to vote to the poor can thus serve as a commitment device of the elites. Extending the right to vote to ever more groups of society is equivalent to an extension of democracy. The authors thus view the transition from autocracy to democracy as the elites' response to threats from the non-elites. In an extended version of their model, a third group – the middle class – is introduced. If it is sufficiently large, more gradual institutional change becomes possible – and also likely.

Democracy as a tool of the elite to make commitments credible

Douglass North, John Wallis, and Barry Weingast (2009) (hereafter, NWW) have published no less than a "conceptual framework for interpreting recorded human history" – the subtitle of their book. They start from the observation that violence has been a major problem for most societies for the whole history of mankind. In other words, more often than not, there has not been a state, at least not one that meets Max Weber's definition, i.e., an organization commanding a monopoly of legitimately using violence. NWW propose that human history has known only three types of social order: (1) foraging, (2) limited access, and (3) open access.

Under this framework, explaining institutional change implies explaining the transition between these three orders. I here focus only on the transition from (2) to (3). **Limited access orders** are based on personal relationships and the ability to form organizations is limited. In limited access orders, violence is controlled by relying on a **dominant coalition**. Members of the dominant coalition share the rents that emerge from the absence of violence. In **open access orders**, cooperation between individuals is based on impersonal institutions that treat all individuals alike. Positions in both politics and the economy are open to everyone and are allocated according to merit. All individuals have the right to found political or economic (e.g., corporations) organizations. In open access orders, all violence is controlled by the state and the military is under civilian control. The authors group the overwhelming majority of today's countries into their second category. Roughly speaking, only the (more established) OECD countries are believed to be open access orders.

NWW's take on the transition from limited to open access orders emphasizes that doing so must be in the interest of the overwhelming majority of the players who make up the dominant coalition. When the elites in the limited access order become able to deal with each other impersonally, then that society will be on the threshold of becoming an open access order. NWW identify three threshold conditions: (1) the rule of law for elites, (2) perpetually existent organizations in both public and private spheres, and (3) consolidated control of the military by politics. If the vast majority of those members of the elite who form the dominant coalition realize that they can make themselves better off – in interactions with each other – by not relying on personal relationships but on general rules, they will be in favor of what NWW call "rule of law for elites." This sounds like a *contradictio in adiecto*, but what they really mean by the term is that no member of the elite enjoys particular privileges; all of them are treated according to the same rules. However, these rules for the elite are not necessarily, indeed not probably, the same rules by which everyone else has to live, hence the awkward-sounding term "rule of law for elites."

When rent seeking is beneficial

In Chapter 4, we saw that rent seeking is conventionally interpreted as wasteful. Lobbyists not only invest resources into
lobbying politicians that could be spent more productively,
but the rules that they lobby for are in all likelihood detrimental
to overall welfare. NWW propose a different take on rent
seeking: according to them, sizable rents are a precondition
for holding the dominant coalition together. As soon as one
of its members suspects that it is not receiving the rents it
deserves, this member might turn to violence – which is likely
to make most everyone worse off.

This idea can be extended even further: all groups that aim to
change institutions in such a way that they will be getting a
better deal can be viewed as seeking rents. Now, if ever more
groups manage to overcome the dilemma of collective action
and, in the end, the overwhelming majority of citizens are
represented by at least one such group, then it is not unlikely
that they will be able to agree only on general rules according
to which all citizens are dealt with in a like manner. This is
nothing else but the rule of law. In other words, even rent
seeking can foster the rule of law and be hugely beneficial
(Voigt, 1999b).

The main difference between NWW and Acemoglu and Robinson is
that the latter basically rely on two actors (the elite vs. the non-
elite), whereas the former model the elite as a coalition of a multitude of actors. In their explanation of transitions, NWW focus on
the bargaining that takes place within the dominant coalition,
hence explicitly giving up the monolithic actor assumption relied
on by Acemoglu and Robinson.

There are other theories regarding the transition from an
authoritarian to a non-authoritarian regime. Assuming that such
a transition is socially beneficial and that revolutions waste
resources, a non-revolutionary transformation path, such as a
negotiated transformation pact, seems superior, although fraught
with difficulty. Sutter (1995) describes a **punishment dilemma**
that the new (non-authoritarian) government faces vis-à-vis the
former (authoritarian) government. Before taking over, the new
government has an incentive to assure the autocrat exemption

from punishment. As soon as the new government is in power, however, the population might demand that the former autocrat be punished. Anticipating this, autocrats have an incentive to block a peaceful transition away from autocracy. This implies that an *optimal political rule is time inconsistent with respect to dictators* (you know about this problem from Chapter 4, where we discussed it in relation to political business cycles). To explain: In order to prevent potential dictators from becoming actual dictators, they have to be threatened with drastic punishments. *Ex ante*, the optimal rule would thus contain a serious punishment threat. As soon as a dictator has taken over – and society would like to get rid of him – it would be desirable to be able to credibly assure exemption from punishment in order to ensure a peaceful transition to a non-authoritarian regime. *Ex post*, the optimal rule would, hence, only threaten very moderate punishment.

When citizens prefer less – rather than more – separation of powers

In general, it is plausible to assume that citizens prefer more, rather than less, separation of powers. If various political actors have only limited powers, misuse of power seems less likely and citizens will consequently be better off. Interestingly, Acemoglu et al. (2013) identify settings under which voters have an interest to dismantle checks and balances. Their model assumes that there are two groups in society, namely, the rich and the poor, and the poor outnumber the rich. If checks and balances function well, the executive's discretion is low, as is its overall income. This enables the rich, who are assumed to have solved their collective action problem, to bribe government into policies furthering the interests of the rich. In such circumstances, the poor might prefer fewer checks and balances; because the overall income of the executive will increase, bribing it will be more difficult, implying that policies are closer to the preferences of the poor. Acemoglu et al. (2013, 859) point out that this result is likely in "weakly institutionalized states," which are described as states in which "the rich lobby can successfully bribe politicians or influence policies using non-electoral means."

The theories presented here emphasize different aspects of regime transformation. We have not presented a comprehensive theory of regime transformation because there is none. In the following section, we discuss a particular approach to explaining institutional change that focuses on the diffusion of institutional change across space.

6.5 Institutional Change via Institutional Competition?

In Section 6.2, we discussed the naïve theory of property rights emergence. One reason why this theory still has many supporters although it is seen by some as naïve could be the mechanism invoking institutional change that is described in this section. Douglas Allen – the same author who makes sense of the seemingly strange habits of British aristocrats – justifies the view of institutions as efficient when he writes: "in the Darwinian struggle between nations, firms, and individuals, societies are driven to find institutions that get the job done best under the circumstances faced at the time" (Allen, 2011, xi). In other words, entire societies can be seen as in competition with each other and only those whose institutions are halfway efficient will survive or prosper.

Although the notion of "institutional competition" can be traced back at least to Kant and Montesquieu, economists consider an essay by Charles Tiebout (1956) as the cornerstone of the notion concerned with the diffusion of institutions across space. The basic idea is very simple: *It is not only the suppliers of traditional goods that are in competition with each other, but also the suppliers of bundles of public goods.* Following Tiebout (1956), mayors can be thought of as providing bundles of public goods that cater to citizens. Citizens are then assumed to move to the place that offers that bundle of public goods which best suits their preferences. (Local) institutions can also be thought of as public goods. This is why Tiebout's theory is directly relevant here. If a mayor now observes that other mayors are able to attract more citizens (or firms, or foreign investment, etc.), she is assumed to have incentives to improve the quality of the institutions offered by her. There is, hence, a competition for citizens and one important action parameter are institutions. Therefore, this process is often referred to as "institutional competition."

In economics, this idea was first raised in regard to the competition between local entities within a country but is now found in the context of nation-states competing for (scarce) mobile resources.

Here, the owners of mobile resources are interpreted as representing the "demand side" for an institutional environment that allows them to reap the returns on their invested capital.

Governments are also in competition with each other

There are two opposing views on institutional competition. On the one side, it is argued that institutional competition can lead to more effective control over governing agents, as the competitive process forces the governing agents to give more thought to the preferences of the governed (see, e.g., Besley and Case, 1995). On the other side, it is argued that institutional competition might lead to a **race to the bottom**: If capital keeps moving to where its returns are highest, states might not enact regulations that are costly to mobile firms (such as environmental regulation), and also reduce social and welfare spending (such as social policy) (see, e.g., Sinn, 1997; see also Mueller, 1998).

Following Albert O. Hirschman (1970), the migration of mobile resources is called exit. Further, it is assumed that *exit* leads to loss of popularity of the government and that the latter thus has an incentive to adjust public goods bundles such that there is a net inflow of mobile resources. Another mechanism for effecting changes in public goods bundles, also according to Hirschman, is **voice**. Voice means that those who are negatively affected by some policy choices speak up and demand improvement. If we assume that – due to globalization – relocation of one's assets to another country is much easier than was the case in the past, *voice* might be sufficient to achieve changes in the supply of public goods because the threat of *exit* is much more credible in the presence of low mobility costs.

Conditions for institutional competition to be socially beneficial

Proponents of the first view of institutional competition often posit that institutional competition increases social welfare by inducing less efficient institutions to be replaced with more efficient ones. Viktor Vanberg (1992, 111) argues that two conditions must be fulfilled in order for institutional competition to be socially beneficial. First, it must be possible to *try out potentially beneficial institutional innovations* in order to ensure that they are likely to be *factually implemented*. Second, there needs to be a **mechanism of selective retention** that reliably eliminates errors, meaning that less efficient practices (routines, tools) are systematically replaced with efficient ones. This is, therefore, an evolutionary view of institutional competition. To show that institutional competition is socially beneficial, one needs to be able to identify the mechanism through which selective retention takes place.

Although the analogy between goods competition and competition with regard to public goods bundles seems convincing at first sight, there are at least *two problems with this analogy*: Problems of the analogy

1. Characteristics of goods.

Competition in goods has to do with individual goods. If supplier and buyer can agree on a price and conclude a contract, mutually beneficial exchange is possible. Conversely, institutional competition refers to public goods that are often intangible. Individual willingness to pay is not sufficient for the provision of such goods. Rather, collective action – based on collective decision-making rules – determines which **bundles of public goods** are actually provided. As soon as one deviates from the unanimity rule with regard to all individual constituent goods, it can happen that the public good is a **collective "bad"** for some individuals, if only for the reason that they have to pay for its provision without ever utilizing it. If I hate soccer and all gatherings of soccer fans but am forced to support the sport because part of my tax bill is used to support it, I might well perceive this good as a "bad."

The possibility of exit is only partially relevant, as the same structural problem is equally present in other jurisdictions. A different picture would emerge if an individual could assemble his or her own individual "menu" of public goods from a variety of suppliers.

2. Communication of preferences.

Following the terminology of Hirschman, the demand-side preferences are communicated to the supply side via *exit* and *voice*. Within the realm of regular goods competition, buyer exit requires some interpretation on the supplier's side, as the buyer usually does not specify a reason for exit. With respect to institutional competition, exit requires a lot more interpretation. After all, the institutional supply side is only one factor determining the expected returns to mobile resources. In the final investment decision, many other, non-institutional factors also play a role, for instance, the number of potential consumers and their purchasing power.

Voice is unlikely to have any effects if it does not occur collectively. Individuals who observe a deterioration in the quality of the provided bundle of public goods will be able to do something about it only if they are able to overcome the **problem of collective action** (Olson, 1965). Due to the asymmetric **organizability of interests**, only certain preferences are articulated via voice. Often, this results in institutions being changed in the manner suggested or demanded by the organized actors. It appears problematic to claim that institutional competition closes the gap between politicians and voter preferences because "the" preferences of the voters might not even exist.

Finally, the signals sent by exit and voice are not always crystal clear. We already stated that the signals induced by institutional competition usually require more interpretation than signals in simple goods competition. Due to the combination of public goods characteristics and the asymmetric organizability of interests, it seems questionable whether consumer preferences (in the traditional sense) can be communicated clearly. Put differently: *Exerting the exit option is by no means sufficient evidence of actual deterioration in the quality of the public goods bundle and neither does the absence of voice necessarily imply that the demand side is satisfied with the quality of the supplied public goods.*

In recent years, the "spatial diffusion" of institutions has been discussed. The idea is that institutions do not spread across space randomly but that factors like geographical proximity, but also cultural or historical closeness, make adoption more likely. This concept is broader than the one just discussed as institutions could also spread across space via coercion. In a paper analyzing the diffusion of constitutional rules, Goderis and Versteeg (2014) explicitly name four instruments that are used for coercion. Whereas colonization and military occupation seem both outdated and outlawed, making membership in international organizations contingent on first implementing certain institutions seems to be a very current practice. This can also be said of making payment of foreign aid conditional on certain institutional reforms. Regarding the spatial diffusion of constitutional rules, Goderis and Versteeg (2014) find that shared legal origins, competition for foreign aid, a shared religion, and shared colonial ties are the main drivers.

6.6 Elements of a General Theory

6.6.1 Preliminary Remarks

In Sections 6.2 to 6.4, we covered several specific aspects of change in external institutions. The aim of this section is to assemble a list of elements that a general theory of institutional change requires. A general theory of institutional change would be able to explain all kinds of institutional change, no matter where or when it occurs. As there is no generally accepted theory on this topic yet, we cannot present one. The book by Acemoglu and Robinson (2005) is probably closest to such a theory.

First, changing external institutions requires an **explicit process of collective decision-making**. This is most obvious in a country with a democratic constitution where at least a parliamentary majority is required to amend the constitution. That the needed majority has been achieved is often due to the efforts of interest groups who demand certain institutional changes. Note that this aspect of institutional change is unique to external institutions; parliaments cannot change internal institutions.

Economics is based on methodological individualism, meaning that in explaining any phenomenon (e.g., a change in external institutions), we need to show that the relevant actors have an incentive to act in a particular manner. Otherwise, we would risk committing the **functionalist fallacy** (Elster, 1984, 28ff.). So, the question is: What role do individual decisions play in regard to the origins and change of institutions?

Definition

Functionalist fallacy: Improper direct linking of the social function of an institution and its origin.

The decision situation of an actor who is subject to any set of external institutions can be schematically illustrated using Matrix 6.1.

Each cell of the matrix describes individual behavior vis-à-vis a set of external institutions. The four letters depicting the four

Matrix 6.1 Individual decision situation with regard to the choice of external institutions

		Choice within rules	
		Comply with institutions	Not comply with institutions
Choice of rules	Not demand institutional change	A	C
	Demand institutional change	B	D

possible combinations are used to structure the arguments in this section. If the behavior of most members of a group can be grouped into cell A, institutional change appears unlikely. If, however, the behavior can be grouped in cell D, institutional change appears a lot more likely.

Here, we combine two levels of analysis that are usually considered separately in constitutional economics: the level of **choice within rules**, where one can either comply or not comply with (given) institutions, and the level of **choice of rules**, where one can either demand or not demand institutional change.

Note

Constitutional economists distinguish between the *choice of rules* and the *choice within rules*.

Determinants of institutional change It would be very useful to be able to predict under which conditions we should expect which behavior, but even if we cannot predict specific behavior – and thus institutional change – six factors should be particularly relevant:

1. The **bounded rationality** of actors.
2. The **problem of collective action**.
3. The **path dependency** of institutional change.
4. **Political transaction costs**.
5. The **relative power** of the relevant actors.
6. Prevalent **internal institutions**.

As we will see right now, more often than not, the first four factors inhibit institutional change. But if they do not inhibit such change, factor 5 can give us a clue regarding its direction: If the power of a certain group has increased relative to the power of all other relevant groups, we expect to see change in line with the interests of the group whose relevance has increased. Finally, factor 6 can be considered a constraint on the set of external institutions that can be enforced.

All six aspects are briefly discussed in the following.

6.6.2 Satisficing Behavior

Recall the concept of bounded rationality discussed in Chapter 1. Within this concept, Herbert Simon (1955) posits a hypothesis regarding the utility function of boundedly rational actors.

He assumes that actors do not attempt to maximize utility in each and every situation, but that they **satisfice**, that is, they are content once they attain a certain utility level. As soon as that threshold is reached, actors have no incentive to change their behavior. Thus, if an actor has so far behaved in conformity with existing institutions, there is no reason to believe he or she will start disobeying rules or insist on institutional change. The necessary condition for changing one's behavior from cell A to any of the other cells in Matrix 6.1 is that the utility experienced from unchanged behavior has significantly decreased in comparison to previous periods. Note that these considerations take place within a single person – and that no cooperation with others is necessary.

6.6.3 Collective Action Problems

Satisficing behavior is not the only reason why not every reduction in utility (relative to the utility associated with other options) is accompanied by a demand for comprehensive institutional change. Institutions are made up of rules that all actors in society are expected to comply with. They can, therefore, be thought of as public goods, the effects of which unfold because a multitude of actors is bound by them. An institutional change would affect not only one person, but all persons with similar preferences. And as you now know, in such a situation, each actor hopes that the – costly – demand for institutional change will be made, and paid for, by someone else, thus allowing him or her to *free-ride.*

Definition

Free-rider: Actor who benefits from a good without contributing to its provision.

As all actors hope to free-ride, collective action is unlikely to happen frequently, even in situations where taking collective action could benefit everyone. The behavior of discontented actors who are not able to overcome collective action problems so as to demand institutional change will either remain unchanged (and can thus be grouped in cell A in Matrix 6.1), or switched to breaking existing rules (i.e., be grouped in cell C). Whether institutional change is more likely to occur if more people break existing rules individually is entirely uncertain. The problem of collective action will only be overcome every now and then and not regularly. This is one way to explain why institutional change does not occur continuously but rather discretely.

6.6.4 Path Dependency of Institutional Change

Definition

Path dependency: Present decisions are influenced and constrained by past decisions.

The concept of **path dependency** is usually employed to explain the diffusion of technologies. However, according to Douglass North (1990a, 92–104), the concept is also very useful in the analysis of institutional change and, with just a few modifications, it is possible to draw an analogy between competing technologies and institutions (for a detailed discussion of this analogy, see Kiwit and Voigt, 1995). The central point of the original path dependency argument is that technologies can persist even though there might be more efficient competing technologies (see, e.g., Arthur, 1989). This is due to **network externalities**: The more people use a technology, the greater is the utility of everyone using the technology. For example, if I am the only person in the world using Facebook, I am never going to have any "friends." If one specific technology enjoys a widespread user base, suppliers of competing and possibly more efficient technologies will find it difficult to capture market share due these network externalities. The most frequently used example to illustrate path dependency is the arrangement of letters on modern keyboards. Supposing that you use an English version, the letters on the upper left hand side of your keyboard are almost certain to read QWERTY. Now, some people claim that a different arrangement of the letters on the keyboard would have been more efficient – but that it never became generally accepted due to substantial switching costs. New keyboards would need to be installed; everybody being accustomed to the current arrangement would need to be retrained and so on.

Proponents of path dependency claim that inefficient technologies can often come out on top and that competing, superior technologies cannot make any headway without government intervention. Thus, a purely market-based solution could lead to sustained inefficiencies. If the concept of path dependency can be applied to institutions and the function of institutions is to reduce uncertainty (and thereby enable economic prosperity), it must be concluded that institutions can originate and change without any improvements being made to economic growth and development. Along these lines, Paul David (1994, 218f.) writes:

[I]nstitutions generally turn out to be considerably less 'plastic' than is technology and the range of diversity in innovations achieved by recombinations of existing elements is observed to be much broader in the case of the latter. Thus, institutional structures, being more rigid and less adept at passively adapting to the pressures of changing environments, create incentives for their members and directors to undertake to alter the external environment. . . . Finally, it may be remarked that because the extent of tacit knowledge[1] required for the efficient functioning of a complex social organization is far greater – in relation to the extent of knowledge that exists in the form of explicit, codified information – than is the case for technological systems, institutional knowledge and the problem-solving techniques subsumed therein are more at risk of being lost when organizations collapse or are taken over and 'reformed' by rivals.

If institutional change is subject to path dependency, this could be part of an explanation why inefficient institutions can survive. As such, the presence of path dependency would rather help to explain the stability of institutions over time rather than their change.

6.6.5 Political Transaction Costs

Under the Coase theorem, scarce goods will be used efficiently given that property rights are well specified (see Chapter 2). Assuming that political markets are analogous to goods markets, does this mean that, in political markets, efficient policies and institutions are always chosen?

Note
Reminder: The Coase theorem only holds if property rights are well defined and transaction costs are zero.

---

[1] The term *tacit knowledge* dates back to Michael Polanyi (1998 [1952]). Tacit knowledge is knowledge that is incorporated in our actions, even though we are not able to articulate this knowledge. With regard to institutions, tacit knowledge implies that institutions also contain knowledge that cannot be articulated. If institutions are abolished, the tacit knowledge contained in them is also lost.

Remember from Chapter 2 that the Coase theorem only holds if there are enforceable property rights and transaction costs are negligibly low. If the Coase theorem is going to work for political markets, it means that these conditions must be met in these markets, too, which is even more doubtful than it is for traditional goods markets.

Transaction costs are the costs of using the market. In turn, political transaction costs are the costs of using the "political market." Binding agreements should be much harder to achieve on political markets than on traditional goods markets. Even defining the exchange will be difficult. Furthermore, in case of contract breach, it is unclear how, or even if, the conflict could be mediated. All in all, there are many reasons to believe that political transaction costs are highly relevant. They constrain the possibilities for changing the status quo, thus contributing to stabilization. Twight (1992) conjectures that politicians deliberately manipulate political transaction costs in order to limit political opposition with respect to certain political domains. *Political transaction costs stabilize efficient as well as inefficient institutions.* Acemoglu (2003) wonders why there is no political Coase theorem. He points out that there is no generally accepted "initial allocation" nor is there a neutral third party endowed with any sanctioning power that could enforce any potential deal between any of the concerned parties. He concludes that the origins and change of institutions can be better explained with recourse to the relative power of the relevant actors. This leads us directly to the next argument, namely the relative power of the relevant actors.

6.6.6 The Relative Power of the Relevant Actors

Until now, we have identified several factors that are obstacles to fast and comprehensive institutional change, rather than being conducive to it. To explain institutional change, it seems plausible that we need to inquire into the incentives of the involved actors. This involves identifying how well they are organized, which resources they can use, which strategies are at their disposal, and so forth. If some group becomes more relevant over time, we would also expect the design of institutions to change. Institutions influence the distribution of incomes. Groups whose relevance for national product has increased and who have managed to overcome the problem of collective action will sooner or later demand that institutions change to better meet their needs. One way to think of it is to contrast *de jure* and *de facto* power. *De jure* power is reflected in external institutions. When the actual power of a relevant group increases relative to that of all other groups, its *de facto* power increases. In order for *de jure* and *de facto* power to be aligned again, the external institutions are likely to be changed to reflect the new situation in the country.

For example, until the sixth century BC in Rome, the cavalry, provided by the nobles, were the only relevant factor in the empire's military strategy. Introduction of the phalanx – which had been invented in ancient Greece – led to a strengthening of the infantry. Use of the phalanx was considered necessary because Rome had suffered a devastating defeat in 477 BC. However, the infantry was composed mostly of plebeians, or plebs, who were not politically involved at all. This resulted in class struggle, as the plebs were burdened with increasing duties (such as military service) without any additional benefits (such as political participation). Due to their increased relative power, the plebs were able to force several institutional changes such as participation in political decisions, lifting of restrictions regarding both occupation and marriage, and some release of debts incurred for buying armor necessary for becoming part of a phalanx (more details and additional examples can be found in Voigt, 1999a, 128–137; Acemoglu and Robinson, 2005 provide a very similar approach).

6.6.7 The Relevance of Internal Institutions

The above-discussed elements of a general economic theory of institutional change emphasize the **demand side**. These elements focus sharply on the ability of potential beneficiaries of institutional change to realize their demands. For a comprehensive theory, however, we also have to account for the **supply side**. In a democracy, political entrepreneurs have an incentive to discover the preferences of unorganized voters and provide suitable legislation. In this context, the norms prevalent in large portions of the population should play a major role. From empirical evidence (Lewis-Beck and Stegmaier, 2019), we know that many citizens do not condition their voting decision solely on their expected individual monetary benefits, but also on their perception of whether groups they care about are treated fairly. This can explain

Institutional change depends both on the demand side and the supply side

why public servants – who usually cannot lose their jobs – might vote for a party that champions the interests of the jobless. In turn, this provides an incentive for politicians to take prevalent justice and fairness norms seriously.

6.6.8 A Short Summary

Institutional change is a rather unlikely event as many conditions need to be met before it occurs. A first necessary condition is that a sufficiently large number of people are unsatisfied with the currently valid institutions and that they are ready to incur costs to demand institutional change. Efficiency-enhancing institutional change is by no means guaranteed, as political transaction costs are likely to be significant. Although institutions tend to be resistant to change, shifts in the relative power of social groups will be reflected in corresponding changes in external institutions. The shifts will also indicate the direction of institutional change. Finally, politicians have an incentive to take into account the justice and fairness norms prevalent in large portions of society as these can be decisive in elections.

6.7 Open Questions

This chapter has made clear that there is a multitude of approaches to explaining specific aspects of institutional origins and change. There is no one comprehensive approach that integrates traditional political economy arguments (relevance of power) as well as specific institutional economics assumptions (bounded rationality, relevance of internal institutions such as justice norms). Thus, one central question raised by this chapter is whether such an integrated approach is possible.

Many other questions also arise: To what degree is a country's current development determined by its past? To what degree is it possible to change a development path?

QUESTIONS

1. It is not very flattering to call a theory "naïve." Explain why the theory proposed by Demsetz (1967) is called a naïve theory.
2. Discuss how North's theory of property rights development bridges the gap between contract theories à la Hobbes and predatory exploitation theories à la Marx.

3. Explain why – using North's theory – maximization of ruler income and maximization of social product can be irreconcilable.
4. What competition and transaction cost restrictions is a ruler subject to according to North's theory? To what degree do both restrictions make likely inefficient property rights?
5. What is the role of collective action for institutional change? How can institutional competition be linked to collective action?

FURTHER READING

The commonalities, but also the differences, between public choice, social choice, and political economy are discussed in Mueller (2015). Tullock (1987) is one of the first monographs to provide an economic theory of autocracy. It contains a number of empirical examples, but no integrated theoretical approach. Wintrobe (1998) offers such a theory, based on the application of simple economic arguments.

The publications of Mancur Olson on the transition from anarchy to autocracy have inspired a number of other essays, including Niskanen (1997). Moselle and Polak (2001) distinguish between anarchy, organized banditry, and the predatory state. In direct contrast to Olson, they argue that "the unbridled predatory state is likely to reduce the welfare of the populace relative to anarchy and organized banditry" (Moselle and Polak, 2001, 5).

Nunn (2014) is an up-to-date survey on how historical events affect current institutions. The various findings of the economic theory of legal origins are summarized in La Porta et al. (2008). Those interested in digging deeper will find Zweigert and Kötz (1998) helpful. Among the very many critical assessments regarding the significance of legal origins, two are particularly helpful: Spamann (2010) recodes the original coding – and ends up with a completely different dataset. Klerman et al. (2011) point out that colonial history might be more important than belonging to a particular legal tradition.

Kirstein and Voigt (2006) discuss the self-interest of rulers. They conjecture that promises to behave in a specific manner are not credible at the constitutional level. The authors argue that constitutional-level promises will be implemented only if all actors involved have an interest in the implementation, not only at the time of signing the contract but also at the time of its implementation. The authors identify parameter constellations under which neither the ruler nor the ruled can increase their payoffs by unilaterally deviating from their promises.

The concept of "spatial diffusion" is described in more detail by Elkins and Simmons (2005).

A critical and entertaining account of the traditional concept of path dependency can be found in Liebowitz and Margolis (1989).

Alesina and Spoalore (2005) discuss the determinants of state size. Dixit (1996) provides a detailed analysis of political markets using the concept of political transaction costs.

7 Explaining Change in Internal Institutions

7.1 Introductory Remarks

In Chapter 6, we asked whether we can use the instruments of economic analysis to inquire into the origins and change of external institutions. We identified factors that are likely to be an explanation of both the choice of external institutions, as well as their change over time. In this chapter, we ask whether economic analysis can contribute to understanding the origins and change of internal institutions. In Chapter 6, we emphasized the role of explicit collective decisions for external institutions. Type 4 internal institutions (those with organized enforcement) can also be changed via explicit collective decision-making. We will not delve further into the topic of type 4 internal institutions, as the factors identified in Chapter 6 are also relevant for them. Type 1 institutions are solutions to coordination games. Lacking any element of conflict, it is easy to imagine their spontaneous emergence and high stability over time. Thus, we will rather address the hard cases in this chapter, that is, the determinants of type 2 and type 3 institutions (ethical rules and customs, respectively).

We will not attempt to explain the origins of specific institutions. Instead, we ask whether we can identify **mechanisms** that contribute to the development of diverse institutions. In a literature survey that appeared nearly 30 years ago, Jon Elster (1989b) did not want to exclude the possibility that norms – which are closely related to type 2 and type 3 institutions – develop randomly. That is equivalent to saying that we simply do not know of a general mechanism underlying their emergence and change over time. Since Elster's survey, in the last few years in particular, there has been an enormous interest among economists in both the determinants and the effects of "culture." No matter how culture is defined, internal institutions are likely to be an important part of it. In this chapter, we develop a "synthetic approach" made up of approaches found in various disciplines. This approach focuses on the conceptual. If relevant empirical evidence is available, we do mention it.

Can we identify mechanisms of institutional development?

> **Chapter Highlights**
> - Frame the emergence of norms as an economic problem.
> - Consider the potential roles of repetition and reputation in norm emergence.
> - See under what conditions (costly) sanctioning can be rational.

We proceed as follows: First, we define the terms "values" and "norms" and discuss their relation to institutions. We proceed by describing the issue of the origins of norms in economic terms (Section 7.2). In Section 7.3, we briefly present and critically discuss different hypotheses concerning the origins of norms. This section also contains the "synthetic approach" just mentioned. Whereas this approach focuses on possible transmission channels by which internal institutions might spread, it is rather silent on potential triggers for the choice of internal institutions and their change over time. In Section 7.4, a number of exogenous factors that might induce change in internal institutions are discussed. These include both geographical factors and external institutions. Section 7.5 concludes the chapter with open questions.

7.2 The Problem in Economic Terms

Type 2 and type 3 institutions are based on values and norms. Conceptions regarding right behavior are presupposed for both types of institutions. For type 3 institutions, behavior that is not compatible with normative conceptions is sanctioned by third parties. In a first step, we need to define both values and norms.

Definition of values

Following the *International Encyclopedia of the Social Sciences* (Darity, 2007), values can be defined as "conceptions of the desirable, influencing selective behavior. Values are not the same as norms for conduct. ... Values are standards of desirability that are more nearly independent of specific situations. The same value may be a point of reference for a great many specific norms; a particular norm may represent the simultaneous application of several separable values" (see Figure 7.1). Thus, justice is a value that can be found in many specific norms, such as concerning the fair share of the pie, fair parental treatment of children, fair treatment of workers, and fair grading of exams.

Values are not equal to norms

Traditionally, the topic of values and norms has been more prominent in sociology than in economics. You might have heard

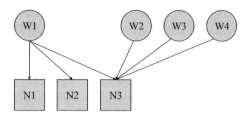

Figure 7.1 One value can be a reference point for multiple norms; one norm can represent the application of multiple values.

James Duesenberry (1960) quipping that "economics is all about how people make choices; sociology is all about why they don't have any choices to make." Well, that was decades ago.

Definition

Homo sociologicus: Behavioral model used in sociology. Put very simply, *homo sociologicus* attempts, by his or her actions, to fulfill role expectations of relevant reference groups.

Nevertheless, traditional sociology does not appear to be the right place to look for explanations of why norms develop, because it deals with the roles assigned to individuals by society while assuming that norms are given. We, however, are interested in the origins of norms here.

In the last few decades, a competing sociological approach has been developed (**rational choice sociology**) which shares with economics the paradigm of rational decision-making. One of its leading representatives was James Coleman. In his *Foundations of Social Theory* (Coleman, 1990), he argues that the *existence of externalities is a necessary condition for the development of norms.* In an earlier work he wrote: "The central premise ... is that norms arise when actions have external effects, including the extreme cases of public goods or public bads. Further, norms arise in those cases in which markets cannot easily be established, or transaction costs are high" (Coleman, 1987, 140). Norms structure social interaction. However, if social interactions do not affect third parties (and thus do not exhibit externalities), there is no need for norms.

Externalities are a necessary condition for the development of norms ...

Unfortunately, it is possible to assign an externality to virtually every action. As a consequence, norms might develop to structure virtually any interaction situation. This necessary condition is almost universally fulfilled, thus making it difficult for us to

... which are almost universally fulfilled

distinguish between situations in which it is plausible that norms
might develop and situations in which it is not. We require a way to
assess whether externalities are perceived as significant by the
parties affected.

Littlechild and Wiseman (1986, 166) provide a nice illustration of
how differently externalities can be perceived:

Consider some [of] the various ways in which smoking by one person
A might be argued adversely to affect a non-smoker B:

a) B's health may be adversely affected, in ways that can be verified by
    persuasive empirical evidence.
b) Even without such evidence, B may *believe* that his health is adversely
    affected.
c) B may be simply annoyed by tobacco smoke.
d) B may be concerned about the effect of smoking on A's health.
e) B may be concerned about the effect of A's smoking on the happiness
    of third party C, who is exposed to A's smoke, or on third party D, who
    is a concerned friend or relative of A.
f) B may be annoyed at what he believes is A's lack of awareness of the
    suffering he is causing.

This example shows how differently one situation can be interpreted and how many possibilities there are to assign externalities
to a simple everyday situation such as this one.

Aside from the existence of externalities, Coleman (1987) mentions a further condition for the development of norms: *the individual willingness to sanction norm-deviant behavior.* If a sanction
can be carried out by a multitude of persons, it represents a public
good. Many people have an interest in sanctioning behavior that
deviates from an accepted norm. Because sanctioning is associated
with costs, however, each individual prefers that someone else
carry out the sanction. Thus, we need to clarify how the associated
free-rider problem can be solved. The involved problem is a classical problem in the provision of public goods. Though this insight
is important, it does not provide an explanation, but is merely a
precise statement of the problem.

In a 1986 essay, Robert Axelrod mentions **meta norms** – norms
concerned with the sanctioning of norm-deviating behavior – as a
solution to the public good problem. However, such recourse to
meta norms does not solve the problem, it merely transfers the
problem to a different level, as one has to show how the free-rider
problem concerning meta norms can be solved, and so on. This line

Willingness to sanction noncompliant behavior

of reasoning thus leads to an **infinite regress**. Sanctioning by third parties is not the only way to ensure compliance with a norm. Individual internalization of a norm represents a further possibility. In our lingo: We need to explain both the development of mechanisms for the enforcement of type 3 institutions and the process of internalization that leads to the development of type 2 institutions.

Definition

An **infinite regress** arises if the truth of a proposition requires the support of a second proposition, the correctness of which requires the support of a third proposition and so on *ad infinitum*.

7.3 Hypotheses on the Origins of Norms

The conditions just sketched represent the basic problem in economic terms, but do not contain any explanation yet. Thus, let us briefly present some explanatory approaches. We will start with evolutionary (game) theory, move on to ask whether we should explicitly take into consideration that interactions can be repeated and that reputations might emerge out of one's behavior, and finally present an attempt to combine theory elements from such thinkers as Hume, Weber, Hayek, and Lewis.

7.3.1 Evolutionary Approaches

In contrast to traditional game theory, evolutionary game theory attempts to avoid demanding assumptions with regard to the rationality of actors. Representatives of evolutionary game theory are not interested in explaining individual decisions, but rather *the survival of competing behavioral strategies*. Imagine a situation in which an individual can either apply the strategy "tell a lie" or the strategy "tell the truth." Evolutionary game theory now inquires into the survival probabilities of these strategies. Actors are not considered as persons, but rather as carriers of strategies. Strategies that factually survive must have functioned *as if* they had pursued the objective to survive (Alchian, 1950; Friedman, 1953). Within evolutionary game theory, arguments exclusively based on genetic evolution are rare. Thus, you will rarely find the argument that humans are genetically determined to be liars or non-liars. If one is interested in explaining the many commonalities that are shared by

Explanation of the survival of competing behavioral strategies mankind all over the planet, this approach might have some merit. Here, however, we are mainly interested in explaining the differences in norms across different societies. For that, recourse to purely genetic arguments is unlikely to be helpful.

An interesting aside

One interesting exception to the general evaluation that arguments based on genetics are unhelpful is the *commitment* approach by Robert Frank (1988). Frank considers the question of how exchange partners can communicate the earnestness of their intent (you have already encountered the dilemma of the strong state – a special case of the more general commitment problem discussed here). Verbal promises such as "Trust me!" are called *cheap talk* by game theorists, as anyone who is interested in exchange is able to make such promises at virtually zero cost. Frank argues that emotions – that is, seemingly irrational expressions – can be of high strategic relevance. Emotions such as anger or guilt can help others assess a person. Emotions that are genetically predetermined – and that are thus not easily imitated – can provide valuable signals for predicting the behavior of others. Thus, the problem of *credible self-commitment* would be lessened. Emotions can allow individuals to categorize other individuals with high reliability as cooperators, allowing cooperators to structure their interactions primarily with other cooperators.

Evolutionary approaches often focus on **memes** instead of genes (Dawkins, 1989). Memes are cultural traits that are transmitted and spread via memory and imitation. Colman (1982, 267) describes it thus: "A meme will spread through a population rapidly if there is something about it that makes it better able than the available alternatives to infect people's minds, just as germs spread when they are able to infect people's bodies. This analogy draws attention to the fact that the fittest memes are not necessarily ones that are beneficial to society as a whole." In their anthropological approach to norm evolution, Boyd and Richerson (1994) argue that memes spread like innovations.

Definition

Meme: Ideas or thoughts that spread via communication.

Definition

Norms: Memes that influence behavioral standards.

Norms can then be defined as memes that influence behavioral standards.

Boyd and Richerson (1994) describe cultural evolution as a process that is driven by three forces. It is driven by: *Cultural evolution as process*

1. **Unbiased transmission** during the childhood of individuals. This implies that children are characterized by the same values and norms as their parents. As long as carriers of different norms exhibit constant and identical birth rates, the population composition remains the same.
2. **Biased transmission.** This takes place when children grow up and come into contact with other systems of values and norms. This type of transmission is thus explicitly influenced by choices of the relevant actors.
3. **Natural selection,** i.e., higher reproduction rates of individuals with specific traits.

Using this approach, Boyd and Richerson attempt to create a bridge between approaches that are frequently perceived as competing: the approach of genetic evolution following Darwin, and the approach of cultural evolution. In fact, they have coined the term "gene–culture coevolution" to indicate that evolution takes place via both culture and genes. According to that concept, culturally transmitted information can lead humans to change both their physical and their social environment which can, in turn, change the selective pressures on genes.

Boyd and Richerson describe biased transmission analogously to the diffusion of innovation. In the same manner that an individual can choose to use an innovation or not, an individual can choose to adopt a meme or not according to his or her preferences. However, this notion is not compatible with the above described diffusion process of memes. From our point of view, the notion that norms are subject to conscious choice is neither practical nor right. Norms can influence our utility even if we do not individually accept or reject specific norms. The analogy is also somewhat misleading, as the use of innovation is subject to conscious choice, while the use of institutions is not. Social interactions that lead to the diffusion of norms are not discussed. However, the discussion of precisely such processes should be the focus of an explanatory approach. Another reason why this approach is not satisfactory is the assumption that individuals can choose from a pool of memes those that they prefer the most. Thus, the emergence of such a pool of memes is entirely random; no further attempts to explain the origins of memes are made.

Similar to gene–culture coevolution, Samuel Bowles and Herbert Gintis (2011) also draw on multilevel selection, just as Boyd and Richerson (e.g., 2005) do. The idea here is that selection takes place on the individual, as well as on the group level. In their account of why humans are a cooperative species, Bowles and Gintis argue that war plays a crucial role. It frequently leads to the extinction of entire groups. Simultaneously, war helps spread the norms of the winners. Wars will regularly be won by those groups who have more altruists in their midst. This is how Bowles and Gintis hope to show that altruism does entail evolutionary advantages. It seems a bit ironic that war – certainly one of the less civilized activities of mankind – is thought to foster altruism.

Critique   Many representatives of evolutionary approaches employ evolutionary game theory for their analysis. In contrast to the theoretical approaches of traditional game theory, evolutionary game theory requires rather lax assumptions regarding the rationality of individuals. Indeed, a bird or a rat that behaves according to trial-and-error is sufficiently rational for the use of this approach. We could also interpret this as a disadvantage of the evolutionary approach, as it does not take into account the human capability to weigh competing hypotheses, anticipate consequences of decisions, and so on.

7.3.2 Repetition or Reputation as Explanatory Factor?

As previously mentioned, repetition can be associated with an immensely increased number of equilibria (you remember the Folk theorem discussed in Chapter 4). This can even be the case if, although interactions are not repeated between the same two individuals, it is possible to obtain and communicate information regarding the behavior of others displayed in previous rounds at low cost. We saw that conditional cooperation (for instance in the form of tit-for-tat) is one of many possible equilibrium strategies in the repeated prisoner's dilemma. If information regarding other players can be easily and reliably communicated, defecting behavior can destroy an individual's reputation and reduce their future chance of finding exchange partners. It follows that each individual is forced to weigh the (one-off and present) benefit from defection against the (repeated and future) cost of not being able to find transaction partners.

In order for **reputation** to be this effective, three conditions have to be met:

1. The respective "case" of defection needs to be **sufficiently public**. It is not only known to the parties involved.
2. The **perception of the relevant facts** is shared by most observers. That is, most observers perceive the case **identically**.
3. The relevant facts are evaluated similarly: **Norms** that are used to evaluate the case are **shared** by most of the observers.

Conditions for reputation to be effective

However, this implies that reputation can only effectively shape behavior if "proto-norms"[1] are already in place. If this is true, we have to conclude that reputation by itself cannot explain the formation of norms, but may be useful for explaining the origins of norm-complying behavior. Moreover, scholars who argue in favor of an evolutionary approach insist that cooperative equilibria will only be sustainable in very small groups (e.g., Boyd and Richerson, 2005).

Critique

7.3.3 An Attempted Synthesis

In the previous two sub-sections, we presented strategies that might be used to explain the formation of norms. We evaluated both rather critically. In this sub-section, we will attempt a third explanatory approach. It is by no means an original one. Rather, you can see it as a synthetic approach that tries to integrate explanations by a variety of thinkers that span several centuries.

7.3.3.1 Regular Behavior

Assume that one person has exhibited distinct behavioral regularities in his exchange with another person. Based on this experience, the exchange partner has formed expectations regarding the first person's future behavior. If these expectations are not met – implying a negative externality for the other person – the result will

---

[1] The prefix means "first."

be anger towards the person who behaved disappointingly. We thus assume that individuals – based on previously observed regularities – form the expectation that this regularity can be extrapolated into the future. Put differently, an individual will expect that another individual who has acted in a certain way in a given situation will continue to act in the same way in the future. Thus, coordination is facilitated when individuals *transform actual regularities into the normative expectation that this regularity will continue into the future.* Assuming that there is a basic human need to be appreciated by others, this mechanism could well provide a reason for continued compliance with the rule which has now attained normative status, even if external factors might have changed in a manner that makes other behavior seem more reasonable.[2]

This notion regarding the origins of norms can be traced back at least to David Hume (1990 [1740]). Robert Sugden (1986, 152) offers a modern interpretation: "Our desire to keep the good will of others ... is more than a means to some other end. It seems to be a basic human desire. That we have such a desire is presumably the product of biological evolution."[3] Introducing a preference as "inherently human" could be criticized as prematurely suspending the search for insights. However, we can justify it with a simple **counterfactual argument**. Let us assume there are two groups of humans. Members of the first group exhibit an inherent preference to seek appreciation by other group members, while members of the second group do not. In consequence, norms that encourage productive activity will evolve in the first group, for instance because honesty is widespread in the first, while it is not in the second group. Sooner or later, the second group will be crowded out by

---

[2] Similarly, Majeski (1990, 276) argues: "The first time a rule that eventually becomes a norm is invoked by an individual in the group it is *not* a norm. It is an individual contextually generated decision rule. ... An individual rule becomes a norm when the application of the rule by other members of the social group is justified by appeal to the precedent application, or when the application is justified by the individual as the expected and/or appropriate behavior of a member of the group. Also, an individual rule becomes a norm when the rule is so established in the group that individuals perceive it to be the only plausible alternative."

[3] Very closely related hypotheses are put forward by Max Weber (1964 [1922], 191f.), Friedrich A. Hayek (1973, 96), William Graham Sumner (1992 [1906], 358), and David Lewis (1969, 99). These arguments can be traced back as far as the *Nicomachean Ethics* of Aristotle.

members of the first group. Notice that, at the end of the day, this is also an evolutionary argument.

However, this line of argumentation should not be overreached. Differences in norms of different groups are too large to be explained solely as the result of genetic dispositions. Furthermore, we need to account for the fact that the circle of persons that we seek acknowledgment from is apparently highly variable. Thus, we need to be clear about the factors that determine the composition and size of the reference group.

7.3.3.2 Interdependent Utility Functions

A very simple way to let costly sanctioning behavior appear straightforward is to claim that evolution has supported other-regarding preferences and that, therefore, they are assumed to exist. Fehr and Schmidt (1999) have chosen a different path; they assume a particular preference function which they christen "**inequity aversion**". Simply put, inequity aversion means that people experience negative utility from unequal outcomes, such as unequal incomes. People are even assumed to suffer utility losses when they are better off than their reference group (although less so than if they are worse off).

Now, many questions can be asked, like how the reference is defined, what the ratio is between being better off than the reference group versus being worse off, etc. But the remarkable consequence of inequity aversion is that punishing non-cooperative behavior can be completely rational. In other words, the sanctioning part of type 3 institutions has been systematically integrated into economic models. A very simple way to think about inequity aversion is to think of it in terms of interdependent utility functions. My utility is influenced by how others do.

Definition

Interdependent utility functions: Utility function in which my utility is also determined by the utility that others enjoy.

Interdependent utility functions can be used to explain the origins of norms. Interdependent utility functions might help us explain why apparently uninvolved third parties are willing to sanction norm-reneging behavior even though this is associated with costs (Figure 7.2). If the utility of person Q is negatively influenced by

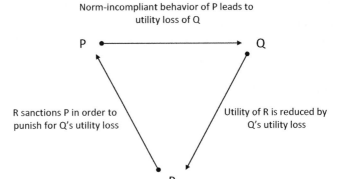

Figure 7.2 Using the concept of interdependent utility functions to explain the existence of costly sanctions.

noncomplying behavior of person P, and Q's utility positively affects the utility of a third person R, one could easily envision situations in which person R has an incentive to sanction person P's noncomplying behavior.

Traditionally, utility functions are assumed to be non-interdependent in economics, such that the utility of others is irrelevant for an individual's utility. Individual utility is then neither positively nor negatively affected by the fact that someone else's utility is reduced.

If, conversely, we assume interdependent utility functions, person R's utility is not only a function of her available bundle of goods p_R, but also of another person's bundle of goods p_Q.

$$U_R = f(\alpha \cdot p_R + \beta \cdot p_Q)$$

Traditionally, it is assumed that β is zero, that is, the utility of R is not affected by the utility of person Q. Introducing interdependent utility functions also has far-reaching consequences for sanctioning and internal institutions. *We can now explain the existence of costly sanctions.* For instance, if your little brother's utility is an argument of your utility function, you might be able to increase your utility by sanctioning his friend who just took away his toy. Within the scope of rational choice, you will carry out a sanction if the costs of sanctioning are lower than additional utility gained from the fact that your brother's utility just increased. Thus, the probability of sanctioning depends on the weight that the other person's utility has in your utility function and the available sanctioning technologies.

Far-reaching consequences of interdependent utility functions for sanctioning

Traditionally, *homo economicus* is modeled to be atomistic, that is, a utility maximizing individual who acts in isolation. If it were possible to formulate the conditions under which interdependent utility functions can be expected to occur, an adequate extension of the concept could be useful in explaining the development of the sanction component of type 3 institutions. The transition from non-interdependent to interdependent utility functions can be justified by the fact that it increases the explanatory and predictive power of models. However, the introduction of modified utility functions is also accompanied by a host of new questions. For instance, one needs to clarify the weight with which other persons' utility affects your utility.

7.3.3.3 Norms of Cooperation

The Folk theorem states that cooperation can evolve in repeated games even for relatively high degrees of conflict. However, the degree to which groups actually manage to cooperate varies significantly. One could suspect a learning process behind this variation. *The better groups of individuals are able to coordinate their behavior in a game with little or no conflict, the more likely they are able to solve games with a higher degree of conflict by cooperating.* This hypothesis is based on a simple consideration: The higher the degree of conflict inherent in a game, the larger the risk to be exploited by the respective other player. If members of a social group are able to solve a game that has a certain degree of conflict in a cooperative manner, the likelihood of solving a game with a degree of conflict just a little bit higher should be greater than if that group was not able to solve the first game (Axelrod, 1970 defines the degree of conflict in games).

The hypothesis just outlined implies that the *development of norms might be path dependent*. The probability that, in a certain situation, a norm of cooperation develops and is sustained depends, among other things, on whether members of a social group were previously able to structure interactions cooperatively. This hypothesis reminds us that we should not neglect the cognitive dimension. Two situations that appear identical to external observers might be reconstructed very differently by the parties involved. The resulting degree of conflict and, in consequence, the probability of solving the game cooperatively might vary significantly.

Path dependency in the development of norms?

North on cognition and beliefs

Nobel laureate Douglass North has been a crucial advocate for relentlessly pushing the research agenda of institutional economics forward. In his 2005 book *Understanding the Process of Economic Change*, he points out the importance of both beliefs and cognition for institutional change. He argues that institutions are created based on the relevant actors' beliefs. If the results of the institutions people create are not as expected, people will update their beliefs – they will learn – and institutional change will continue. To understand the process of institutional change, then, one must understand how beliefs come into being, receive updating, and form the basis of human action.

North tries to deal with the question by delving into cognitive science. To understand how beliefs are formed and how humans learn, he asserts, we must first understand better how our brains work. Thus, he enters territory where, owing to the academic division of labor, economists are amateurs. Here, North comes very close to an argument made by Friedrich A. Hayek in the early 1950s in a book called *The Sensory Order* (Hayek, 1952). In that book, Hayek developed a number of hypotheses about how the brain works and how external sensations are structured in ways that allow the experiencing being to make sense of them. Although North makes frequent references to Hayek, his own excursion into cognitive science remains largely unsatisfactory.

Many questions regarding the relationship between cognition, beliefs, and institutions remain to be answered. For example, institutions are collective phenomena whereas beliefs are individual phenomena, and updating beliefs – learning – is an individual experience. If institutional change is interpreted as a consequence of changing beliefs, an aggregation problem needs to be explicitly dealt with: How are individual beliefs transformed into modified institutions?

The Israeli social scientist Edna Ullman-Margalit (1977, 121–127) proposes an explanation that is close to the above-sketched hypothesis. She discusses the so-called stag–hunt game. It is a game in which the degree of conflict lies somewhere between a pure coordination game and the prisoner's dilemma. She argues that the prisoner's dilemma can be transformed into a stag-hunt game if there is a general expectation that the actions of individual actors are stabilized by habit, and if there is a favorable starting point at which, somehow, cooperation is established.

Let us briefly explain the nature of the stag-hunt game: In order to catch a stag, two hunters need to cooperate. One hunter flushes the stag out, which allows the other hunter to shoot it. If the two hunters do not cooperate, each can merely catch a hare. Both hunters prefer catching a stag to catching a hare. Catching a hare, however, is preferable to catching nothing, which is the case if one hunter attempts to cooperate while the other hunter is off hunting a hare. This results in the payoffs depicted in Matrix 7.1 (the first number respectively denotes the payoff for the row player, the second the payoff for the column player). _{The stag-hunt game}

As opposed to the prisoner's dilemma, this game does not have a dominant strategy, that is, the best response of the row player (R) depends on the choice of the column player (C) – and vice versa. The game is characterized by two symmetric Nash-equilibria in pure strategies: (R1, C1) and (R2, C2). At first glance, it should be easy to switch from the non-cooperative equilibrium (R2, C2) to the cooperative equilibrium (R1, C1), as both hunters would be better off. However, each hunter depends on the respective other hunter's cooperation in order to achieve the cooperative equilibrium, while non-cooperation yields a payoff of 2 with certainty. In his discussion of the game, Binmore (1994, 120–125) describes players that achieve (R1, C1) as players that have learnt to trust each other.

Matrix 7.1 The stag-hunt game

		Hunter C	
		C1 (stag)	C2 (hare)
Hunter R	R1 (stag)	3 ⟋ 3	2 ⟋ 0
	R2 (hare)	0 ⟋ 2	2 ⟋ 2

The original stag-hunt game

The game we just discussed can be traced back to Geneva philosopher Jean-Jacques Rousseau (1992 [1755]). In the second part of his *Discourse on the Origen of Inequality*, he writes:

This is how men could imperceptibly acquire some crude idea of mutual commitments and of the advantages to be had in fulfilling them, but only insofar as present and perceptible interests could require it, since foresight meant nothing to them, and far from concerning themselves about a distant future, they did not even give a thought to the next day. Were it a matter of catching a deer, everyone was quite aware that he must faithfully keep to his post in order to achieve this purpose; but if a hare happened to pass within reach of one of them, no doubt he would have pursued it without giving a second thought, and that, having obtained his prey, he cared very little about causing his companions to miss theirs. (Rousseau, 1992 [1755], 46f.)

Our basic argument is that cooperation is more likely in a game with a higher degree of conflict if the players are part of a social group in which the equilibrium (R1, C1) is a commonly accepted social norm. However, this also means that we are leaving the safe grounds of game theory, as the solution to the game in question depends on the solution of other previously played games that are not explicitly considered in the analysis.

Trust and internal institutions

By now, there is a huge body of literature on the effects of trust on economic outcomes. In a word, since high levels of trust can save individuals a lot of transaction costs, high trust societies are better off in many dimensions compared to low trust societies. But what is the relationship between trust and internal institutions?

We propose to think of trust as a consequence of internal institutions – and not as an internal institution in and of itself. If I trust someone, I essentially expect that the person I am trusting behaves according to the values and norms embedded in the relevant internal institutions. Interestingly, trust levels have been shown to remain amazingly stable over generations. The offspring of migrants who came to the USA two or even

> three generations ago still display trust levels very similar to those found in the originating country. Since all of the migrants were subject to the same external institutions – namely, those of the USA – the internal institutions underlying different trust levels must have remained unchanged over a number of generations. Fernández (2010) nicely summarizes the relevant literature.

Let us summarize the argumentation developed so far:

1. Individual decision rules and habits can attain normative status.
2. Principally, it appears reasonable to work with interdependent utility functions. However, the question how another person's utility and how the utilities of any number of other people exactly affect individual utility remains open.
3. The development of cooperation norms might be path dependent. The more stable such norms are in games of a given level of conflict, the more likely it is that members of a social group are able to solve games designed with a high level of conflict.

We have not yet discussed in detail how the sanction component of type 2 internal institutions might evolve. (Type 2 internal institutions are those ethical rules to which the actors commit themselves.) This entails bad conscience or the psychological costs that can arise, even if one is sure that no one is watching.

7.3.3.4 Concerning the Sanctioning Component

Dennis Mueller (1986) argues that actors who have been taught to cooperate by threat of sanctions will continue to cooperate in the absence of sanctions. This argument can help us explain how type 2 internal institutions are transmitted. Mueller proposes to modify the commonly used behavioral assumption of rational egoism to an assumption of **adaptive egoism**. In doing so, Mueller supports the Adaptive egoism acknowledgment of psychological research results in economics. However, proposing that norm-complying behavior learned in childhood is fully retained in adulthood would be equivalent to abandoning the economic approach. After all, the basic premise of economics is that virtually any action can be invoked by incentives. Thus, it appears reasonable to introduce a **two-stage** A two-stage **behavioral model**. In the first stage, the decision problem is behavioral model classified as involving little or high costs. In the second state and given that the costs of norm-compliance are rather low, there is a high chance that the individual will comply with the norm. But if the costs of complying are high, the individual is more likely to think the entire problem through systematically. Framed differently: *The higher the costs of norm-compliance, the higher the likelihood that the decision problem is subjected to a rational choice calculus.* Now, the apparent problem is how to identify regularities in the transition from one to the other decision-making procedure.

7.3.3.5 Outlook

Many attempts to explain the origins of internal institutions presuppose the existence of some explanatory factors such as the existence of shared values. A natural corollary is to ask whether one is able to use an economics approach to explain the origins of these presupposed factors. In recent years, more and more researchers have concluded that the economics approach by itself is not sufficient for this purpose, and that results from studies conducted by other disciplines, such as cognitive science, need to be accounted for. We argued above that one condition for the existence of shared values and norms is that the actors involved perceive a given situation in a similar manner. Representatives of the cognitive sciences primarily inquire into questions of exactly that nature, which is why there is hope that economists might be able to learn from them.

7.4 Potential Triggers for Change in Internal Institutions

7.4.1 Introductory Remarks

Whereas in Section 7.3 we were primarily interested in identifying possible mechanisms for determining the origin of internal institutions, here we focus on potential determinants of their change. A precondition for observing changes in internal institutions seems to be that the environment must have changed, somehow implying that the net benefits of complying with the internal institutions must also have changed. Changes in the environment might include natural disasters or changes in the microclimate, but also technological advances that allow for different and more useful cultivation methods. But since there is no explicit procedure for changing internal institutions, it seems quite possible that they remain unchanged. In other words, changes in the environment are a necessary, but not sufficient, condition for systematic changes in internal institutions. This implies that although society as a whole would be better off if institutions changed, such change often does not take place. We now set out to discuss two factors of external change that could trigger change in internal institutions, namely, geography and change in external institutions.

7.4.2 Geography Again

In Chapter 6, we saw that geographic conditions can have an impact on the likelihood of state formation, as well as on the kind of regime that is likely to emerge. Here, we ask whether geographic conditions can be one determinant for the internal institutions used by societies. Even in Chapter 5, we discussed an example of such possibility. We brought up the work of Alesina et al. (2013) who demonstrated that in societies where the use of the plough was suitable (a geographic aspect) the status of women is affected until today, measured by the percentage of women in the workforce or the percentage of female parliamentarians. Norms regarding the role of women in society are elicited by the consent – or not – to statements like: "When jobs are scarce, men should have more right to a job than women."

Platteau (2000) is particularly interested in possible explanations for the (non-)development of many African societies. Most of these societies have internal institutions that aim at a high degree of equality among their members. Today, the growth-retarding effect of these institutions is widely acknowledged. Investments that are both sizable and obvious are less likely to be made. Promotions to better paying jobs are frequently turned down because the additional income would have to be shared with one's relatives. But equality-enhancing, i.e., redistributive, institutions not only lead to a suboptimal allocation of resources, they can also drive up transaction costs which can cause more growth-retarding effects. For example, to hide the size of my financial assets from my environment, I might prefer not holding a bank account, or putting only a fraction of my assets there. To hide how wealthy a farmer I am, I might disperse my cattle geographically, which implies, however, higher monitoring costs (chapter 5 of Platteau's book contains more examples).

Given that most observers agree that these institutions are inhibiting growth, two questions need to be dealt with. First, how could these institutions ever emerge in the first place, and second, how come they have survived until today? Traditional agrarian societies heavily depend on the climate, the weather in particular. In such societies, the pooling of risks, i.e., mutual insurance, is an important means to reduce uncertainty. According to Platteau, it is the very structure of tribal society that makes the emergence of strongly egalitarian norms seem beneficial. Interestingly, this is not the full story. If (economic) success was primarily attributable to entrepreneurial skills and effort, then unequal outcomes might appear justified. To cut the strong link between effort and success, tribal societies have often rationalized the unpredictable aspect of nature by resorting to magical practices. Individuals who are too successful are often constrained through witchcraft. As soon as a single person believes in it, it already has a factual effect. This is another example for the relevance of beliefs already alluded to earlier.

Internal institutions might survive although they are making society worse off

So how can these norms survive given that they are inhibiting growth and development today? Well, simply because once established, such norms are extremely difficult to change. After all, many people appear to benefit; each time a relative gets an increase in pay, they can claim their share. Individual evasion seems frequently easier than collective change. In some regions, "stranger" entrepreneurs are not subject to the equality norms, hence some entrepreneurs move away from home. Sometimes, individuals convert to religions that are less strict about equality. So this is one example where, due to many changes in the environment, a society would be better off if its internal institutions changed, but this change simply does not occur.

Trust has been mentioned a number of times throughout this book as an important resource for keeping transaction costs low. Trust itself is not an institution – but can be a consequence of institutions. Since the evidence is almost undisputed that trust has important effects on many walks of life (Algan and Cahuc, 2014 is a recent review), it is of interest to ask why trust levels differ so dramatically across the world. One explanation is closely connected to the climate–insurance nexus just probed into with regard to Africa. Ruben Durante (2010) conjectures that mutual trust developed in pre-industrial times as a consequence of farmers insuring each other because they had to cope with climatic risks.

He simply assumes that farmers in areas with higher variability of weather conditions were more likely to set up mutual insurance schemes and learned to trust each other. Today, weather conditions have become a lot less important for agricultural output. Still, Durante is able to show that in those European areas subject to higher year-to-year variability in precipitation and temperature, people still display higher trust levels. A particular aspect of geography has, therefore, induced mutual insurance schemes that have taught people to trust each other. The enhanced levels of trust help people in these regions to save on transaction costs to this very day.

Trust levels might have geographic origins

7.4.3 External Institutions

So far, we have discussed what an economic explanation for the origins of norms might look like. We have ignored, however, the possibility that the development of norms might also be influenced by existing external institutions. To be able to further delve into this possibility, we need to clarify whether and how external institutions that were in place a long time ago can still impact on individuals' behavior today.

Italy is characterized by marked differences in behavior between the north and the south. In the north, the likelihood that people trust each other and cooperate with each other is markedly higher than in the south. Putnam (1993) (whom you encountered in Chapter 2) ascribes these differences to differences in history. More precisely, to differences in the history of how cities gained their independence between the years 1000 and 1200. In a nutshell, the argument is that having gone through the experience of becoming an independent city-state implies having had the experiences of self-administration, of being responsible for one's own *res publica*. Having successfully mastered the administration of one's own affairs was likely to lead people to trust each other. So the argument essentially is that a particular set of external institutions – namely, those involved in becoming an independent city-state – has very long-lasting effects on how people deal with each other. Putnam refers to this as trust and social capital; we would refer to it as internal institutions.

Then again, trust might also be the consequence of external institutions

The argument, as such, might sound plausible but a thousand years is a very long time so the story also sounds rather far-fetched. It is fortunate for us that Guiso et al. (2008) tested it empirically. They identified the 400 largest Italian cities in 1871 (the year of the first census after Italy became a nation-state) and traced their history back to the beginning of the last millennium. And indeed, they found that cities that became independent almost a thousand years ago are still very different from cities that did not. There are more not-for-profit organizations in the former, participation in referendums is higher, and the likelihood that an organ donor organization exists is also higher. The authors claim that at least half of the differences in social capital can be explained by referring to the history of the specific city.

A similar point has been made more recently by Sascha Becker and his co-authors (Becker et al., 2016) who look into the long-term effects of the Habsburg Empire. Compared to neighboring empires such as the Russian or the Ottoman, the Habsburg Empire is said to have had a fairly efficient, little corrupted, and widely accepted bureaucracy. The Empire ceased to exist in 1918, and Becker et al. are interested to find out whether it lives on in how citizens think of the state and its representatives. They are able to do this because the Empire's borders cut through five currently existing states: Montenegro, Poland, Romania, Serbia, and Ukraine (Figure 7.3). In other words, today, at least formally, populations in each of these countries live under identical external institutions. But distinct parts of these countries were "treated" by the Habsburg administration before 1918, while other parts were not. Is the amount of trust that citizens in these five countries display towards their bureaucracy affected by whether they live in a region that was formerly run by the Habsburg Empire? Yes, trust levels are significantly higher in those regions than in other parts of the country, and the degree to which today's administration is perceived as corrupt is significantly lower in regions that had been run by the Habsburgs a century ago.

Now, are citizens in regions formerly governed by the Habsburgs simply more naïve because they put more trust in their local bureaucracy and perceive it to be less corrupt? This is, of course, not what Becker and his co-authors have in mind. The argument is that due to the constraints established by an administration more than a hundred years ago, today's administrations still function better than those administrations that were never governed by the Habsburgs. Since the former borders of the Habsburg Empire do not play any role in the five countries, external institutions can be excluded as a potential reason for these differences. In all likelihood, the external institutions put in place by the Habsburgs more than a hundred years ago had an effect on the internal institutions

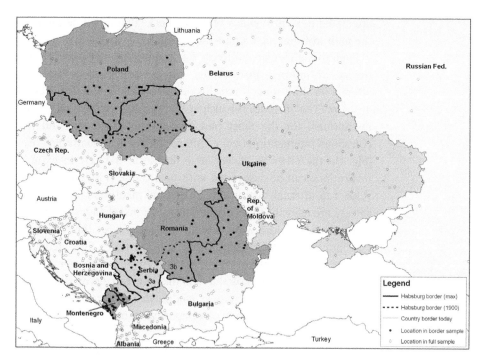

Figure 7.3 The Habsburg Empire in Eastern Europe.
Source: Becker et al. (2016)

that constrain the bureaucracy even today, making it more efficient and less corrupt.

7.5 Open Questions

That external institutions can influence the development of internal institutions was shown, for the most part, using an example. Even though we know that case studies cannot replace a precise theory, we simply do not possess such a theory yet. Developing such a theory is associated with some difficulties, as economists are used to being able to cleanly distinguish between dependent and independent variables. Here, there is ample potential for mutual interactions. Internal institutions can affect the development of external institutions, while external institutions can also influence internal institutions. Undoubtedly, we are dealing with very complex relationships that require further analysis. We still have a long way to go in order to arrive at an "economic theory of the origins of internal institutions." In this chapter, we attempted to identify a few building blocks that might be useful on the path towards such a general theory.

Even though we are still very far from a fully-fledged economic theory of internal institutional change, we can, nevertheless, attempt to draw policy conclusions based on the few things we do know. This includes the insight that the development of internal institutions, for the most part, occurs spontaneously, and that conscious interventions via economic policy are usually not feasible. On the other hand, we have just seen that certain external institutions can be associated with predictable consequences with respect to internal institutions. If internal institutions present in a society are relevant for economic transactions, changes in external institutions should always attempt to account for this relevance. Furthermore, we have emphasized multiple times that incompatibilities between internal and external institutions can lead to increased transaction costs. From this, we can derive the policy conclusion that *(consciously modifiable) external institutions should not be completely incompatible with existing internal institutions.*

In Chapters 8 and 9, we will offer a more detailed discussion of the consequences for economic policy that can be drawn from the NIE.

QUESTIONS

1. Give additional examples of behavior that follows instrumental rationality and behavior that is belief-oriented.
2. Following the smoking example from Section 7.2, discuss the problem of externalities with respect to a situation on a train where a passenger who is suffering from a cold sits down next to a passenger who is talking very loudly on his mobile phone.
3. Think of further examples for the development of social norms via factual behavioral regularities.
4. Discuss determinants that might be relevant for explaining the development of internal institutions which are not accounted for by evolutionary game theory.
5. Why might the (original) development of social norms not be sufficiently explained with recourse to the concepts of repetition and reputation?
6. Clarify the attempted explanatory approach sketched in Section 7.3.3 using an example.

FURTHER READING

A critical discussion of *homo sociologicus* can be found in Dahrendorf (1968) who actually coined the term.

Weibull (1997) is probably still the best introduction to evolutionary game theory. Boyd and Richerson (2005) is a volume comprising 20 of their papers. Bowles and Gintis describe their approach in detail in *A Cooperative Species* (Bowles and Gintis, 2011) The book is also extremely useful because it summarizes the insights of a half a century of research in sociobiology using a unified notation which allows the reader to see commonalities and differences between the various approaches very easily.

Bowles and Gintis are not the only social scientists who ascribe to war an important function in the development of institutions. Tilly (1992), for example, made the argument that fighting war increases the odds of successful state-building. More recently, John Ferejohn and Frances Rosenbluth (2014) have argued that traditional forms of war-making, involving a large percentage of the population, have fostered democracy because those fighting demanded a say in decisions regarding public goods. More recently, however, war has become a high-tech affair and it might no longer foster the advent of democracy.

In various publications, Alberto Bisin and Thierry Verdier have dealt with the question of how values are transmitted across generations. It is important to identify the transmission mechanism to understand why some populations seem to converge in their values whereas others remain heterogeneous for a long time. Their contribution in *The New Palgrave Dictionary of Economics* (Bisin and Verdier, 2008) is a very accessible survey to that literature.

Jack Knight has dealt with the issue of internal institutional change in several publications. Here, let us merely mention *Institutions and Social Conflict* (1992), which focuses on the relevance of power to the development of institutions.

Alesina and Giuliano (2015) is an excellent survey on the relationship between culture and institutions. A recent contribution by Algan and Cahuc (2014) reviews the contributions regarding the impact of trust on various economic outcomes. Fehr (2009) critically discusses the various ways trust has been used to explain the origin of a number of effects and convincingly demonstrates the endogeneity of trust. This supports the position taken in this chapter that trust is determined by both internal and external institutions.

The contributions dealing with possible interrelationships between (both external and internal) institutions and historical development are summarized in Nunn (2014). Nunn puts particular emphasis on the observed historical persistence of institutions.

8 On the Need for Normative Theory

8.1 Introductory Remarks

So far, we have dealt mainly with positive questions. In Chapters 2–5, we discussed the consequences of different institutions on economically relevant variables. In Chapters 6 and 7, we explored the origins of institutions and how they change, from an economic perspective. We now consider normative questions. Which institutions should be implemented? Which institutions can be legitimized and with what methods? Chapters 8 and 9 will examine some of these normative questions. In Chapter 9, we will investigate how the perspective of the NIE might influence policy decisions. However, in order to be able to derive policy consequences, we need a normative foundation. By that, we mean establishing criteria that will enable us to judge what is "good" or desirable. In this chapter, we delve into the necessity for, and the possibilities of, such a normative foundation.

We have seen throughout this book that good institutions cause high levels of prosperity. Private property rights and the possibility to exchange them voluntarily can lead to enormous gains in welfare, which is assumed to be an important goal. Nevertheless, we observe many institutions which limit private autonomy and the freedom of contract. Could it be that private autonomy (or freedom of contract) must be limited in order to secure the very existence of private autonomy (or freedom of contract)? Should the sale of human organs be limited and, if yes, how? Should female genital mutilation be prohibited? Should there be constraints on selling hard or soft drugs?

Chapter Highlights
• Familiarize yourself with arguments that support the importance of a normative approach.
• Get to know the "coordination approach" as an alternative to the more standard way of thinking about welfare economics.
• Become acquainted with different ways to explicitly deal with bounded rationality.

We proceed as follows. In Section 8.2, we define normative theory and explain why it is important. In Section 8.3, we encounter arguments that are useful in determining whether an institution (or an institutional arrangement) is legitimate. In Section 8.4, we discuss requirements for a normative theory that are based on insights that arise from the NIE and, thus, differ from more established normative theories.

8.2 What is Normative Theory and Why Should We Study It?

In a series of essays written at the beginning of the twentieth century, Max Weber argued that value judgments can never be thought of as scientific. The freedom-from-value-judgment postulate has since been associated with his name. In 1904 he wrote: "An empirical science cannot tell anyone what he *should* do – but rather what he *can* do – and under certain circumstances – what he *wishes* to do" (Weber, 2011, 54). Before we deal with the need for normative theory, let us first consider why Weber denies normative theories scientific status.

Value judgments are statements about how something should be, in contrast to how something is. While positive statements can be tested empirically (given that all relevant terms are defined), normative statements cannot. If we define the goal of science as the search for truth and if statements are considered to be true only if they match reality,[1] *normative statements* cannot be described as scientific, because they *cannot be falsified*. In other words, it is impossible to show that they do not match reality.

| Definition |

Value judgments cannot be falsified

In the social sciences, **falsification** refers to proving a conjecture, hypothesis, or theory as false or not in accordance with reality. According to Karl Popper, a philosopher of science, proving conjectures wrong is a central element of scientific progress (Popper, 1959). Falsifiability is a precondition for falsification. It presupposes that conjectures have empirical content. This, however, is not the case with regard to normative statements.

[1] This definition of truth can be traced back to the philosopher Alfred Tarski (1902–1983) and is also referred to as the **correspondence theory of truth**.

Why, then, are we dealing with the "need for normative theory" in this chapter? If economists are not content with explaining the world as it is, but are interested in giving advice on how the world could be made "better," they require a benchmark so that they can compare the "better" world to the actual state of the world. To be able to identify deviations of the actual world from some ideal world and then be able to formulate proposals concerning how to reduce these deviations, conceptions of how the world should be are required.

How are we to arrive at such normative conceptions? Naturally, we could justify certain values by meta-values or fundamental values. An example could be: "Government should support the poor to keep them from starving because this is an imperative of basic justice." In this example, a normative statement ("government should support the poor") is based on a more fundamental value ("justice"), which seems capable of achieving widespread consensus. The idea of supposed general consensus will be dealt with in Section 8.3. Here, let us point to the **problem of ultimate justification**, which has been discussed in philosophy for millennia. Philosophers also refer to it as **Agrippa's trilemma**. The term "trilemma" implies that we are dealing with an unsolvable problem. According to this trilemma, the attempt to justify norms and values with higher-level norms and values has to result in one of three unsatisfactory options. One can run into a **circular argument** (that is, at some point, having to "justify" some fundamental value with recourse to a lower-level value), an **infinite regression** (that is, referring to a higher-level norm *ad infinitum*), or cancel the process with **recourse to a dogma** (that is, a set of beliefs that is accepted without explicit justification). Thus, one is forced to choose between three unsatisfactory options.

The problem of ultimate justification

In Section 8.3, we encounter an attempt at practicing normative institutional economics as satisfactorily as possible. But before we move on, let us mention two pitfalls of normative theorizing:

1. Many thinkers are liable to commit a **naturalistic fallacy**. This involves wrongly deducing an "ought" from an "is." Because something *is* the way it is, there must be a good reason that it *ought* to be thus. This fallacy has already been dealt with in detail by David Hume.
2. Economists are also prone to committing an **instrumentalist fallacy**. This fallacy assumes that some politically mandated goals

Pitfalls of normative theorizing

are "given," and economists are required to identify the means by which these goals can be best attained. It is a fallacy because tools can also be goals in themselves (and goals can be tools if we think of vertical tool–goal relationships), but also because tools can have effects not only on the one goal under consideration but also on other goals (often called side effects or spillover effects). This fallacy was criticized back in the 1930s by Gunnar Myrdal. It implies that means (or instruments) are value-free.

As we move on to our encounter with two competing normative concepts, be careful not to be seduced by either of the two fallacies just described, regardless of which concept you prefer.

8.3 Two Competing Normative Concepts

8.3.1 The Welfare Theoretical Approach

The dominant normative approach in economics – the so-called **welfare economics** – was developed around 100 years ago. Welfare economists are interested in **optimal allocation**, which they describe as the *maximization of a social welfare function under constraints*. It is easy to see that welfare economics is derived from utilitarianism.

Definition

Utilitarianism is the ethical – normative – theory that justifies behavior if it is conducive to maximizing utility – or happiness – of the greatest possible number of people. It was first proposed by Jeremy Bentham in the late eighteenth century and then refined during the nineteenth century by John Stuart Mill.

In economics, allocation refers to the assignment of scarce resources and goods to competing uses. If the market does not establish an "optimal" allocation, economists often support government intervention, which is supposed to bring the actual allocation closer to the optimal one. Due to this clear focus on optimal allocation, we could also refer to this approach as the **allocation approach**. Under this approach, cases when the market process does not lead to an optimal allocation are referred to as market failure. The allocation approach is based on a number of assumptions, the most important of which are: (a) that a social maximand can be identified, (b) that government representatives intervene in the market, and (c) that representatives of the state face incentives to maximize social

Assumptions of the allocation approach

welfare. Whether or not these assumptions are useful has been doubted regularly by representatives of different normative programs. Here, we briefly present three points of criticism put forward by Harold Demsetz back in 1969 about the link between **market failure** and the demand for governmental intervention.

The welfare economic ideal is based on assumptions that will never be met. If this ideal state of the world is compared to reality, reality will regularly fare very badly. The attempt to realize a state of the world which is impossible to realize has been dubbed the **Nirvana approach** by Demsetz (1969).

Nobel laureate George Stigler describes the approach of welfare economics by telling an ironic story. He compares welfare economists to jurors of a piano competition between two players who after listening to the first, bad, piano player, immediately crown the second player the winner without bothering to listen to the latter play. This is like crowning state intervention as the winner of a contest without having taken the possibility of government failure explicitly into account. Some representatives of the NIE claim that attempts to establish an optimal allocation are fundamentally flawed. According to them, the economy is not some organic unit which can be maximized meaningfully. Instead, these critics are interested in the question of how interactions of a great number of actors can be coordinated so that order – and prosperity – result. Within this approach, coordination is emphasized by asking what set of institutions is best at enabling citizens to develop expectations that stand a high chance of turning out to be correct. These expectations should develop outside the framework of some central plan, implying a situation where actors are able to pursue a host of different individual goals. This approach could be labeled the **coordination approach**. Whereas the allocation approach has its philosophical roots in utilitarianism, the coordination approach has its roots in social contract theory.

The coordination approach

Definition

Social contract theory is the notion that the legitimacy of the state – and the behavior of its representatives – can be legitimized only by the consent – be it explicit or tacit – of the individuals living under it. One of its best-known representatives, Thomas Hobbes, describes the state of nature not only as a state being absent, but where life is "solitary, poor, nasty, brutish and short." To leave the war of all against all behind, rational individuals would have incentives to establish a state through voluntary consent. Other well-known representatives of social contract theory are John Locke, Jean-Jacques Rousseau, and in the twentieth century John Rawls and James Buchanan.

To some degree, representatives of the coordination approach operate on a different level of analysis than representatives of the allocation approach. Representatives of the coordination approach are interested in institutions that facilitate (or impede) economic exchange. They are, therefore, interested in describing rules that enable different actors to coordinate their behavior. Representatives of the allocation approach are more interested in evaluating the outcomes of different allocation mechanisms. Coined differently, representatives of the allocation approach strive to achieve specific results, while representatives of the coordination approach are interested in creating the necessary preconditions to establish a process that helps individuals reach their individual goals.

In Chapter 1, we mentioned that representatives of the NIE do not agree on whether the NIE is primarily located within the realm of the allocation approach, asking questions that have not been asked yet by its more mainstream representatives, or whether the NIE is based on a fundamentally different normative approach. A description of the welfare theoretic allocation approach is contained in most introductory economics textbooks. Instead of describing it yet again, we rather focus on a more detailed description of the coordination approach which has been described far less often but is preferred by some representatives of the NIE.

Definition

Welfare economics is a branch of economics concerned with maximization of welfare on the group (often the nation-state) level. To make various feasible outcomes comparable in terms of their welfare implications, it is based on a social welfare function.

8.3.2 Hypothetical Consent: A Heuristic to Derive Normative Statements

In this sub-section, we discuss whether the notion of hypothetical consent can be used as a heuristic to derive normative statements.

Definition

"Heureka!" is Greek and means "I have found it." A **heuristic** is a pragmatic approach to finding hands-on solutions to problems. Heuristics are used to identify sensible solutions in little time. Relying on a rule of thumb is an example.

James M. Buchanan is a constitutional economist. He is a scientist who utilizes the instruments of economics in order to analyze fundamental rule systems, specifically, constitutions. Constitutions consist of institutions, thus, one can consider constitutional economics to be part of the NIE. Buchanan's central aim is to explain the origins of institutions and to develop norms for evaluating existing legal systems (Buchanan, 1975, 50ff.). In this effort, without recourse to external norms, he attempts to derive the logical structure of social interactions solely from the perspective of a self-interested desire to maximize one's utility (Buchanan, 1975, 80).

In Section 8.2, we saw that the problem of ultimate justification is unsolvable. Buchanan also needs to presuppose norms. The central normative pillar of his theory is that goals and values of any one individual should *a priori* not be more important than those of another individual. This position is also referred to as normative individualism. You have encountered methodological individualism as one of the cornerstones of economics. According to this concept, only individuals can act, not organizations, systems, or other entities. According to normative individualism, *individuals are the only source of values* or value judgments. This implies that there are no external sources of norms, such as divine commands or natural laws. As soon as we allow for the possibility that individuals have different values or pursue different goals, it is very difficult to apply the allocation approach we just discussed.

Normative individualism

It is possible to derive a **procedural norm** from the assumption of methodological individualism. Buchanan adopts this argument from Knut Wicksell (1896), a Swedish economist. Economic exchange of private goods is considered to be beneficial if the involved exchange partners voluntarily agree to it. Everyone involved expects to gain from it, otherwise they would not agree to it voluntarily. Frequently, exchange activity is conceptualized as involving merely two parties, the buyer and the seller. Buchanan follows Wicksell, who applied the same valuation criterion for

Derivation of a procedural norm

decisions which affect more than two parties, extending the criterion to an entire society. Rules that are supposed to be valid for all members of society can only be assumed to be beneficial for all members of society if one can reasonably assume that each societal member would agree to these rules. Rules are considered to be legitimized if no rational individual is expected to oppose their introduction. Thus, we are *applying the Pareto criterion to the whole of society.*

Achieving unanimity can be associated with enormous costs, particularly in large groups. No rational individual will insist on requiring unanimity for all collective decisions as long as the expected consequences of a decision are not very costly. I might never use the local swimming pool but still be willing to bear some of the costs incurred for its maintenance. Still, I am unlikely to insist on being involved in making decisions regarding the local swimming pool, because the costs I expect to bear are simply not worth it. But there are policy areas in which potential costs can be huge. Imagine a majority decision that implies I cannot practice an important part of my religion anymore (like coloring my hair green). This involves basic human rights, and at least conceptually, they should only be changeable if everybody agrees to the proposed change. More generally speaking, constitutional rules can be considered the most basic rules of society. Changing them can have important consequences for many people. This is why the decision rule regarding constitutional rules should be more inclusive than the decision rule on the opening hours of the local swimming pool. In most countries, this is indeed the case.

Definition

Interdependence costs: In their *The Calculus of Consent* (1962), James Buchanan and Gordon Tullock propose a simple way to derive optimal decision rules. Assume that the least costly way of providing some good is by making it available to the public (this implies that both private provision and provision by a club are more expensive). But what proportion of people should optimally vote in favor of some proposal? How inclusive should the decision rule be?

Buchanan and Tullock propose to frame the issue as a trade-off between two cost categories, namely, decision-making costs on the one hand and external costs on the other. Decision-making costs are at their minimum when a single individual can decide. The larger the number of individuals involved in consenting to a proposal, the higher the decision-making costs. External costs are the costs individuals must bear as a consequence of being outvoted. When the decision rule is unanimity, external costs are by definition zero – as nobody is outvoted. Buchanan and Tullock propose to add the two cost curves and call the resulting curve an "interdependence cost curve." According to them, the minimum of this curve is equivalent to the optimal decision rule. If this logic is shared by everybody, there will be unanimous consent in favor of making some decisions with a decision rule that is below unanimous consent. In Figure 8.1, interdependence costs have their minimum at k, implying that the optimal decision rule should be k/n.

Unanimity is costly

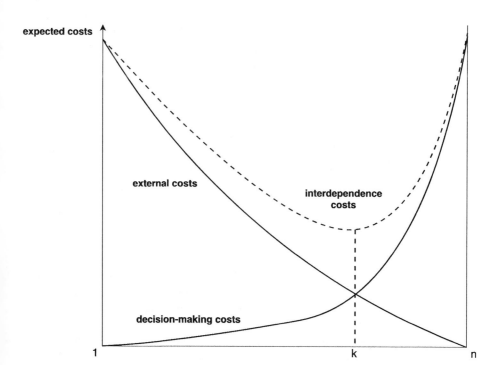

Number of individuals who need to agree for collective action

Figure 8.1 The interdependence cost calculus.

The normative approach at hand utilizes the Pareto criterion which is fundamental to welfare economics, but offers an alternative interpretation of it:

1. The criterion is not used to evaluate specific results, but rather rules or institutions, the use of which lead to certain results. If a rule can be considered to be legitimized, there is no reason to consider the results that arise from it to be "unjust" (Hayek, 1976 argues very similarly).
2. Furthermore, "Pareto optimality" is replaced by "Pareto superiority." Conceptually, an optimum is a situation that cannot be improved any further. However, if we identify a rule to be Pareto superior, we are merely applying comparative institutional analysis. If, at any point in time, we find that there is general approval of a rule other than the rule in place, the status quo is being compared to an alternative rule. If the alternative is able to generate unanimous consent, it can be considered superior to the existing rule. However, this does not exclude the possibility that there might be yet another rule which is even better.
3. This approach questions whether a single welfare economist is able to evaluate if a specific state of affairs is Pareto optimal. If this was the case, one would ascribe a specific kind of omniscience to the evaluating welfare economist, as he or she would need to know all of the preferences of all of the actors. Buchanan considers this position to be "wholly unacceptable" (Buchanan, 1959, 126). He argues that just because a group of scientists considers a policy to be Pareto superior does not make it so; the explicit consent of everyone who is affected by the policy is required to make it so.

Thus, Buchanan's normative approach does not tell us which institutions should be implemented in society. Instead, it provides a procedure to determine whether there are specific institutions that individuals might be willing to accept under certain circumstances. If this is the case, these institutions are legitimized and should be implemented. Taken as heuristic, this procedure is quite convincing. It focuses on the individual and does not require recourse to external sources of values or value judgments. Nevertheless, let us discuss some weaknesses of this heuristic.

8.3.3 Some Critical Comments on the Unanimity Test

Many years back, Buchanan himself explicitly recognized that the actual implementation of the unanimity test just described was fraught with some difficulties (Buchanan, 1959, 134ff.). To avoid these difficulties, Buchanan pleads to replace the concept of factual consent by the concept of **hypothetical consent**. Buchanan uses speed limits as an example of hypothetical consent: "it seems clearly possible that general agreement on the imposition of some limits might well have emerged ... within reasonable boundaries" (Buchanan, 1978, 35). The general consent presumed by Buchanan is based on hypothetical reasons alone. A purely hypothetical consent concerning institutions gets us very close to the omniscient scientist that was criticized regarding the allocation approach. The fragility of such a "conceptual consent" is revealed as soon as different external observers do not agree on which rule a population might have consented to. Thus, the attempt to evaluate and legitimate collective goods decisions beyond the formal procedural norm is also confronted with very serious problems.

Hypothetical vs. factual consent

The possibility of a hypothetical consent also depends on the assumptions regarding the information available to the actors. If actors are precisely aware of their individual socioeconomic status, they can use this information to extrapolate their future status. Proposed rule changes that are associated with anticipated utility decreases are unlikely to be supported, thus failing the test of consent. Uncertainty regarding one's own future position is also referred to as the veil of uncertainty. John Rawls (1971), who is interested in identifying universal principles that rational people could agree on, introduced a slightly different perspective, namely the **veil of ignorance**. Rawls asks whether individuals could (or would) consent to a set of basic rules if they did not possess relevant information that they actually possess. In this manner, one could assume individuals do not know whether they are rich or poor, young or old, strong or weak, and so on. This thought experiment is supposed to ensure that the only rules that can be considered as legitimized are those that do not disadvantage (or reversely privilege) certain social groups. It remains, however, a bit unclear what can be learned from this exercise in terms of possible consequences. Imagine an existing institutional arrangement that could not be legitimized (because certain groups simply do not consent) while a supposed change of this arrangement

Veil of ignorance following Rawls

passed the hypothetical consent. If the supposed reform could not be supported by political and actual majorities, the non-legitimized status quo would remain in place.

To sum up, the coordination approach is concerned with the rules of the game, rather than with its outcomes. To ascertain whether specific changes in basic institutions can be considered an improvement – and hence normatively desirable – one needs to ask whether all individuals affected by such change could agree to them. As a heuristic, the coordination approach seems an improvement over the allocation approach, although it also suffers from a number of important weaknesses.

8.4 Requirements for a Normative Theory from the Perspective of Institutional Economics

As a central assumption of the NIE, we have repeatedly noted that the bounded rationality of actors implies positive transaction costs. It follows that this central assumption should also be reflected in a normative theory of institutions, i.e., that part of the NIE that is concerned with identifying what institutions are desirable for a society. In this section, we present two possibilities to explicitly account for this assumption. Unfortunately, the two approaches lead to completely different conclusions. This goes to show that a mere accounting for the central assumption of the NIE is not sufficient to derive generally agreeable statements.

8.4.1 The Approach of Williamson

Efficiency according to Williamson

Oliver Williamson adheres to the concept of "efficiency," but defines it in a very unconventional manner: "*An outcome for which no feasible superior alternative can be described and implemented with net gains is presumed to be efficient*" (Williamson, 1996, 195, italics in original). Remember that Demsetz (1969) accuses welfare economists of comparing perfect government action with imperfect market results. This leads Williamson to propose his modified definition of efficiency. In this view, only realized or realizable alternatives can be compared with each other. Thus, an institutional change can only be evaluated as beneficial if the costs of implementing it are accounted for, based on the current status quo (which is already in place). *If the relevant transaction costs are so high that there is no superior policy which can be implemented,* then Williamson refers to the current state of affairs as *"efficient."* The deduction of theoretical optima often disregards factual political restrictions, such that states of the world in which there is no implementable improvement are incorrectly regarded to be inefficient.

8.4.2 The Approach of Hayek

During his entire academic life, Friedrich August von Hayek was always concerned with the quality of rules that would enable people to live together not only peacefully but also in prosperity. He can, therefore, be considered a new institutional economist before the advent of the NIE. Hayek always emphasized that we are suffering from **constitutional ignorance**. With that term, he meant that human ignorance cannot be reduced by any amount of research, because it is inherent in humans. Taking constitutional ignorance seriously, he warned against a **pretense of knowledge**. With that term, he meant to say that due to the fact that a large part of our ignorance is constitutional, humans often attempt to create social order based on knowledge they do not possess or cannot possess. Although Hayek does not explicitly refer to transaction costs, his insistence on constitutional ignorance indicates that the assumption of bounded rationality played an important role in his work.

Constitutional ignorance and the pretense of knowledge

If ignorance is constitutional, the question arises how we can best cope with it. Hayek's answer to this is neither new nor very original. Echoing Kant (1991 [1797]), Hayek demands that rules – as one part of institutions – should be characterized by certain properties that can be summarized by the term **universalizability**. According to this criterion, rules should be:

1. *General*, that is, applicable to a non-foreseeable multitude of persons and cases.
2. *Abstractly* (or negatively) formulated, that is, they should prohibit certain behavior rather than demanding a specific behavior.
3. *Specific* in the sense that individuals can always ascertain whether a behavior is prohibited or not.

Universalizability

According to Hayek, universalizable rules are associated with at least two desirable consequences. On the one hand, they reduce uncertainty, a trait highly appreciated in institutions. This is

Consequences of universalizable rules

primarily ensured by the trait of specificity.[2] On the other hand, innovations are possible due to the trait of abstractness, which is very important for an open and dynamic economy. The utilization of universalizable rules implies that policymakers, for the most part, refrain from corrective interventions, as the latter are not universalizable. Hayek (1964) is aware that the use of universalizable rules can lead us to ignore knowledge that we actually possess in some cases. Apparently, he places more value on the stability of law resulting from universalizable rules, than on potential gains sacrificed by not using knowledge which is actually available.

8.4.3 Consequences of the Two Approaches

Both Williamson and Hayek emphasize the limits of human knowledge and rationality; however, they draw different conclusions. An interpretation of Williamson could be: *Ex ante*, we cannot be sure that we have found the best possible rules. Over time, our knowledge concerning the effects of rules can improve and it is in our best interest to be able to make use of that newly gained knowledge. One way for us to make use of the newly gained knowledge is to formulate rules – in this case laws – so generally that we are able to reinterpret their contents in the light of newly gained knowledge. If, however, despite having framed legislation in a general fashion open to very different interpretations it is necessary to reform a law formally, the costs of doing so should not be too high, in order to not delay the use of newly acquired rule-relevant knowledge.

Hayek: bounded rationality of all actors

Hayek, on the other hand, emphasizes that all actors are boundedly rational. This not only pertains to lawyers who have to interpret abstract and openly formulated law, but also to legislators who transform new knowledge into institutional bodies via

---

[2] Nevertheless, the observation of one of the authors of the *Federalist Papers* – the collection of essays which advertised the acceptance of the new US constitution of 1787 – should be valid even today. Alexander Hamilton wrote that "All new laws, though penned with the greatest technical skill, and passed on the fullest and most mature deliberation, are considered as more or less obscure and equivocal, until their meaning be liquidated and ascertained by a series of particular discussions and adjudications" (Hamilton, Madison, and Jay, 1961 [1788], no. 37). This observation in conjunction with the desire for less uncertainty leads to the recommendation of changing rules and institutions as seldom as possible.

amendments. Because the level of complexity that all relevant decision-makers can deal with is limited, it appears advisable to formulate rules in general and simple terms.

Williamson might counter that it would be foolhardy to consciously refrain from utilizing existing knowledge. It appears that his recommendations are characterized by the hope that our knowledge concerning the functions of institutions can be expanded and is thus not subject to constitutional ignorance. However, the question of how we can be sure of whether we have attained new knowledge remains. Experiences from economic policy seem to suggest that seemingly certain knowledge can be proven wrong very quickly.

Hayek and Williamson differ in their assumptions concerning what humans are capable of knowing. Their diverging conclusions on how to cope with our ignorance could be interpreted as a consequence of differently weighed sub-goals. While Williamson hopes that new knowledge is embodied in institutions as quickly as possible, Hayek is primarily interested in reducing the legal uncertainty of all actors involved. Here, we will not further pursue the question of whether it is possible to dissolve the sketched trade-off using (meta-)theoretical arguments.

8.5 Open Questions

In this chapter, we introduced welfare economics as the dominant normative approach to economics. Our discussion included a treatment of several problems with arguments based on welfare economic theory that concern representatives of the NIE. We then encountered an alternative approach that is for the most part attributed to James Buchanan. It should be clear by now that this approach also exhibits several problems and weaknesses. Thus, in a further step, we presented two approaches in which bounded rationality and positive transaction costs play a role. However, the conclusions that Hayek and Williamson draw are by no means identical. In Chapter 9, we will present policy recommendations that representatives of the NIE can give at this point.

QUESTIONS

1. Illustrate the meaning of the naturalistic and the instrumentalist fallacy with a respective example of your own choosing.

2. Try to use the heuristic of hypothetical consent to legitimize constitutional rules in a policy area of your own choosing.

FURTHER READING

Audi (2010) is a contemporary introduction to epistemological questions. Johansson (1991) offers an accessible introduction to welfare economics. The Nobel Prize in economics was awarded to James M. Buchanan in 1986. His prize lecture (Buchanan, 1987) is an accessible summary of what I have called the coordination approach in this chapter.

9 Consequences for Economic Policy

9.1 Introductory Remarks

In Chapter 8, we dealt with the problem of deriving normative statements regarding institutions. In this chapter, we consider whether the NIE does and should have consequences for the theory of economic policy. The latter traditionally deals with the description and identification of policy goals, the identification of means to attain those goals, and the identification of the respective actors responsible for implementing policy measures.

Representatives of the NIE assume that it makes sense to explicitly account for bounded rationality and the ensuing positive transaction costs in economic models. In this chapter, we inquire into the consequences of accounting for these assumptions with regard to policy recommendations from economists to policymakers. Put differently, how does the optimal use of policy instruments change if we explicitly account for the fact that actors are boundedly rational and that transaction costs are larger than zero?

Chapter Highlights
• Discuss policy recommendations based on insights from the NIE.
• Ask whether internal institutions can be activated by government action.
• Study an example of far-reaching institutional reforms.

In Section 9.2, we proceed in a traditional manner. We begin by assuming that policymakers are benevolent and attempt to maximize some kind of social welfare function. By doing so, we ignore a number of arguments that have occupied center stage in previous chapters. In Section 9.3, one specific aspect is analyzed in more detail. Namely, can external institutions be utilized to activate latent and functional internal institutions? In other words, we ask whether policies can be designed such that they help to alter internal institutions in an intended direction. Section 9.4 presents a case study. We describe how New Zealand has implemented in practice far-reaching reforms. New Zealand was chosen, because time and again observers refer to the NIE when explaining the reforms there.

9.2 Policy Recommendations: The Traditional – Naïve – Approach

Economic policy consequences

In this section, we present several consequences for economic policy that can be derived from the NIE. These recommendations are not naïve in and of themselves. However, they do not account for the incentives of policymakers. Thus, it would be naïve to expect policymakers to immediately implement these suggestions. Nevertheless, this traditional approach has a right to exist. It shows which measures would be implemented by policymakers if they were either benevolent or subject to restrictions that make them behave as if they were benevolent.

The policy recommendations we name here are derived from the preceding chapters. Let us describe them in detail:

Recommendation #1: It is not sufficient to strive for improvements of physical and human capital. It is at least equally important to install institutions that are conducive to economic growth.

This suggestion represents an extension of economic growth theory. In economic growth theory, institutions were neglected almost entirely for a long time. In the long term, economic growth is only possible through growth of total factor productivity. In Chapter 5, we found that total factor productivity decisively depends on the quality of institutions.

Recommendation #2: Institutional change should be the exception, not the rule. If institutional change promises net gains, it should be carried out as transparently as possible to enable actors to formulate expectations that have a good chance of being confirmed.

The function of institutions is to enable actors to formulate expectations that have a good chance of turning out to be true. Any type of institutional change, even with the best of intentions, runs, however, the risk of *increasing* uncertainty. Institutions need to be enforced by administrators, police officers, judges, and so on. Newly created or modified institutions can increase uncertainty because the specific way in which the content of the institutions is interpreted by the enforcers is unclear initially and needs to develop over time. An increase in uncertainty seems, therefore, very possible, at least during some initial period. Conversely, the longer certain institutions remain unchanged, the easier it becomes to formulate adequate expectations. Institutions exhibit capital-like characteristics if they increase in value with age (see Buchanan, 1975, chapter 7).

Transparency is desirable at all levels of legislation, as it reduces uncertainty. This is true for the process in which new legislation is produced, for the immediate publication of laws newly passed (not the norm in many countries), and for transparency concerning their implementation. Many countries have introduced freedom-of-information acts which are supposed to enable citizens to know how laws are implemented. If these freedom-of-information acts are factually implemented, they can increase transparency.

Recommendation #3: When trying to implement institutional change, governments should strive to commit to this change as much as possible.

If the goal of economic policy is to increase per capita income, and external and internal institutions are crucial for per capita income, the demand for installing growth-enhancing institutions is certainly not surprising. Naturally, the implementation of this recommendation is subject to great difficulties. Otherwise, why would so many dysfunctional institutions exist? Institutions are of little use if they are merely formally in place, and do not enhance the ability of interacting partners to form stable expectations. One of the goals of economic policy should be to work towards a convergence of *de facto* and *de jure* institutions. However, the government typically has trouble committing credibly to the rules it sets in place (you recognize this as the **dilemma of the strong state**). Why, then, should private citizens believe any of the promises of a government to safeguard private property rights, when at the same time the government has the power to expropriate? One suggestion in the literature is to consolidate the security of property rights by making them (legally) part of the constitution of a country (Gwartney and Holcombe, 1999). Again, we can ask why a governmental promise should be believed to be more credible solely because it is part of a written document with a different name. It has been argued that – at the end of the day – constitutional rules need to be self-enforcing (Hardin, 1989; Ordeshook, 1992). One way to make institutional change credible is, therefore, to install self-enforcing institutions. If that is not possible, an alternative is to create a high number of stakeholders that are likely to oppose the

[margin note: Institutional change and economic growth]

government if it does not comply with its promises. An example for such behavior is described in Chapter 4. One way to privatize state-owned companies consists in selling shares to large segments of the population. Any expropriation attempt by the government would be very costly, as many of the shareholders are likely to protest against such government behavior.

If the government of a country simply cannot credibly commit to institutional change domestically, Levy and Spiller (1994, 210) propose that governments have the option of binding their hands by making commitments to international organizations. Whether the World Bank or other international organizations are suitable for this, needs to be considered case by case.

Recommendation #4: When reforming external institutions, the existing internal institutions need to be accounted for. By and large, the external institutions should be compatible with the internal institutions of society.

Institutional change that enlarges the gap between *de jure* and *de facto* institutions tends to imply higher transaction costs and is thus counter-productive. Keefer and Shirley (1998) point out that policies aimed at inducing change in external institutions have often proven ineffective in the past. The authors consider the alternative approach of focusing on change in internal institutions.[1] However, they point out that adequate internal institutions are, in and of themselves, not sufficient to induce sustainable economic growth. Attempts to induce change in internal institutions have frequently failed. If change is attempted nevertheless – for instance by establishing external institutions that sanction the use of specific internal institutions – there will be an increase in enforcement costs. If private actors continue to use these internal institutions that are now sanctioned, they need to be more careful, which amounts to an increase in transaction costs.

This insight has been expressed by different authors in different ways. For instance, North (1990a, 140) writes: "When there is a radical change in the formal rules that makes them inconsistent with the existing informal constraints, there is an unresolved tension between them that will lead to long-run political instability."

---

[1] Whether, and if so to what degree, this can be achieved will be discussed in Section 9.3.

Recommendation #5: The untapped productive potential of internal institutions should be identified and private actors should be encouraged to function as catalysts to spread these institutions.

Recommendation #4 seems to imply that governments should not even attempt to tinker with the internal institutions of a society. However, this might be a premature conclusion. In many parts of the world, farming communities are responsible for the maintenance of their irrigation systems. Some communities have managed to develop internal institutions that ensure a steady flow of water, while others have failed to develop such institutions. This is described in more detail in Chapter 4. Following her research on irrigation systems, Ostrom (1996, 226) proposes that farmers whose irrigation system does not work properly should be given the chance to visit communities in which it does work well, to learn from them and to create adequate internal institutions.

Recommendation #6: When implementing institutional change via deregulation, it is advisable to implement comprehensive packages simultaneously, in order to give actors who suffer losses due to deregulation in their respective industry the opportunity to realize gains due to deregulation in other industries.

This recommendation is less naïve, as it accounts for political economy aspects. Assume a government aims to increase economic growth and at the same time strives for re-election. To improve growth prospects the government might want to implement institutional reform. But if reforms are met with opposition from potential voters, the government will need to make trade-offs. The popularity of a government also depends on the sequencing of institutional change.

Institutional change and political sustainability

In the 1980s, the government of New Zealand implemented a whole series of far-reaching reforms to encourage renewed growth in the country. Observers of the reforms in New Zealand (Evans et al., 1996) report that the simultaneous implementation of a multitude of reforms helped the government to remain reasonably popular. While some industries suffered losses due to the reforms (e.g., through reductions in subsidies and protectionism), reforms implemented in other industries increased competition, prompting higher quality products and potentially lower prices for consumers. The widespread implementation of reforms across industries was likely to make people both worse off (as producers) as well as better off (as consumers). In the case of New Zealand, industries in which comprehensive deregulation was implemented early on often demanded similar deregulation for other industries. They became, therefore, stakeholders in favor of institutional change.

Recommendation #7: Only feasible alternatives should be compared with each other. This involves explicitly accounting for the implementation costs of new institutions.

One of the fundamental insights of the NIE is that the allocation and coordination mechanisms can never be perfect or without cost.

Institutional change and government failure

Before policymakers decide to correct some market failure previously identified using abstract criteria, they need to consider the possibility of government failure. As discussed in Chapter 8, institutional change only makes sense if the benefits of change outweigh the cost. These include not only the set-up and operational costs of institutions, but also the political costs that are incurred to get a sufficient number of parliamentarians to vote in favor of new institutions.

9.3 Activation of Internal Institutions through Government Action?

Throughout this textbook, we have emphasized the relevance of internal institutions. Some of the policy recommendations just developed are concerned with the relationship between internal and external institutions, primarily their compatibility with each other. In this section, we build on our previous reflections and ask if there are situations where the state can act as a catalyst for activating internal institutions. Imagine the existence of some internal institutions that encourage people to provide themselves with a public good. Further imagine that if a minimum number of people participate in the private provision of a public good, many others would also do so. In such a situation, an actor able to help a group of individuals meet that threshold could act as a catalyst, inducing private actors to rely upon those internal institutions. We will analyze whether government action, or even the mere announcement of a specific action, can affect the activation of what could be termed "latent" internal institutions. These "latent" internal institutions will only be used if somebody kicks off their use and the question is whether the government can be that somebody.

Assume that virtually all citizens of a country perceive environmental pollution to be a grave problem and that – in principle – all citizens are willing to do something to reduce pollution. *Moral suasion* – that is, the attempt by policymakers to induce changed

behavior by moral pressure – is, however, ineffective. Even if we   Moral pressure: a
assume that basically all citizens are willing to bear the costs   dubious tool
for better environmental protection, there is little reason to believe
that citizens will reduce their individual pollution without any
external incentives. Individual reduction of pollution is associated
with costs, but the effect of this individual effort on aggregate
environmental quality is virtually zero. Thus, the activation of
internal institutions requires different forms of governmental
intervention.

Reducing environmental pollution is equivalent to the provision   The state can help
of a public good. Everyone gains from a cleaner environment and   citizens to
no one can be excluded from this benefit. Robert Sugden (1986,   coordinate
behavior
137) shows that the voluntary provision of public goods often fails
because of the great difficulty in creating a simple and transparent
rule which allocates the individual contributions required for the
production of the public good. Thus, we need a rule that informs
individual polluters about their respective new level of pollution.
By doing this, we would take an important first step towards
overcoming the social dilemma.

9.3.1 A Specific Example: Voluntary Commitment Declarations

Let us now turn to voluntary commitment declarations (VCDs)
as an example of how internal institutions can be activated by
appropriate government action. VCDs are declarations by groups
of polluters (usually associations) to achieve some environmental
goal within a specific time frame. VCDs are often induced by
governmental announcements to pass certain decrees. The fact that
associations prefer VCDs to direct regulation shows that they
anticipate lower costs from the former. Often, VCDs involve some
form of exchange in which the government commits to refrain
from using regulatory instruments for the duration of the VCD.
Prominent examples for VCDs include the declaration by automakers to reduce CO_2 emissions, take back scrap cars, and to
develop and produce a three-liter car. These declarations have been
made on the European level, as well as in various nation-states
such as Germany, Japan, and Korea. Within the framework of this
particular example, we will examine the potential of all four types
of internal institutions to channel the behavior of polluting firms.
In terms of game theory, agreements between the government and

Problems of
voluntary
commitment
declarations.

associations would be declared as *cheap talk* as neither side can credibly commit to its respective promises. Formulated differently, there are *strong incentives for ex post opportunism* on both sides. The government could break its promise to not use regulatory instruments, while firms within the association could break their promise to stick to self-declared environmental goals. Game theorists would, therefore, predict that such agreements are unlikely to induce any change of behavior.

| Definition |

Cheap talk: Game theory term which describes the ability to costlessly communicate declarations of intent. As the prisoner's dilemma has an equilibrium in dominant strategies, such communication should be without consequence for the outcome of the game.

Self-enforcing
agreements

In Section 9.2, it was argued that one way to make promises credible is to design them as self-enforcing agreements, i.e., agreements in which all involved parties have *ex post* incentives to stick to their *ex ante* agreed upon commitments: in the language used in this book, to design them as type 1 institutions. Clearly, VCDs do not represent such agreements. Both parties have trouble credibly committing to their promises given as part of the VCD. Thus, the political transaction costs of VCDs appear to be rather high. For those individuals who are critical of VCDs, the story ends here. As no sanctions are to be expected, none of the involved parties has an incentive to change their behavior.

Activation of
internal
institutions as
solution?

For those familiar with the NIE, the story goes on. One could ask whether VCDs could induce behavioral change by activating internal institutions in the members of the association. Assume the pollution reductions committed to at an association level are broken down to its member firms, thus, "allocated." If member firms perceive the rule of allocation to be fair, we could already expect certain behavioral changes even if noncompliance has no legal consequences. A breach against the rule *pacta sunt servanda* (agreements must be kept) can induce (psychical) costs for the breaching party if they have been socialized accordingly. In the typology you have come to know, type 2 internal institutions are able to channel behavior. The sanction against a member firm that does not comply with the agreed upon reduction in pollution consists of lowered utility due to the breach of an ethical rule (in this case the rule that promises ought to be kept).

On the other hand, some of those who are willing to contribute in principle might only contribute for real if others also contribute an amount that is perceived to be appropriate.[2] It appears that the regular *monitoring* of VCDs fulfills just this function. By permitting monitoring at regular intervals, contributors can assure themselves that they are not suckers,[3] but rather part of a functioning private provision of a public good. Frey (1997) argues that voluntary contributions can transform intrinsic motivation into action, while governmental distrust can lead to *crowding out* and evasive behavior. It might make sense to have the monitoring overseen by independent third parties, not suspicious government officials. For instance, the RWI Institute for Economic Research – a German economics think tank – is commissioned to *monitor* the VCD declared by a broad range of German industries to reduce CO_2 emissions. Any individual firm can assure itself by the numbers provided by its association that they are contributing to a functioning public good. The track records of all associations that participate in the VCD are collected and documented by the RWI. The degree to which these associations comply with the promises is, therefore, easily visible by all interested parties – not only within an association, but also across associations.

Monitoring by independent third parties

Advocates of VCDs often argue that when a vast majority of a society's members care about the environment, noncompliance with the agreed upon environmental goals would be associated with reputational damage. The possibility of incurring this damage represents incentives for firms to comply with publicly agreed upon goals. The **reputation mechanism** can be interpreted as part of an institution that informally sanctions the noncompliant party by revoking its social recognition and reducing its social interaction with third parties. We have, thus, arrived at type 3 institutions.

Further incentives via type 3 institutions

However, the recourse to the environmentally responsible society might be hasty and imprecise for two reasons. First, we need to assume the presence of a critical public that follows up on the compliance of VCDs in the medium to long term. For now, let us take this as given. Then, reputation would be relevant only if noncomplying parties could be specifically targeted with costs that

---

[2] Sugden (1986) describes this as a "reciprocity principle." Weimann (1994) refers to a strong "exploitation aversion" which is found in experiments.

[3] In the prisoner's dilemma, *suckers* are actors who cooperate while the other party is defecting and thus realizing gains at the cost of the sucker.

they could avoid by complying with the VCD. If we take a look at the German CO_2 reduction VCD, it includes associations from very different industries. The potential of individual consumers to sanction such associations by exit or the like is rather low.

Even if such a withdrawal of approval was possible, we cannot exclude the possibility that just a few free-riders within an association are responsible for noncompliance of the association as a whole. This means we have come round to the association-internal prisoner's dilemma. *Costs through deprivation of reputation* should be imposed on free-riders primarily by other association members. This is probably easier too, as the frequency of interaction is higher within an association. Put differently, association members are playing a repeated game. Whether the internal sanctioning mechanism reputation works – thus increasing the likelihood of compliance with the VCD – depends, among other things, on the number of association members, the precision with which members can assess the environment-related actions of other members, and the time preference of individual members.

Loss of reputation

Furthermore, it is at least possible for an association to formally sanction defecting member firms, that is, utilizing type 4 institutions. This is more likely to occur if rule compliance cannot be adequately ensured by informal sanctions alone. At this point, it is important to explicitly inquire into the kind of relationship that member firms have with their association. Is membership voluntary? Is membership important for the business success of the member firms? Does the association have any kind of power it can exert on a noncomplying firm? Should the answer to the last question be yes, type 4 institutions might, indeed, play an important role.

Type 4 institutions could also be relevant

We can conclude that *a latently present willingness to voluntarily contribute to the production of a public good can be activated by representatives of the state by: (a) threatening to pass external institutions (in this case, regulatory requirements) in the case of non-activation, and (b) supporting private actors to overcome relevant social dilemmas.* Before representatives of the state attempt to move in this direction, however, it needs to be verified whether the necessary conditions exist or can be created. For the case of VCDs, one necessary condition is that a high percentage of the respective harmful substance is emitted by a relatively small number of polluters and that they can be divided into sufficiently small groups to allow the application of some allocation rule. Referring to necessary conditions more generally, for the state to be able to act as catalyst: (a) appropriate type 2 institutions need to be present for the majority of the individuals involved, and (b) sanctioning mechanisms for type 3 institutions can be activated (if they already exist) or be created (if they do not exist yet).

9.4 Policy Reforms in Practice: Case Study of New Zealand

9.4.1 The Initial Situation in New Zealand

In 1840, New Zealand was annexed by Great Britain. As an agriculturally oriented country, it primarily exported meat, wool, and dairy products to Great Britain, which enabled it to attain an excellent standard of living for decades. Starting in the 1930s, New Zealand set in place comprehensive social security systems. The economic collapse of New Zealand began in 1973, when the UK joined the European Community (EC). After this, the potential to export agricultural products from New Zealand to Europe became more and more restricted. The potential for New Zealand producers to spread into other markets was limited by both protectionist policies of other countries, as well as subsidized agricultural exports from EC producers.

As a response to the two oil crises in 1974 and 1979, the New Zealand government began a policy of **import substitution**. This policy was intended to encourage the domestic production of goods that were previously imported. A similar policy was attempted by many Latin American countries and has mostly proven to be of little use as it involves deliberately refraining from exploiting specific comparative advantages. Because domestic producers were protected from foreign competition both by high tariff and high non-tariff barriers, competitiveness was even further decreased. In the 1970s and 1980s, the growth of both productivity and GDP remained well below the OECD average. While New Zealand's per capita income in 1950 was 26 percent above the OECD average, in 1990 it was 27 percent below the OECD average (Bollard, 1994).

Import substitution

9.4.2 Overview of the Most Important Reforms

In 1984, the Labour Party emerged victorious in New Zealand's parliamentary elections. The incumbent conservative Prime

Minister Robert Muldoon was replaced by David Lange. Immediately after the change of government, comprehensive reforms were implemented, initiated primarily by Minister of Finance Robert Douglas. In 1987, Labour was re-elected. Compared to the first Labour legislative period, the speed of reforms decelerated significantly. Even though there was another change of government in 1990, the newly elected Conservative government continued the comprehensive reform efforts of the Labour government. In 1994, the Conservative government was re-elected. Similar to the Labour government, the Conservative government significantly decelerated their reform efforts in their second legislative period.

Over a period of more than ten years, New Zealand's governments passed and implemented a multitude of reforms. Naturally, we cannot describe them in detail here (for a comprehensive account, see for instance Bollard, 1994 or Evans et al., 1996). Instead, here is a brief overview:

- *Deregulation of the financial sector*: The government abolished interest rate regulation, capital transaction control, and minimum reserve requirements.
- *Clear priorities in monetary policy*: In 1989, the Bank of New Zealand became independent, its sole purpose being to maintain price stability. Central bankers are responsible for meeting the goal of price stability, risking dismissal if failing to meet the goal.
- *Fiscal policy*: From the beginning of the reform period, the government's efforts at generating surpluses in order to amortize debts were successful. By broadening the tax base, the government managed to reduce the top income tax rate from 66 to 33 percent. Indirect taxes were unified by the introduction of a value-added tax. Government expenditures were reduced by drastically cutting the level of subsidies.
- *Civil service*: Some departments were converted into state-owned enterprises that were later sold. Employment was reduced in the civil service sector. The management of state-owned enterprises was established on merit-based contracts. State-owned firms were made subject to the same competition law as private firms, and are, for the most part, subject to the same competitive pressures.
- *Labor market deregulation*: Master contracts were replaced by firm-level contracts. This change disempowered labor unions

practically overnight. Within three years, there was a 38 percent reduction in union membership. The incidence of labor strikes has decreased significantly.

- *Industry and trade*: Widespread trade barriers were rapidly reduced. This has led to an increase in the proportion of imported goods. Consumers now face a much broader selection of products, often at lower prices.
- *Agriculture*: Deregulation and liberalization of agriculture was one of the first steps the Labour government took in 1984. Previous subsidies were abolished almost completely.

For some of the measures, the delay until there was noticeable improvement in the respective indicators was remarkable. For instance, the GDP share of public expenditures continued to rise until 1988. It took ten years for GDP to begin growing again.

9.4.3 Explaining the Reforms

The New Zealand reforms are noteworthy for two reasons. First, it is remarkable that they were implemented at all. Second, it is extraordinary that the respective governments were re-elected (the last time a Labour government had achieved this before 1987 was in 1946!). We will identify four factors that together facilitated the implementation of the reforms: (1) the **ideas** and **theories** upon which the reforms were built; (2) the **persons** who promoted the implementation of the reforms; (3) the **institutions** and **organizations** which supported – or at least did not impede – the reforms; and (4) the **specific circumstances** under which the reform process was initiated.

9.4.3.1 Underlying Theories

The encompassing interventionist policy administered until the mid-1980s was, for the most part, founded on the predominant economic theories of the time– a welfare economic approach that subscribed to the ideal of perfect competition and demanded state intervention if the optimal results of welfare economic models were not attained. The import substitution policies following the oil crises in the 1970s were induced by the same underlying theories.

In the meantime, more recent theoretical approaches had spread within the New Zealand Treasury, which comprises not only the ministry of finance, trade and industry, but also acts as the prime economic advisor to the government (we will come back to this later). Bollard (1994, 90f. and 94f.) describes the theories that began to assert themselves in the mid-1980s:

- The market failure approach was replaced by the **transaction cost approach** which explicitly accounts for the fact that political and bureaucratic coordination is associated with costs. Thus, it is not only markets that can fail, but also bureaucracies and even the government. The immediate consequence is the use of comparative institutional analysis (Evans et al., 1996, 1862). The publications of Ronald Coase, Harold Demsetz, and Oliver Williamson probably played an important role in this regard.
- The usual arguments in favor of state-owned enterprises ("national interests") lost most of their appeal. Instead, and drawing on **principal–agent theory**, it was now argued that state-owned enterprises are particularly plagued by inefficiencies due to incentive and monitoring problems.
- In addition, the rationality of relying on the government to provide services was doubted more and more. Supply-oriented theories that pointed to **crowding out effects** of a large public sector replaced the incumbent theories.
- At the beginning of the 1980s, strongly influenced by the work of William Baumol, the traditional regulatory approach was replaced by the approach of **contestable markets**. According to this approach, the number of competitors in a market is irrelevant to market outcomes (such as price and quantity), as long as potential competitors are not prevented from entering the market. Often, however, state-issued regulations are a serious kind of entry barrier that keep innovative firms from entering a market.

Beyond these, Bollard (1994, 90f.) names the theories of James Buchanan and Gordon Tullock as relevant concerning the functioning of political processes and the theories of Armen Alchian as relevant with regard to private property rights.

9.4.3.2 Persons Involved

In the past, one could observe again and again that the successful passing and implementation of comprehensive reform packages was closely linked to specific persons. The introduction of the social market economy in Germany is inseparably linked to Ludwig Erhard, and the 1980s reforms in Great Britain and the USA to

Margaret Thatcher and Ronald Reagan respectively. The same is true for the New Zealand reforms. Roger Douglas was chief of the Treasury for the Labour party; for the national party it was Ruth Richardson. Interestingly, both stepped down during the respective second legislature period of their parties.

Economic theory categorizes actors with recourse to a very simplified behavioral model. Using this behavioral model, a great number of different behavioral outcomes can be predicted with surprising reliability. However, the economic model is less suitable for the explanation – and even less so for the prediction – of innovations. The behavior of firms that engage in creative destruction in the Schumpeterian sense and create completely new products by recombination of resources is very difficult to integrate into the economic model. The same restrictions apply to the analysis of **political entrepreneurs** who – in the realm of politics – conduct recombinations, leaving aside trodden paths.

9.4.3.3 Behavior-Channeling Institutions, Relevant Organizations

Although we have just emphasized the importance of political entrepreneurs for the successful implementation of comprehensive reforms, these political entrepreneurs require an appropriate institutional framework to implement these reforms. Not all institutional frameworks are equally suited for this purpose. Different observers point out that the framework in New Zealand was very accommodating for reform-minded policymakers.

The New Zealand system, like the English system, is characterized by the so-called **Westminster model**. When the reforms were initiated, New Zealand had a majority voting system. For each electoral district, there is one representative, the candidate with the majority of votes is sent to parliament, and all other votes are disregarded. Such a voting system regularly leads to a two-**party system**. The party with the parliamentary majority creates the government. The New Zealand political system is **unicameral**. There is no second chamber that needs to approve the passing of proposed laws. As New Zealand does not have a written constitution, even far-reaching modifications of the legal system are possible by simple majority.

Westminster model

This type of system gives great power to the respective government. This power can be used to adopt a high degree of interventionism and regulation, like in the years before 1984, or to push deregulation and opening up, like in the years after 1984. In the meantime, New Zealand has introduced a proportional representation system similar to the system used in Germany. A number of splinter parties have formed on both the left and right of the political spectrum. Majority voting rules very regularly lead to two-party systems, implying that a single party will form the government. To gain the majority of the popular vote, party platforms need to cater to general interests rather than to small special interest groups. Proportional voting rules regularly lead to multiple party systems implying the need to form coalition governments. Party programs are more likely to cater to smaller groups with less general interests. To remain in government, coalition governments need to agree on many compromises between the coalition partners. In this sense, the change of the New Zealand voting system is an indicator that reforms would not continue at the same pace. However, since a proportional representation system limits the scope for government-induced change in all directions, it also should be (rather) difficult to take back the reforms achieved.

We already mentioned the Treasury as a relevant organization. Knorr (1997, 145) points out that it is mostly staffed by economists rather than lawyers, as in many other countries.

9.4.3.4 Favorable Circumstances

John Williamson (1994) claims there are a number of factors that influence whether or not newly elected governments are able to implement reform packages. These include:

1. The "crisis hypothesis."
2. The "mandate hypothesis."
3. The "honeymoon hypothesis."
4. The "presence of a fragmented and demoralized opposition."

Bollard (1994) argues that three of these factors were present in New Zealand during the period of reform. Both the long-term worsening of the terms of trade and the short-term deterioration of the balance of payments (which led to the replacement of the Muldoon government) were perceived as a **crisis** by the population. Times of crisis can be used by governments to implement reform packages.

The **mandate hypothesis** claims that the size of the parliamentary majority over the minority is an indicator of the legitimacy with which the new government implements comprehensive reforms. The

Labour victory of 1984 appeared to be a landslide victory with Labour winning 56 out of 95 seats, 13 more than in the previous election. Thus, the second factor was also present in New Zealand.[4]

The **honeymoon hypothesis** states that the electorate attributes negative outcomes to the former government and gives newly elected governments a certain period of time to change course. This, too, could have been the case in New Zealand.

Finally, the losing national party was indeed in a state of dissolution after the loss in 1984. For a long time, it was occupied with trying to find a successor for Muldoon and formulating the party's future programs. Its reconsolidation lasted till 1990 when it succeeded in defeating the Labour party. Thus, one could characterize the **opposition** as **fragmented and demoralized**.

Another lucky circumstance named in the literature is that the Labour government was confronted with a remarkable number of foreign policy incidents during its first legislative period. This could mean that the attention of the public and the prime minister were diverted from the radicalness of domestic economic reforms (Knorr, 1997, 143f.). These incidents include disputes within the then existent defense alliance ANZUS (Australia, New Zealand, USA), the sinking of the Greenpeace ship *Rainbow Warrior* by the French secret service, and the sinking of a Soviet warship to the south of New Zealand.

9.5 Open Questions

The example of New Zealand constitutes empirical evidence that reform proposals that are based on institutional economic insights can be realized politically. But the somewhat detailed account of the New Zealand case shows that beyond the insight that improving institutions is important, the likelihood of seeing any such improvements implemented depends on the specific context as just pointed out.

QUESTIONS

1. Illustrate the logic of the argument developed in Section 9.3 concerning VCDs in environmental policy using the prisoner's dilemma.

---

[4] With 93.7 percent the turnout at this election was the highest ever recorded in New Zealand. This has been interpreted as a desire by voters in favor of change.

2. Analyze reforms undertaken in your country using the framework provided in this chapter.

FURTHER READING

Freedom-of-information acts have been implemented in many countries with the aim of making the behavior of an administration and its bureaucracy more transparent and accountable. Whether freedom-of-information acts actually achieve these goals, remains doubtful. Costa (2013) deals with the issue. Blume and Voigt (2013) inquire into the consequences of transparency in the way budget laws are produced and implemented, and find that transparency is significantly correlated with the effectiveness of government.

The use of voluntary commitment declarations among European automobile manufacturers is discussed in Fontaras and Samaras (2007). The OECD report "Voluntary Approaches for Environmental Policy: Effectiveness, Efficiency and Usage in Policy Mixes" (OECD, 2003) is a more general overview of voluntary commitments. The monitoring reports by the RWI are available online but only in German (http://en.rwi-essen.de/media/content/pages/publikationen/rwi-projektberichte/RWI_PB_Monitoringbericht-2011-und-2012.pdf).

The possibility to induce change in internal institutions via external institutions is discussed in Aldashev et al. (2012).

New Zealand offers an example of very comprehensive national reforms. Naturally, insights from the NIE can also be applied to different situations. Every amendment is associated with the hope of changing incentives for the relevant actors in order to achieve better outcomes. Lawyers refer to this as a "regulatory impact assessment." In the past, empirical social studies have not been an area of expertise for lawyers, but we see great potential and manifold reasons for economists and lawyers to cooperate. Economists can support lawyers by predicting potential effects of changed laws and in analyzing factually induced behavioral changes *ex post*. In some jurisdictions, this is firmly established as regulatory impact assessment. Comparative studies on the experiences with regulatory impact assessment have been put forward by the OECD (2004) and the European Council (2004).

10 Outlook

10.1 Introductory Remarks

The previous nine chapters can be grouped into four broad parts. In the first part (Chapter 1), we encountered the questions that institutional economists pose and the instruments that can be used to answer those questions. In the second part (Chapters 2–5), we assumed that institutions are exogenously given. We then considered how different institutions affect different subjects: simple transactions (Chapter 2), firm structure (Chapter 3), and collective decisions (Chapter 4). In Chapter 5, we looked at the effects of institutions on economic growth and development. In the third part (Chapters 6 and 7), we proceeded to "endogenize" institutions, that is, consider institutions as determined by other factors. We asked how an economics approach can help us explain the evolution and change of external institutions (Chapter 6) and internal institutions (Chapter 7). In the fourth part, we turned to potential policy implications (Chapters 8 and 9). In Chapter 8, we discussed the need for a normative theory. In Chapter 9, we examined specific policy implications.

In this chapter, we will review the questions posed in the Introduction and examine whether we have gotten any closer to answering them.

If you are indeed one of those readers who reads this book from front to back, please re-read the Introduction and try to answer the questions posed there using what you have learned. If you choose to proceed immediately, you will miss a nice opportunity for repetition.

Let us proceed to the questions posed in the Introduction and potential answers.

We asked why the majority of humans worldwide command a low per capita income. One way to answer this is using property rights theory. But we can also resort to the relationship between institutional quality and economic growth discussed in Chapter 5, as well as the theories of institutional change presented in

Why are so many people malnourished?

Chapter 6. We cannot truly understand why it is so difficult to implement institutions that are commonly known to be conducive to economic development unless we accept that there are individuals in low-income countries who profit from the status quo and expect to suffer from growth-enhancing institutions. As we have seen repeatedly, it does not suffice to implement a set of adequate external institutions to promote economic development. Rather, a set of internal institutions is required that, at the least, does not fundamentally conflict with those external institutions.

Why is it so difficult to transplant constitutions successfully? Another question was why the import of constitutions that have proven to be successful elsewhere often does not yield the desired results, such as prosperity and stability. The easiest way to answer this is with recourse to the compatibility between external and internal institutions. If the imported institutions are not compatible with conventions and traditions prevalent in a society (internal institutions), any imported constitution (external institution) will remain a mere piece of paper. Another answer could be that conditionality imposed by the IMF and World Bank can lead to *window dressing*. Conditionality basically means that the IMF offers credits to a government conditional on implementing a number of reform measures. Frequently, these reforms are unpopular among the population and governments will therefore only pretend to implement them in order to receive the credits needed from the IMF. Laws are passed *de jure* in a country that no one in that country *de facto* considers enforcing.

On the relationship between individual liberty and economic growth We discussed several studies in Chapter 5 that addressed the question whether there is a relationship between individual liberties and per capita income, all of which point to the conclusion that this is not a mere correlation, but a causal relationship.

Is there a silver bullet for transforming entire countries? Then there was the question whether there is one correct way of reforming previously socialist societies, namely fast and far-reaching privatization. This topic has not been explicitly discussed in this book. You might know that, initially, there was serious dispute about whether transformation should occur as a *big bang* or rather more gradually. From discussions in numerous chapters of this book, two potentially contradictory arguments can be derived. On the one hand, the necessity that external institutions must not be fundamentally at odds with internal ones might suggest that reforms should only take place gradually. On the other hand, there are many aspects belonging to the political economy of reform that we discussed with regard to the example of New Zealand in

Chapter 9. There, we saw that fast and encompassing reform can be conducive to a large pro-reform coalition across very different interest groups. In the meantime, we have assembled a lot of empirical evidence regarding the effects of slow vs. fast transition. The evidence suggests that nations that undertake rapid reforms have managed to increase their living standards far more readily than nations that pursue more gradual reforms.

At this point, you might wonder why this chapter is called Open questions "Outlook" if all we have done so far is remind ourselves of all the puzzle pieces that we have encountered in the first nine chapters. That is why we now proceed to presenting several areas in which there is both need and potential for further development. If you are interested in what you have read so far, why not consider conducting your own research in this exciting area?

Let us start off with several unexplained aspects you might remember from previous chapters. We have discussed internal and external institutions more or less equitably. Giving equal weight to internal and external institutions is not common in most current economics research. The vast majority of studies deal exclusively with external institutions. The few studies that consider internal institutions treat them neither equally nor exclusively.

In Chapters 8 and 9, you probably noticed that the normative foundations of institutional economics are still rather thin. Most scholars within the NIE have some quarrels with the established welfare approach. But refusal of an established approach does not in itself represent an alternative, no matter how good the reasons for the refusal. The alternative approach we presented in Chapter 8 does suffer from many caveats. As soon as we attempt to apply that approach to economic policy, there is uncertainty how exactly that should be done.

In what remains of this concluding chapter, we briefly address four areas that have not received much attention so far, but that we expect to play a far greater role in the future. We start with the role of cognition for the relevance of institutions, which represents a rather abstract aspect. We then discuss the role of ideas for the emergence of novel institutions. The question whether the personal traits of individuals can be decisive in policy outcomes is taken up in Sections 10.3 and 10.4. In Section 10.5, we inquire into possible consequences of globalization for the relevance of institutions. Section 10.6 deals with the most serious challenge for empirically validated institutional economics, namely, identification, a technical term used by econometricians to ask how observational data can be used as if they had been produced by a real experiment. In a sense, we inquire into the relevance of "four i's" – namely ideas, individuals, internationalization, and identification – for the relevance of "the fifth i" – namely institutions. At the very end of this chapter, we have a few suggestions where to turn to in case you are enthusiastic about the NIE and want to start your own research right away.

10.2 Institutions and Mental Models

The role of mental models

Mental models crucially affect how we view the world. Naturally, we need to ask how they develop, how they spread socially, and so on. Human cognition is a necessary part of this investigation. Due to cognitive constraints with respect to information reception and processing, information is received and processed selectively. Perceptions and experiences that are culturally passed on or based on direct experimental learning lead to the forming of neuronal links. These structures include classifications that are used to select information. However, this also implies path dependency in that previous perceptions and expectations determine which information is received in the future.[1] How is this relevant for institutional economics?

The relevance of communication and culture

1. Our considerations make it clear how important communication and cultural background can be. The interpretation of new information depends on which internal model an actor has of his or her environment. If that is the case, we could well assume that different and totally separated groups will, at best, randomly achieve converging internal models. Given that there is a multitude of institutional arrangements to structure repeated interactions and the above mentioned cognitive path dependency, it seems probable that institutions might differ significantly between different groups.[2] This clarifies the relationship between institutional change and perceptions. Roughly speaking, cognitive path dependency leads to converging internal models, which assume rule character if they are associated with

---

[1] Hayek's *The Sensory Order* (1952) is an early attempt at utilizing this association for economic analysis.

[2] For a similar argument, see Denzau and North (1994, 14f.).

behavioral regularities within the group in question. At the same time, institutions that are culturally passed down from one generation to the next can modify human perception by excluding certain courses of action. This is obvious for type 2 and type 3 institutions.

2. The second aspect is closely related to the first. Path dependencies in learning can help prevent conflicts if they provide a shared pre-understanding or common ground. The set of available actions is perceived through this filter. By this filtering, the amount of information that needs to be received and processed is reduced. This reduction, for its part, is relevant for interactions and potentially resulting conflicts in that individuals only perceive a subset of all possible actions from which the optimal one is chosen. Consequently, the risk of conflict is less prevalent than the model of a perfectly informed utility maximizer might suggest. However, a shared cultural common ground can also turn out to be a disadvantage with regard to institutional change. Shared views and convictions of how the world is to be interpreted can hardly be changed overnight, as they result from a learning process that is characterized by path dependencies. Modifications are possible in principle, but if prevalent approaches lead to "satisfying" results (relative to one's individual acceptability threshold), there is no incentive to look for new courses of action. Thus, the notion that perception is based on path dependency reveals a social friction between stability and flexibility. This has to be accounted for when attempting to steer social processes.

Shared common grounds can reduce conflicts

3. Finally, the limitation of human perception can have different effects, depending on the institutions under consideration. Culturally transmitted institutions such as social rules concerning customs, morality, and decency (type 2 and 3 internal institutions) directly affect external institutions via the interpretation of laws. Some of the implications resulting from this interaction on the controllability of social processes have already been discussed in different parts of this book.

Cognition and internal institutions

A number of branches of the study of economics have started to delve into these issues. The most prominent branch is definitely behavioral economics whose representatives not only want to observe how real people behave, but why they behave as they do. Some behavioral economists have even gone one step further, examining the brain activity of individuals while they make their choices. This research is often referred to as "neuro economics." If we are able to determine why people behave the way they do, we will get closer to a better understanding of why some institutions work better than others.

10.3 Institutions and Ideas

Ideas as "imagined institutions"

Cognition – the topic of Section 10.2 – and ideas are closely interrelated. In this brief section, we deal with the possible relevance of "imagining institutions," that is, the capacity of the human mind to think up institutions that have never been implemented in reality before. For the sake of brevity, we refer to this possibility as "ideas." If we want to understand why some institutions undergo considerable change over time, it might not be sufficient to point to the interests of the relevant actors. Sometimes, completely new institutions seem to pop up in almost no time. After these new institutions are implemented in various places, one might wonder why now, why not before, or where did the impetus come from?

For institutional economists, the interplay between institutions and ideas is an interesting challenge.

Is a certain institutional environment a precondition for the genesis of new and innovative ideas? Are ideas really an important causal factor for institutional change? Is institutional change driven by a set of determinants other than ideas, only to be theorized after the change has taken place? Are general statements regarding causality possible at all?

These questions are, of course, not new. Karl Marx, for one, famously claimed that (political and ideological) consciousness is determined by the relevant class structure (in German: "*das gesellschaftliche Sein bestimmt das Bewußtsein*"). It is the mode of production that determines one's consciousness and, hence, ideas. It is well known that Marx developed many of his arguments in direct opposition to German philosopher Friedrich Wilhelm Hegel who insisted on the primacy of ideas. Whether or not this evidence supports Marx, there are many cases in which institutions emerged or changed, and their theoretical underpinning or even justification was only delivered *ex post*. Historian Paul Kennedy (1987, 20), for instance, has this to say: "Long before Adam Smith had coined the exact words, the rulers of certain societies of western Europe were tacitly recognizing that little else is requisite to carry a state to the highest degree of opulence from the lowest barbarism, but peace, easy taxes, and tolerable administration of justice." In other words, it was not the ideas of Adam Smith that laid out the core institutional features of a prosperous market economy before they were implemented but, rather, Smith was able to astutely observe, evaluate, and describe those crucial ingredients after they had been implemented. Myriad other examples led science writer Stephen Jay Gould (1985, 335) to conclude that "Pristine originality is an illusion."

On the other side of the spectrum there is the belief that creative minds are capable of imagining views of the world that do not need to be based on the status quo. If their ideas are able to infiltrate the minds of many who use them to coordinate their behavior in novel ways, institutional change becomes a possibility. Of course, the status quo has the simple advantage of being realized already. To make novel ideas the new status quo requires, however, some sort of collective action as extensively discussed in Chapter 7. Oftentimes, new ideas will therefore not have important effects but, as John Stuart Mill observes, there might be exceptions: "Ideas, unless outward circumstances conspire with them, have in general no very rapid or immediate efficacy in human affairs; and the most favorable outward circumstances may pass by, or remain inoperative, for want of ideas suitable to the conjecture. But when the right circumstances and the right ideas meet, the effect is seldom slow in manifesting itself" (Mill, 2006 [1845], 370).

The potential role of ideas for economic development has long been neglected entirely by economists. More recently, some economists have begun to deal with the topic. One of the better-known advances is called *Identity Economics* written by Rachel Kranton and Nobel Prize winning economist George Akerlof (Akerlof and Kranton, 2010).

10.4 Institutions and Individuals

This book has presented many different arguments making the case that "institutions matter." This does not, however, imply that nothing else matters. For a long time, economists simply ignored the possibility that personal traits of politicians could matter too. This is astonishing, as it seems straightforward to assume that notwithstanding the binding constraints introduced via institutions, politicians are left with some discretionary leeway that they can use in very different ways. The decision to go to war or not is only one of the many decisions that might be impacted by specific personal traits. Others are the willingness to run huge deficits, the quality of public goods provided, the degree to which policies improving the rule of law are pursued, and many others.

Institutions matter – but individuals matter too

Over the last decade or so, economists have begun to fill this research gap. A very ingenious approach was chosen by Jones and Olken (2005) who wanted to know if individual leaders make a difference with regard to the growth path of the countries they govern. Leadership change is usually not a random event. Important parts of one's own faction might be unhappy with the decisions of their prime minister and might, therefore, try to agree on a different one. This makes it almost impossible to claim a causal relationship between the leader and the subsequent growth path. To account for this possibility, Jones and Olken decide to analyze only one particular kind of change (or non-change) in political leaders, namely those resulting from assassination (attempts). The underlying rationale is that whether such an attempt is successful or not depends on a number of chance events and the result can, therefore, be considered a random event. Based on this identification strategy they show that the unexpected death of a leader can have substantial repercussions for the country's economic growth.

Quite a few studies have since followed suit. Besley et al. (2005) show that more highly educated politicians are less likely to use power opportunistically. Building on their earlier work, Besley et al. (2011) also find that more highly educated politicians are good for economic growth and are less likely to enroll their country into military conflicts. Göhlmann and Vaubel (2007) analyze the impact of the professional background of central bankers on inflation. Dreher et al. (2009) provide evidence suggesting that the professional background of a nation's political actors has an impact on the likelihood of implementing market-liberalizing reforms.

Taking the potential influence of individuals explicitly into account can have important consequences for the NIE. As spelled out before, some scholars point out that many studies purporting to measure institutions and their impacts really only measure policies. Now, policies are chosen by politicians. If it is possible to adequately control for the influence of politicians, we might be able to unbundle policies from institutions. This is closely related to the issues raised in Sections 10.2 and 10.3, because the behavior of politicians (individuals) is heavily influenced by their mental models, as well as the ideas that they have or that are communicated to them.

10.5 Institutions beyond the Nation-State

In economics (including institutional economics), the sovereign nation-state is usually considered to be exogenously given. It is frequently assumed that the government of the nation-state possesses the exclusive monopoly on the use of force within the boundaries of a certain territory. Theories of economic policy are traditionally concerned with representatives of governments that are territorially defined. There are different statistical methods for measuring prosperity on the level of the nation-state, such as GDP. The primacy of the concept of the sovereign nation-state is not restricted to state matters; firms are usually headquartered and associated with one or another nation-state. Societies are often defined by nation-state boundaries. We then speak of the French society, the Italian society, and so on.

Sociologist Ulrich Beck (2000) distinguishes between the nation-state and the nation society. He points out that societies are conceptually subordinate to nation-states (Beck, 2000, 23): "This is expressed in a vision of societies as (by definition) subordinate to states, of societies as *state* societies, of social order as state order." In a similar context, historian Anthony Smith (1983) has coined a specific way of thinking as "methodological nationalism." That the concept of a nation-state, both sovereign and identified by territorial boundaries, has become so successful in economics might seem rather unlikely. True, Adam Smith's most famous work is called *The Wealth of Nations*, but the central subject of economics is the individual. In the light of how economics has evolved, it appears all the more difficult to understand how the concept of "nation-state" could achieve such undisputed primacy. While Adam Smith's individuals still possess social ties to other individuals, the individual of twentieth-century economics is modeled as an atomistic unit.

The term "globalization" has become popular in the last few decades. It is beyond the scope of this work to analyze whether increasing globalization is associated with fundamental changes in the relationships between state governments, transnational firms, and international non-governmental organizations. However, it is apparent that the number of significant international and supranational organizations has increased in the last decades. The basic rules that govern the EU constitute an unprecedented institutional arrangement beyond the nation-state. But there are also other international organizations that have contributed to an increased institutionalization (in our sense). Rather than provide a comprehensive list of international organizations here, the WTO offers us an excellent example. The WTO provides certain rules for the design of national trade policies, the breaking of which is subject to sanctions. Thus, the WTO rules are institutions as defined in this book.

There is a host of new questions regarding institutions beyond the nation-state that have yet to be answered in institutional economics:

- How can we explain that nation-state level politicians are willing to cede part of their competencies to international organizations? *Prima facie*, less competency equals less power. One approach to answering this is already known to you. Politicians might be willing to cede part of their power in order to have a better shot at dealing with the dilemma of the strong state.
- How can we explain the high degree of stability found in international trade rules? After all, the argument for the nation-state is that stability can only be ensured by the state's monopoly on the use of force. Intriguingly, the international trade order is characterized by the absence of a super state or a world government.
- How can we explain that private firms, in cases of cross-border exchange disputes, often resort to private arbitration (a type 4 internal institution) instead of state arbitration?
- Are there alternative institutional arrangements that might provide a substitute to the nation-state? How might such institutions be designed? Would they be complementary or conflicting?
- Will the increase in international links affect the design of nation-state institutions? For instance, could we expect presently non-democratic states to transition towards democracy?
- How do differences in corporate culture affect fusions of firms from different countries? Could these differences help explain why sometimes desired synergies are not realized? Consider the case of Daimler-Chrysler! We could also apply the concept of

corporate culture to international organizations. Employees of international organizations are from different societies with different internal institutions; this could affect the manner in which such employees communicate with each other.

Hopefully, you are realizing that globalization-induced developments of organizations and institutions lead to a great number of (so far) open questions, a few of which we have formulated above. These questions will increasingly be the subject of institutional economics research in coming years.

Globalization implies new questions for the NIE

10.6 Institutions and Identification

We have saved the most serious challenge for the NIE for last: identification. The term is used by Angrist and Krueger (1999) to ask how a researcher uses observational data to approximate a real experiment. To firmly establish causal relationships, one would ideally run an experiment in which some societies are "treated" and others remain "untreated." Whether a society is treated or remains untreated would be decided randomly. If outcomes in the treated societies change relative to the untreated ones, we can be relatively confident that this effect has been caused by the treatment. For institutional economics, an ideal type of treatment would be the random introduction of a new institution or a significantly changed institution in comparison to what has been used in that society.

Since experiments with real institutions will certainly remain the exception, identification becomes a crucial problem for empirical institutional economics. This is because institutions are not exogenously given but humanly devised. This raises, *inter alia*, the question whether the observed outcome has been caused by an institution, or by those choosing this institution. In the appendix at the end of Chapter 5, we briefly explained the use of instruments in the NIE. Ideally, one would like to address this problem by "instrumenting" institutions with some exogenous variables. Convincing instruments are, however, very rare. On top of that, the more narrowly defined the institution under scrutiny, the less likely it is that the exclusion restriction regarding instruments will be fulfilled. This is one pragmatic reason why many empirical analyses regarding the effects of institutions do not focus on single institutions but rather on the quality of entire bundles of institutions.

10.7 Where to Turn to Start Your Own Research?

In this book, I have tried to summarize the most important findings of the NIE without, however, concealing that many questions revolving around the relevance of institutions have not yet been answered convincingly. Having read this book, you might feel that the NIE is an important field and that you could also contribute something to its development. We offer just two or three suggestions that are topics that you could possibly find interesting.

By now, the NIE has turned mainstream. This implies that many important contributions are carried by many different journals in economics, but also in political science and other disciplines. But if you are interested in methodological issues regarding the NIE, then there is a specialized journal that you might want to consult, namely the *Journal of Institutional Economics*. The contributions found in that journal originate from very different authors and it is easy to grasp what a lively field of research the NIE is engaged in by thumbing through the last couple of issues of this journal. The journal likes to be referred to as JOIE, implying that it is, indeed, a pleasure to read it.

In the 1990s, a group of institutional economists who wanted to promote the NIE founded the International Society for the New Institutional Economics, ISNIE in short. Institutional economists with very different interests assembled under the ISNIE umbrella, including those who are interested in the choice of governance structures (as described in Chapter 3), and those interested in the growth effects of institutions (as described in Chapter 5). A number of years back, the society renamed itself as the Society of Institutional and Organizational Economics (SIOE) and my impression is that those primarily interested in the choice of governance structures clearly prevail. Almost simultaneously, a new annual conference was established. It was also given a nice acronym, namely WINIR for World Interdisciplinary Network for Institutional Research. Compared to SIOE, its initiators seem less strict regarding the approaches of the papers admitted to their conference.

FURTHER READING

Voigt (2019) is a survey on "Institutions and Transition." It spells out the most important issues and briefly summarizes the most important empirical findings.

Camerer et al. (2005) is a very early overview of neuro economics. A very accessible survey of how economists have begun to incorporate "ideas" into their models is Rodrik (2014).

For a long time, the non-availability of data might have inhibited studies that take personal characteristics of leaders explicitly into account. Currently, a number of attempts to collect individual traits of political leaders are underway. The Archigos dataset introduced by Goemans et al. (2009) is one such attempt, the LEAD dataset by Ellis et al. (2015) another one. Outside the realm of research motivated by economic and political inquiry, the individual traits of judges has been the subject of intensive analysis for a number of years in literature dealing with legal issues. Segal and Spaeth (2002) is one of the most important contributions to this line of research.

Rodrik's (2011) *Globalization Paradox* is a fascinating account of the inherent tensions and incompatibilities involved in globalization. In particular, he describes what he calls the "fundamental political trilemma of the world economy" arguing that democracy, national determination, and economic globalization cannot be achieved simultaneously.

The journal, as well as the conferences mentioned in Section 10.7, can be easily found in the web. Here are their addresses: http://journals .cambridge.org/action/displayJournal?jid=JOI; www.sioe.org/; http:// winir.org/. Finally, throughout this book, I have often referred to the work of Daron Acemoglu and James Robinson. They run their own blog. You might find it enlightening to follow their blog if you are interested in current discussions. The blog is called whynationsfail.com.

References

Acemoglu, D. (2003). Why Not a Political Coase Theorem? Social
Conflict, Commitment, and Politics. *Journal of Comparative Economics*
31: 620–652.

Acemoglu, D. (2008). *Introduction to Modern Economic Growth*. Princeton
University Press.

Acemoglu, D., D. Cantoni, S. Johnson, and J. Robinson (2011). The
Consequences of Radical Reform: The French Revolution. *American
Economic Review* 101: 3286–3307.

Acemoglu, D. and S. Johnson (2005). Unbundling Institutions. *Journal of
Political Economy* 113: 949–995.

Acemoglu, D., S. Johnson, and J. Robinson (2001). The Colonial Origins of
Comparative Development: An Empirical Investigation. *American
Economic Review* 91: 1369–1401.

Acemoglu, D., Johnson, S., and Robinson, J. A. (2002). Reversal of Fortune:
Geography and Institutions in the Making of the Modern World Income
Distribution. *Quarterly Journal of Economics* 117: 1231–1294.

Acemoglu, D., S. Johnson, and J. Robinson (2005a). Institutions as the
Fundamental Cause of Long-Run Growth. In P. Aghion and S. Durlauf
(eds.), *Handbook of Economic Growth, Vol. 1A*. Amsterdam: Elsevier,
pp. 385–472.

Acemoglu, D., S. Johnson, and J. Robinson (2012). The Colonial Origins of
Comparative Development: An Empirical Investigation: Reply.
American Economic Review 102: 3077–3110.

Acemoglu, D., S. Johnson, J. Robinson, and P. Yared (2005b). From
Education to Democracy? *American Economic Review* 95: 44–49.

Acemoglu, D., S. Naidu, P. Restrepo, and J. Robinson (2014). *Democracy
Does Cause Growth*. Working Paper No. 20004. Cambridge, MA:
National Bureau of Economic Research.

Acemoglu, D. and J. Robinson (2005). *Economic Origins of Dictatorship
and Democracy*. Cambridge University Press.

Acemoglu, D. and J. Robinson (2012). *Why Nations Fail: The Origins of
Power, Prosperity, and Poverty*. New York: Crown Business.

Acemoglu, D., J. Robinson, and R. Torvik (2013). Why Do Voters Dismantle
Checks and Balances? *Review of Economic Studies* 80: 845–875.

Aghion, P. and R. Holden (2011). Incomplete Contracts and the Theory
of the Firm: What Have We Learned over the Past 25 Years? *Journal
of Economic Perspectives* 25: 181–197.

Ahern, K., D. Daminelli, and C. Fracassi (2015). Lost in Translation? The Effect of Cultural Values on Mergers around the World. *Journal of Financial Economics* 117: 165–189.

Aidt, T. S. (2016). Rent Seeking and the Economics of Corruption. *Constitutional Political Economy* 27: 142–157.

Akerlof, G. A. (1970). The Market for Lemons: Quality Uncertainty and the Market Mechanism. *Quarterly Journal of Economics* 84: 488–500.

Akerlof, G. A. and R. E. Kranton (2010). *Identity Economics: How Identities Shape Our Work, Wages, and Well-Being.* Princeton University Press.

Albouy, D. Y. (2012). The Colonial Origins of Comparative Development: An Empirical Investigation – Comment. *American Economic Review* 102: 3059–3076.

Alchian, A. (1950). Uncertainty, Evolution, and Economic Theory. *Journal of Political Economy* 58: 211–221.

Alchian, A. (1984). Specificity, Specialization, and Coalitions. *Journal of Institutional and Theoretical Economics* 140: 34–39.

Alchian, A. and H. Demsetz (1972). Production, Information Costs, and Economic Organization. *American Economic Review* 72: 777–795.

Alchian, A. and S. Woodward (1988). The Firm is Dead; Long Live the Firm: A Review of Oliver E. Williamson's 'The Economic Institutions of Capitalism'. *Journal of Economic Literature* 26: 65–79.

Aldashev, G., Chaara, I., Platteau, J. P., and Wahhaj, Z. (2012). Using the Law to Change the Custom. *Journal of Development Economics* 97: 182–200.

Alesina, A. and P. Giuliano (2015). Culture and Institutions. *Journal of Economic Literature* 53: 898–944.

Alesina, A., P. Giuliano, and N. Nunn (2013). On the Origins of Gender Roles: Women and the Plough. *Quarterly Journal of Economics* 128: 469–530.

Alesina, A. and E. Spolaore (2005). *The Size of Nations.* Cambridge, MA: MIT Press.

Alessi, L. de (1980). The Economics of Property Rights: A Review of the Evidence. *Research in Law and Economics* 2: 1–47.

Algan, Y. and P. Cahuc (2014). Trust, Growth, and Well-Being: New Evidence and Policy Implications. In P. Aghion and S. Durlauf (eds.), *Handbook of Economic Growth, Vol. 2.* Amsterdam: Elsevier, pp. 49–120.

Allen, D. (1998). Transaction Costs, and Coase: One More Time. In S. Medema (ed.), *Coasean Economics: Law & Economics and the New Institutional Economics.* Boston, MA: Kluwer, pp. 105–118.

Allen, D. (2000). Transaction Costs. In B. Bouckaert and G. de Geest (eds.), *Encyclopedia of Law and Economics, Volume I: The History and Methodology of Law and Economics.* Cheltenham: Edward Elgar, pp. 893–926.

Allen, D. (2011). *The Institutional Revolution: Measurement and the Economic Emergence of the Modern World*. University of Chicago Press.

Alston, L. (2008). The "Case" for Case Studies in New Institutional Economics. In E. Brousseau and J.-M. Glachant (eds.), *New Institutional Economics: A Guidebook*. Cambridge University Press, pp. 103–121.

Angrist, J. and A. Krueger (1999). Empirical Strategies in Labor Economics. In O. Ashenfelter and D. Card (eds.). *Handbook of Labor Economics, Vol. 3A*. Amsterdam: North Holland, pp. 1277–1366.

Angrist, J. and J.-S. Pischke (2009). *Mostly Harmless Econometrics: An Empiricist's Companion*. Princeton University Press.

Arruñada, B. (2007). Pitfalls to Avoid when Measuring Institutions: Is Doing Business Damaging Business? *Journal of Comparative Economics* 35: 729–747.

Arthur, B. (1989). Competing Technologies and Lock-in by Historical Small Events. *Economic Journal* 99: 116–131.

Audi, R. (2010). *Epistemology: A Contemporary Introduction to the Theory of Knowledge*. London: Routledge.

Axelrod, R. (1970). *Conflict of Interest: A Theory of Divergent Goals with Applications to Politics*. Chicago: Markham.

Axelrod, R. (1984). *The Evolution of Cooperation*. New York: Basic Books.

Axelrod, R. (1986). An Evolutionary Approach to Norms. *American Political Science Review* 80: 1095–1111.

Baker, G., R. Gibbons, and K. Murphy (2002). Relational Contracts and the Theory of the Firm. *Quarterly Journal of Economics* 117: 39–84.

Barro, R. and D. Gordon (1983). Rules, Discretion, and Reputation in a Model of Monetary Policy. *Journal of Monetary Economics* 12: 101–121.

Barzel, Y. (1977). Some Fallacies in the Interpretation of Information Costs. *Journal of Law and Economics* 20: 291–307.

Barzel, Y. (1987). The Entrepreneur's Reward for Self-Policing. *Economic Inquiry* 25: 103–116.

Beck, U. (2000). *What is Globalization?* Trans. Patrick Camiller. Cambridge: Polity Press.

Becker, G. (1968). Crime and Punishment: An Economic Approach. *Journal of Political Economy* 76: 169–217.

Becker, G. (1976). *The Economic Approach to Human Behavior*. University of Chicago Press.

Becker, G. (1983). A Theory of Competition among Pressure Groups for Political Influence. *Quarterly Journal of Economics* 98: 371–400.

Becker, S., K. Boeckh, C. Hainz, and L. Woessmann (2016). The Empire Is Dead, Long Live the Empire! Long-Run Persistence of Trust and Corruption in the Bureaucracy. *The Economic Journal* 126: 40–74.

Becker, S. and L. Woessmann (2009). Was Weber Wrong? A Human Capital Theory of Protestant Economic History. *Quarterly Journal of Economics* 124: 531–596.

Benham, A. and L. Benham (2000). Measuring the Costs of Exchange. In
C. Menard (ed.), *Institutions, Contracts, and Organizations.* Cheltenham:
Edward Elgar, pp. 367–375.

Berggren, N. and C. Bjørnskov (2011). Is the Importance of Religion in
Daily Life Related to Social Trust? Cross-Country and Cross-State
Comparisons. *Journal of Economic Behavior & Organization* 80:
459–480.

Berkowitz, D., K. Pistor, and J. Richard (2003). Economic Development,
Legality, and the Transplant Effect. *European Economic Review* 47:
165–195.

Besley, T. and A. Case (1995). Incumbent Behavior: Vote-Seeking,
Tax-Setting, and Yardstick Competition. *American Economic Review*
85: 25–45.

Besley, T., J. G. Montalvo, and M. Reynal-Querol (2011). Do Educated
Leaders Matter? *The Economic Journal* 121: F205–F227.

Besley, T., R. Pande, and V. Rao (2005). Political Selection and the Quality
of Government: Evidence from South India. CEPR Discussion Paper
5201. London: Centre for Economic Policy Research.

Binmore, K. (1994). *Game Theory and the Social Contract, Vol. 1: Playing
Fair.* Cambridge, MA: MIT Press.

Bisin, A. and T. Verdier (2008). Cultural Transmission. In S. Durlauf and
L. Blume (eds.), *The New Palgrave Dictionary of Economics.*
Basingstoke: Palgrave Macmillan.

Bjørnskov, C. (2010). How Does Social Trust Lead to Better Governance?
An Attempt to Separate Electoral and Bureaucratic Mechanisms. *Public
Choice* 144: 323–346.

Block, W. (ed.) (1991). *Economic Freedom: Toward a Theory of
Measurement.* Vancouver: The Fraser Institute.

Blume, L., J. Müller, and S. Voigt (2009). The Economic Effects of Direct
Democracy: A First Global Assessment. *Public Choice* 140: 431–461.

Blume, L. and S. Voigt (2013). The Economic Effects of Constitutional Budget
Institutions. *European Journal of Political Economy* 29: 235–251.

Bollard, A. (1994). New Zealand. In J. Williamson (ed.), *The Political
Economy of Policy Reform.* Washington, DC: Institute for International
Economics, pp. 73–110.

Bolton, P. and M. Dewatripont (2005). *Contract Theory.* Cambridge, MA:
MIT Press.

Boserup, E. (1970). *Women's Role in Economic Development.* London:
Allen & Unwin.

Bowles, S. and H. Gintis (2011). *A Cooperative Species: Human Reciprocity
and Its Evolution.* Princeton University Press.

Boyd, R. and P. Richerson (1994). The Evolution of Norms: An
Anthropological View. *Journal of Institutional and Theoretical
Economics* 150: 72–87.

Boyd, R. and P. Richerson (2005). *The Origin and Evolution of Cultures.* Oxford University Press.

Brennan, G. and A. Hamlin (2000). *Democratic Devices and Desires.* Cambridge University Press.

Brewer, M. and R. Kramer (1986). Choice Behavior in Social Dilemmas: Effects of Social Identity, Group Size and Decision Framing. *Journal of Personality and Social Psychology* 3: 543–549.

Brousseau, E. and J.-M. Glachant (eds.) (2008). *New Institutional Economics: A Guidebook.* Cambridge University Press.

Brunetti, A., G. Kisunko, and B. Weder (1998). Credibility of Rules and Economic Growth. *The World Bank Economic Review* 12: 353–384.

Buchanan, J. (1959). Positive Economics, Welfare Economics, and Political Economy. *Journal of Law and Economics* 2: 124–138.

Buchanan, J. (1975). *The Limits of Liberty: Between Anarchy and Leviathan.* University of Chicago Press.

Buchanan, J. (1978). A Contractarian Perspective on Anarchy. In J. Roland Pennock and John W. Chapman (eds.), *Anarchism.* New York University Press, pp. 29–42.

Buchanan, J. M. (1987). The Constitution of Economic Policy. *American Economic Review* 77: 243–250.

Buchanan, J. and R. Congleton (1998). *Politics by Principle, Not Interest: Toward Nondiscriminatory Democracy.* Cambridge University Press.

Buchanan, J. and G. Tullock (1962). *The Calculus of Consent: Logical Foundations of Constitutional Democracy.* Ann Arbor, MI: University of Michigan Press.

Camerer, C., G. Loewenstein, and D. Prelec (2005). Neuroeconomics: How Neuroscience Can Inform Economics. *Journal of Economic Literature* 43: 9–64.

Cameron, L. (1999). Raising the Stakes in the Ultimatum Game: Experimental Evidence from Indonesia. *Economic Inquiry* 37: 47–59.

Cantoni, D. (2015). The Economic Effects of the Protestant Reformation: Testing the Weber Hypothesis in the German Lands. *Journal of the European Economic Association* 13: 561–598.

Carlsson, F. and S. Lundström (2002). Economic Freedom and Growth: Decomposing the Effects. *Public Choice* 112: 335–344.

Chaudhuri, A. (2011). Sustaining Cooperation in Laboratory Public Goods Experiments: A Selective Survey of the Literature. *Experimental Economics* 14: 47–83.

Cheibub, J., J. Gandhi, and J. Vreeland (2010). Democracy and Dictatorship Revisited. *Public Choice* 143: 67–101.

Clague, C., P. Keefer, S. Knack, and M. Olson (1999). Contract-Intensive Money: Contract Enforcement, Property Rights, and Economic Performance. *Journal of Economic Growth* 4: 185–211.

Coase, R. H. (1937). The Nature of the Firm. *Economica* 4: 386–405.

Coase, R. H. (1960). The Problem of Social Cost. *Journal of Law and Economics* 3: 1–44.

Coase, R. H. (1964). The Regulated Industries: Discussion. *American Economic Review* 54: 194–197.

Coase, R. H. (1988). *The Firm, the Market, and the Law*. University of Chicago Press.

Coase, R. H. (1992). The Institutional Structure of Production. *American Economic Review* 82: 713–719.

Coleman, J. (1987). Norms as Social Capital. In G. Radnitzky and P. Bernholz (eds.), *Economic Imperialism*. New York: Paragon House Publishers, pp. 133–155.

Coleman, J. (1990). *Foundations of Social Theory*. Cambridge, MA: Belknap Press.

Colman, A. (1982). *Game Theory and Experimental Games: The Study of Strategic Interaction*. Oxford: Pergamon Press.

Congleton, R. D., A. L. Hillman, and K. A. Konrad (2008). *Forty Years of Research on Rent Seeking*, 2 vols. Heidelberg: Springer.

Cooter, R. and T. Ulen (2012). *Law and Economics*, 6th edition. New York: Addison-Wesley.

Costa, S. (2013). Do Freedom of Information Laws Decrease Corruption? *Journal of Law, Economics, & Organization* 29: 1317–1343.

Dahlman, C. (1979). The Problem of Externality. *Journal of Law and Economics* 22: 141–162.

Dahrendorf, R. (1968). *Essays in the Theory of Society*. Stanford University Press.

Darity, W. (ed.) (2007). *International Encyclopedia of the Social Sciences*. London: Macmillan Library Reference

David, P. (1994). Why Are Institutions the 'Carriers of History'? Path Dependence and the Evolution of Conventions, Organizations, and Institutions. *Structural Change and Economic Dynamics* 5: 205–220.

Davis, D. and C. Holt (1993). *Experimental Economics*. Princeton University Press.

Davis, L. (1986). Comment. In R. Gallman (ed.), *Long-Term Factors in American Economic Growth*. University of Chicago Press, pp. 149–161.

Dawkins, R. (1989). *The Selfish Gene*. Oxford University Press.

De Soto, H. (1990). *The Other Path: The Invisible Revolution in the Third World*. New York: Harper & Row.

Demsetz, H. (1967). Toward a Theory of Property Rights. *American Economic Review* 57: 347–359.

Demsetz, H. (1969). Information and Efficiency: Another Viewpoint. *Journal of Law and Economics* 12: 1–22.

Denzau, A. and D. North (1994). Shared Mental Models: Ideologies and Institutions. *Kyklos* 47: 3–31.

Diamond, J. M. (1998). *Guns, Germs and Steel: A Short History of Everybody for the Last 13,000 Years.* New York: Random House.

Dixit, A. (1996). *The Making of Economic Policy: A Transaction-Cost Politics Perspective.* Cambridge, MA: MIT Press.

Dixit, A. and B. Nalebuff (1991). *Thinking Strategically: The Competitive Edge in Business, Politics, and Everyday Life.* New York: W. W. Norton.

Dreher, A., M. J. Lamla, S. M. Lein, and F. Somogyi (2009). The Impact of Political Leaders' Profession and Education on Reforms. *Journal of Comparative Economics* 37: 169–193.

Dreher, A., H. Mikosch, and S. Voigt (2015). Membership Has its Privileges: The Effect of Membership in International Organizations on FDI. *World Development* 66: 346–358.

Duesenberry, J. (1960). Comment on "An Economic Analysis of Fertility." In Report of the National Bureau of Economic Research, *Demographic and Economic Change in Developed Countries.* New York: Columbia University Press, pp. 231–234.

Durante, R. (2010). Risk, Cooperation and the Economic Origins of Social Trust: An Empirical Investigation. Available at http://papers.ssrn.com/sol3/papers.cfm?abstract_id=1576774.

Duverger, M. (1954). *Political Parties.* London: Methuen.

Easterly, W. and R. Levine (2003). Tropics, Germs, and Crops: How Endowments Influence Economic Development. *Journal of Monetary Economics* 50: 3–39.

Easton, S. and M. Walker (eds.) (1992). *Rating Global Economic Freedom.* Vancouver: Fraser Institute.

Eggertsson, T. (1990). *Economic Behavior and Institutions.* Cambridge University Press.

Elkins, Z. and B. Simmons (2005). On Waves, Clusters, and Diffusion: A Conceptual Framework. *Annals of the American Academy of Political and Social Science* 598: 33–51.

Ellickson, R. (1986). Of Coase and Cattle: Dispute Resolution among Neighbors in Shasta County. *Stanford Law Review* 38: 623–687.

Ellickson, R. (1991). *Order Without Law.* Cambridge, MA: Harvard University Press.

Ellickson, R. (1994). The Aim of Order Without Law. *Journal of Institutional and Theoretical Economics* 150: 97–100.

Ellis, C. M., M. C. Horowitz, and A. C. Stam (2015). Introducing the LEAD Data Set. *International Interactions* 41: 718–741.

Elster, J. (1984). *Ulysses and the Sirens: Studies in Rationality and Irrationality,* revised edition. Cambridge University Press.

Elster, J. (1989a). *The Cement of Society: A Study of Social Order.* Cambridge University Press.

Elster, J. (1989b). Social Norms and Economic Theory. *Journal of Economic Perspectives* 3: 99–117.

Ensminger, J. (1997). Changing Property Rights: Reconciling Formal and Informal Rights to Land in Africa. In J. Drobak and J. Nye (eds.), *The Frontiers of the New Institutional Economics*. San Diego, CA: Academic Press, pp. 165–196.

Ensminger, J. (1998). Fairness in Cross-Cultural Perspective: Evidence from Experimental Economics in a Less Developed Society. Paper presented at the second annual conference of the International Society for the New Institutional Economics, Paris, September.

European Council (2004). A Comparative Analysis of Regulatory Impact Assessment in Ten EU Countries: A Report Prepared for the EU Directors of Better Regulation Group, Dublin. Available at www.betterregulation.ie/attached_files/Pdfs/Report%20on%20RIA%20in%20the%20EUa.pdf.

Evans, L., A. Grimes, B. Wilkinson and D. Teece (1996). Economic Reform in New Zealand 1984–1995: The Pursuit of Efficiency. *Journal of Economic Literature* 34: 1856–1902.

Falk, A. and J. Heckman (2009). Lab Experiments are a Major Source of Knowledge in the Social Sciences. *Science* 326: 535–538.

Fehr, E. (2009). On the Economics and Biology of Trust. *Journal of the European Economic Association* 7: 235–266.

Fehr, E., S. Gächter, and G. Kirchsteiger (1997). Reciprocity as a Contract Enforcement Device: Experimental Evidence. *Econometrica* 65: 833–860.

Fehr, E., L. Götte, and C. Zehnder (2009). A Behavioral Account of the Labor Market: The Role of Fairness Concerns. *Annual Review of Economics* 1: 355–384.

Fehr, E. and K. M. Schmidt (1999). A Theory of Fairness, Competition, and Cooperation. *Quarterly Journal of Economics* 114: 817–868.

Feld, L. and S. Voigt (2003). Economic Growth and Judicial Independence: Cross Country Evidence Using a New Set of Indicators. *European Journal of Political Economy* 19: 497–527.

Ferejohn, J. and F. Rosenbluth (2014). Arms and Men: Technology's Shadow over Democracy. *Yale Global Online*. Available at http://yaleglobal.yale.edu/content/arms-and-men-technology%E2%80%99s-shadow-over-democracy.

Ferguson, A. (1995 [1767]). *An Essay on the History of Civil Society*. Ed. F. Oz-Salzberger. Cambridge University Press.

Fernández, R. (2010). Does Culture Matter? Working Paper No. 16277. Cambridge, MA: National Bureau of Economic Research.

Fontaras, G. and Z. Samaras (2007). A Quantitative Analysis of the European Automakers' Voluntary Commitment to Reduce CO_2 Emissions from New Passenger Cars based on Independent Experimental Data. *Energy Policy* 35: 2239–2248.

Frank, R. (1988). *Passions Within Reason: The Strategic Role of the Emotions*. New York: W. W. Norton.

Frey, B. (1997). A Constitution for Knaves Crowds Out Civic Virtues. *The Economic Journal* 107: 1043–1053.

Friedman, D. (1991). The Swedes Get It Right. *Reason Magazine*: 1–4.

Friedman, M. (1953). The Methodology of Positive Economics. In M. Friedman, *Essays in Positive Economics*. University of Chicago Press, pp. 3–44.

Fudenberg, D. and E. Maskin (1986). The Folk Theorem in Repeated Games with Discounting or with Incomplete Information. *Econometrica* 54: 533–545.

Furubotn, E. and S. Pejovich (1972). Property Rights and Economic Theory: A Survey of Recent Literature. *Journal of Economic Literature* 10: 1137–1162.

Furubotn, E. and R. Richter (1998). *Institutions & Economic Theory: The Contribution of the New Institutional Economics*. Ann Arbor, MI: University of Michigan Press.

Gächter, S., E. Kessler, and M. Königstein (2011). *Do Incentives Destroy Voluntary Cooperation?* Working Paper, University of Nottingham.

Galanter, M. (1981). Justice in Many Rooms: Courts, Private Ordering, and Indigenous Law. *Journal of Legal Pluralism and Unofficial Law* 19: 1–47.

Garrouste, P. and S. Saussier (2008). The Theories of the Firm. In E. Brousseau and J.-M. Glachant (eds.), *New Institutional Economics: A Guidebook*. Cambridge University Press, pp. 23–36

Gibbons, R. (2005). Four Formal(izable) Theories of the Firm? *Journal of Economic Behavior & Organization* 58: 200–245.

Glaeser, E., R. La Porta, F. Lopez-de-Silanes, and A. Shleifer (2004). Do Institutions Cause Growth? *Journal of Economic Growth* 9: 271–303.

Goderis, B. and M. Versteeg (2014). The Diffusion of Constitutional Rights. *International Review of Law and Economics* 39: 1–19.

Goemans, H. E., K. S. Gleditsch, and G. Chiozza (2009). Introducing Archigos: A Dataset of Political Leaders. *Journal of Peace Research* 46: 269–283.

Göhlmann, S. and R. Vaubel (2007). The Educational and Professional Background of Central Bankers and its Effect on Inflation: An Empirical Analysis. *European Economic Review* 51: 925–941.

Gould, S. J. (1985). *The Flamingo's Smile: Reflections in Natural History*. New York: W. W. Norton.

Greif, A. (1992). Institutions and International Trade: Lessons from the Commercial Revolution. *American Economic Review* 82: 128–133.

Greif, A. (2006). *Institutions and the Path to the Modern Economy: Lessons from Medieval Trade*. Cambridge University Press.

Greif, A. and D. Laitin (2004). A Theory of Endogenous Institutional Change. *American Political Science Review* 98: 633–652.

Greif, A., P. Milgrom, and B. Weingast (1994). Coordination, Commitment, and Enforcement: The Case of the Merchant Guild. *Journal of Political Economy* 102: 745–776.

Guiso, L., P. Sapienza, and L. Zingales (2004a). Cultural Biases in Economic Exchange. Working Paper No. 11005. Cambridge, MA: National Bureau of Economic Research.

Guiso, L., P. Sapienza, and L. Zingales (2004b). The Role of Social Capital in Financial Development. *American Economic Review* 94: 526–556.

Guiso, L., P. Sapienza, and L. Zingales (2006). Does Culture Affect Economic Outcomes? *Journal of Economic Perspectives* 20: 23–48.

Guiso, L., P. Sapienza, and L. Zingales (2008). Long Term Persistence. Working Paper No. 14278. Cambridge, MA: National Bureau of Economic Research.

Güth, W. and M. Kocher (2014). More than Thirty Years of Ultimatum Bargaining Experiments: Motives, Variations, and a Survey of the Recent Literature. *Journal of Economic Behavior & Organization* 108: 396–409.

Güth, W., R. Schmittberger, and B. Schwarze (1982). An Experimental Analysis of Ultimatum Bargaining. *Journal of Economic Behavior & Organization* 3: 367–388.

Gwartney, J. and R. Holcombe (1999). Economic Freedom, Constitutional Structure, and Growth in Developing Countries. In M. Kimenyi and J. Mbaku (eds.), *Institutions and Collective Choice in Developing Countries*. Aldershot: Ashgate, pp. 33–59.

Gwartney, J., R. Lawson, and W. Block (1996). *Economic Freedom of the World: 1975–1995*. Vancouver: Fraser Institute.

Gwartney, J., R. Lawson, and J. Hall (2017). *Economic Freedom of the World: 2017 Annual Report*. Vancouver: Fraser Institute.

Haan, J. de and J. E. Sturm (2000). On the Relationship between Economic Freedom and Economic Growth. *European Journal of Political Economy* 16: 215–241.

Hamilton, A., J. Madison, and J. Jay (1961 [1788]). *The Federalist Papers*. Introd. Clinton Rossiter. New York: Mentor.

Hardin, G. (1968). The Tragedy of the Commons. *Science* 162: 1243–1248.

Hardin, R. (1989). Why a Constitution? In B. Grofman and D. Wittman (eds.), *The Federalist Papers and the New Institutionalism*. New York: Agathon Press, pp. 100–120.

Harrison, G. and J. List (2004). Field Experiments. *Journal of Economic Literature* 42: 1009–1055.

Hart, O. (1989). An Economist's Perspective on the Theory of the Firm. *Columbia Law Review* 89: 1757–1774.

Hayek, F. A. (1952). *The Sensory Order: An Inquiry into the Foundations of Theoretical Psychology*. University of Chicago Press.

Hayek, F. (1964). Kinds of Order in Society. *New Individualist Review* 3: 3–12.

Hayek, F. (1973). *Law, Legislation and Liberty, Vol. 1: Rules and Order.* University of Chicago Press.

Hayek, F. (1976). *Law, Legislation and Liberty, Vol. 2: The Mirage of Social Justice.* University of Chicago Press.

Hayo, B. and S. Voigt (2008). Inflation, Central Bank Independence and the Legal System. *Journal of Institutional and Theoretical Economics* 164: 751–777.

Heiner, R. (1983). The Origin of Predictable Behavior. *American Economic Review* 4: 560–595.

Henisz, W. (2000). The Institutional Environment for Economic Growth. *Economics and Politics* 12: 1–31.

Henrich, J. (2000). Does Culture Matter in Economic Behavior? Ultimatum Game Bargaining Among the Machiguenga of the Peruvian Amazon. *American Economic Review* 90: 973–979.

Henrich, J., R. Boyd, S. Bowles, C. Camerer, E. Fehr, H. Gintis, and R. McElreath (2001). In Search of Homo Economicus: Behavioral Experiments in 15 Small-Scale Societies. *American Economic Review* 91: 73–78.

Henrich, J., R. Boyd, S. Bowles, C. Camerer, E. Fehr, H. Gintis, R. McElreath, et al. (2005). "Economic Man" in Cross-Cultural Perspective: Behavioral Experiments in 15 Small-Scale Societies. *Behavioral and Brain Sciences* 28: 795–855.

Herrmann, B., C. Thöni, and S. Gächter (2008). Anti-Social Punishment across Societies. *Science* 319: 1362–1367.

Hirschman, A. (1970). *Exit, Voice and Loyalty: Responses to Decline in Firms, Organizations, and States.* Cambridge, MA: Harvard University Press.

Hobbes, T. (1982 [1651]). *Leviathan.* Harmondsworth: Penguin Classics.

Hodgson, G. (1998). The Approach of Institutional Economics. *Journal of Economic Literature* 36: 166–192.

Holcombe, R. (2016). *Advanced Introduction to Public Choice.* Cheltenham: Edward Elgar.

Hume, D. (1987 [1777]). *Essays: Moral, Political, and Literary.* Ed. E. F. Miller. Indianapolis, IN: Liberty Classics.

Hume, D. (1990 [1740]). *A Treatise of Human Nature.* Ed. L. A. Selby-Bigge. Oxford: Clarendon Press.

Jensen, M. and W. Meckling (1976). Theory of the Firm: Managerial Behavior, Agency Costs and Ownership Structure. *Journal of Financial Economics* 3: 305–360.

Johansson, P.-O. (1991). *An Introduction to Modern Welfare Economics.* Cambridge University Press.

Jolls, C., C. Sunstein, and R. Thaler (1998). A Behavioral Approach to Law and Economics. *Stanford Law Review* 50: 1471–1550.

Jones, B. and B. Olken (2005). Do Leaders Matter? National Leadership and Growth since World War II. *Quarterly Journal of Economics* 120: 835–864.

Kahneman, D. (2011). *Thinking, Fast and Slow*. New York: Farrar, Straus & Giroux.

Kahneman, D., J. Knetsch, and R. Thaler (1986). Fairness as a Constraint on Profit Seeking: Entitlements in the Market. *American Economic Review* 76: 728–741.

Kant, I. (1991 [1797]). *The Metaphysics of Morals*. Ed. Mary Gregor. Cambridge University Press.

Kennedy, P. (1987). *The Rise and Fall of the Great Powers*. New York: Vintage.

Keefer, P. and M. Shirley (1998). From the Ivory Tower to the Corridors of Power: Making Institutions Matter for Development Policy. Paper presented at the second annual conference of the International Society for the New Institutional Economics. Paris, September.

Kirchgässner, G. (2008). *Homo Oeconomicus: The Economic Model of Behaviour and its Applications in Economics and Other Social Sciences*. Dordrecht: Springer.

Kirstein, R. and S. Voigt (2006). The Violent and the Weak: When Dictators Care About Social Contracts. *American Journal of Economics and Sociology* 65: 863–890.

Kiwit, D. and S. Voigt (1995). Überlegungen zum institutionellen Wandel unter Berücksichtigung des Verhältnisses interner und externer Institutionen. *ORDO: Jahrbuch für die Ordnung von Wirtschaft und Gesellschaft* 46: 117–148.

Klerman, D., P. Mahoney, H. Spamann, and M. Weinstein (2011). Legal Origin or Colonial History? *Journal of Legal Analysis* 3: 379–409.

Knack, S. and P. Keefer (1995). Institutions and Economic Performance: Cross-Country Tests Using Alternative Institutional Measures. *Economics and Politics* 7: 207–227.

Knack, S. and P. Keefer (1997). Does Social Capital Have an Economic Payoff? A Cross-Country Investigation. *Quarterly Journal of Economics* 112: 1251–1288.

Knight, F. (1922). *Risk, Uncertainty, and Profit*. Boston, MA: Houghton-Mifflin.

Knight, J. (1992). *Institutions and Social Conflict*. Cambridge University Press.

Knorr, A. (1997). *Das ordnungspolitische Modell Neuseelands. Ein Vorbild für Deutschland?* Tübingen: Mohr Siebeck.

Korobkin, R. and T. Ulen (2000). Law and Behavioral Science: Removing the Rationality Assumption from Law and Economics. *California Law Review* 88: 1051–1143.

Kovač, M. and R. Spruk (2016). Institutional Development, Transaction Costs and Economic Growth: Evidence from a Cross-Country Investigation. *Journal of Institutional Economics* 12: 129–159.

Kreps, D. (1990). *A Course in Microeconomic Theory.* Princeton University Press.

Kreps, D. (1996). Corporate Culture and Economic Theory. In P. J. Buckley (ed.), *Firms, Organizations and Contracts.* Oxford University Press, pp. 221–275.

Kreps, D. (1998). Bounded Rationality. In S. Durlauf and L. Blume (eds.), *The New Palgrave Dictionary of Economics*, 2nd edition. Basingstoke: Palgrave Macmillan, pp. 168–173.

Kreps, D., P. Milgrom, J. Roberts, and R. Wilson (1982). Rational Cooperation in the Finitely Repeated Prisoners' Dilemma. *Journal of Economic Theory* 27: 245–252.

Krueger, A. (1974). The Political Economy of the Rent-Seeking Society. *American Economic Review* 64: 291–303.

Kydland, F. and E. Prescott (1977). Rules Rather than Discretion: The Inconsistency of Optimal Plans. *Journal of Political Economy* 85: 473–491.

La Porta, R., F. Lopez-de-Silanes, and A. Shleifer (2008). The Economic Consequences of Legal Origins. *Journal of Economic Literature* 46: 285–332.

La Porta, R., F. Lopez-de-Silanes, A. Shleifer, and R. Vishny (1997). Trust in Large Organizations. *American Economic Review: Papers and Proceedings* 87: 333–338.

La Porta, R., F. Lopez-de-Silanes, A. Shleifer, and R. Vishny (1998). Law and Finance. *Journal of Political Economy* 106: 1113–1155.

La Porta, R., F. Lopez-de-Silanes, A. Shleifer, and R. Vishny (1999). The Quality of Government. *Journal of Law, Economics, and Organization* 15: 222–279.

Ledyard, J. (1995). Public Goods: A Survey of Experimental Research. In J. Kagel and A. Roth (eds.), *The Handbook of Experimental Economics.* Princeton University Press, pp. 111–194.

Levitt, S. and J. List (2009). Field Experiments in Economics: The Past, the Present, and the Future. *European Economic Review* 53: 1–18.

Levy, B. and P. Spiller (1994). The Institutional Foundations of Regulatory Commitment: A Comparative Analysis of Telecommunications Regulation. *Journal of Law, Economics & Organization* 10: 201–246.

Lewis, D. (1969). *Convention: A Philosophical Study.* Cambridge, MA: Harvard University Press.

Lewis-Beck, M. and M. Stegmaier (2019). Economic Voting. In B. Grofman, R. Congleton, and S. Voigt (eds.), *The Oxford Handbook of Public Choice.* Oxford University Press.

Libecap, G. (1978). Economic Variables and the Development of the Law: The Case of Western Mineral Rights. *Journal of Economic History* 38: 338–362.

Liebowitz, S. and S. Margolis (1989). The Fable of the Keys. *Journal of Law and Economics* 33: 1–25.

Lipset, S. M. (1959). Some Social Requisites of Democracy: Economic Development and Political Legitimacy. *American Political Science Review* 53: 69–105.

Littlechild, S. and J. Wiseman (1986). The Political Economy of Restriction of Choice. *Public Choice* 51: 161–172.

Macher, J. and B. Richman (2008). Transaction Cost Economics: An Assessment of Empirical Research in the Social Sciences. *Business and Politics* 10: 1210.

Macneil, I. (1974). The Many Futures of Contracts. *Southern California Law Review* 47: 691–816.

Majeski, S. (1990). Comment: An Alternative Approach to the Generation and Maintenance of Norms. In K. Coo and M. Levi (eds.), *The Limits of Rationality*. University of Chicago Press, pp. 273–281.

Martynova, M. and L. Renneboog (2008). Spillover of corporate Governance Standards in Cross-Border Mergers and Acquisitions. *Journal of Corporate Finance* 14: 200–223.

Massell, G. (1968). Law as an Instrument of Revolutionary Change in a Traditional Milieu: The Case of Soviet Central Asia. *Law and Society Review* 2: 179–214.

Matsusaka, J. G. (2005). Direct Democracy Works. *Journal of Economic Perspectives* 19: 185–206.

McCloskey, D. (1998). The So-Called Coase Theorem. *Eastern Economic Journal* 24: 367–371.

Meltzer, A. and S. Richard (1981). A Rational Theory of the Size of Government. *Journal of Political Economy* 89: 914–927.

Milgrom, P., D. North, and B. Weingast (1990). The Role of Institutions in the Revival of Trade: The Law Merchant, Private Judges, and the Champagne Fairs. *Economics & Politics* 2: 1–23.

Milgrom, P. and J. Roberts (1992). *Economics, Organization, and Management*. Englewood Cliffs, NJ: Prentice Hall.

Milinski, M., D. Semmann, H. J. Krambeck, and J. Marotzke (2006). Stabilizing the Earth's Climate is Not a Losing Game: Supporting Evidence from Public Goods Experiments. *Proceedings of the National Academy of Sciences* 103: 3994–3998.

Mill, J. S. (2006 [1845]). The Claims of Labour. In J. S. Mill, *The Collected Works of John Stuart Mill, Vol. 4: Essays on Economics and Society 1824–1845*. Indianapolis, IN: Liberty Fund.

Moe, T. (1990). Political Institutions: The Neglected Side of the Story. *Journal of Law, Economics, & Organization*, 6: 213–253.

Montesquieu, C. de (1989 [1748]). *The Spirit of the Laws*. Cambridge University Press.

Moselle, B. and B. Polak (2001). A Model of the Predatory State. *Journal of Law, Economics, & Organization* 17: 1–33.

Mueller, D. (1986). Rational Egoism versus Adaptive Egoism as Fundamental Postulate for a Descriptive Theory of Human Behavior. *Public Choice* 51: 3–23.

Mueller, D. (1998). Redistribution and Allocative Efficiency in a Mobile World Economy. *Jahrbuch für Neue Politische Ökonomie* 17: 172–190.

Mueller, D. (2003). *Public Choice III.* Cambridge University Press.

Mueller, D. (2015). Public Choice, Social Choice, and Political Economy. *Public Choice* 163: 379–387.

Nelson, R. and S. Winter (1982). *An Evolutionary Theory of Economic Change.* Cambridge, MA: Harvard University Press.

Niskanen, W. A. (1971). *Bureaucracy and Representative Government.* New Brunswick, NJ: Transaction Publishers.

Niskanen, W. A. (1997). Autocratic, Democratic, and Optimal Government. *Economic Inquiry* 35: 464–479.

North, D. (1981). *Structure and Change in Economic History.* New York: W. W. Norton.

North, D. (1990a). *Institutions, Institutional Change and Economic Performance.* Cambridge University Press.

North, D. (1990b). A Transaction Cost Theory of Politics. *Journal of Theoretical Politics* 2: 355–367.

North, D. (1993). Institutions and Credible Commitment. *Journal of Institutional and Theoretical Economics* 149: 11–23.

North, D. (1994). Economic Performance through Time. *American Economic Review* 84: 359–368.

North, D. (2005). *Understanding the Process of Economic Change.* Princeton University Press.

North, D., J. Wallis, and B. Weingast (2009). *Violence and Social Orders: A Conceptual Framework for Interpreting Recorded Human History.* Cambridge University Press.

North, D. and B. Weingast (1989). Constitutions and Commitment: The Evolution of Institutions Governing Public Choice in Seventeenth-Century England. *Journal of Economic History* 49: 803–832.

Nunn, N. (2009). The Importance of History for Economic Development. *Annual Review of Economics* 1: 65–92.

Nunn, N. (2014). Historical Development. In P. Aghion and S. Durlauf (eds.), *Handbook of Economic Growth, Vol. 2A.* Amsterdam: Elsevier, pp. 347–402.

OECD (2003). *Voluntary Approaches for Environmental Policy: Effectiveness, Efficiency and Usage in Policy Mixes.* Paris: OECD.

OECD (2004). Regulatory Impact Assessment (RIA) Inventory – Note by the Secretariat. Paris OECD. Available at www.oecd.org/gov/regulatory-policy/35258430.pdf.

Olson, M. (1965). *The Logic of Collective Action.* Cambridge, MA: Harvard University Press.

Olson, M. (1982). *The Rise and Decline of Nations.* New Haven, CT: Yale University Press.

Olson, M. (1996). Big Bills Left on the Sidewalk. *Journal of Economic Perspectives* 10: 3–24.

Olsson, O. and D. A. Hibbs Jr. (2005). Biogeography and Long-Run Economic Development. *European Economic Review* 49: 909–938.

Oosterbeek, H., R. Sloof, and G. van de Kuilen (2004). Cultural Differences in Ultimatum Game Experiments: Evidence from a Meta-Analysis. *Experimental Economics* 7: 171–188.

Ordeshook, P. (1992). Constitutional Stability. *Constitutional Political Economy* 3: 137–175.

Ostrom, E. (1986). An Agenda for the Study of Institutions. *Public Choice* 48: 3–25.

Ostrom, E. (1990). *Governing the Commons: The Evolution of Institutions for Collective Action.* Cambridge University Press.

Ostrom, E. (1996). Incentives, Rules of the Game, and Development. In M. Bruno (ed.), *Annual World Bank Conference on Development Economics.* Washington, DC: World Bank, pp. 207–234.

Ostrom, E. (2000). Collective Action and the Evolution of Social Norms. *Journal of Economic Perspectives* 14: 137–158.

Ostrom, E. (2010). Beyond Markets and States: Polycentric Governance of Complex Economic Systems. *Transnational Corporations Review* 2: 1–12.

Pejovich, S. (ed.) (2001). *The Economics of Property Rights II.* International Library of Critical Writings in Economics. Cheltenham: Edward Elgar.

Pénard, T. (2008). Game Theory and Institutions. In E. Brousseau and J.-M. Glachant (eds.), *New Institutional Economics: A Guidebook.* Cambridge University Press, pp. 158–179.

Pistor, K. (2002). The Demand for Constitutional Law. In S. Voigt and H.-J. Wagener (eds.), *Constitutions, Markets and the Law.* Cheltenham: Edward Elgar, pp. 65–82.

Platteau, J. P. (2000). *Institutions, Social Norms, and Economic Development.* Mahwah, NJ: Psychology Press.

Plott, C. and V. Smith (2008). *Handbook of Experimental Economics Results, Vol. 1.* Amsterdam: North Holland.

Polanyi, M. (1998 [1952]). *The Logic of Liberty.* Indianapolis, IN: Liberty Classics.

Popper, K. R. (1959). *The Logic of Scientific Discovery.* London: Hutchinson.

Przeworski, A. and F. Limongi (1993). Political Regimes and Economic Growth. *Journal of Economic Perspectives* 7: 51–69.

Putnam, R. (1993). *Making Democracy Work: Civic Traditions in Modern Italy.* Princeton University Press.

Rawls, J. (1971). *A Theory of Justice.* Cambridge, MA: Belknap Press.

Riker, W. (1975). Federalism. In F. I. Greenstein and N. Polsby (eds.), *The Handbook of Political Science, Volume V: Government Institutions and Processes.* Reading, MA: Addison-Wesley, pp. 93–172.

Rodrik, D. (2011). *The Globalization Paradox: Democracy and the Future of the World Economy.* Cambridge University Press.

Rodrik, D. (2014). When Ideas Trump Interests: Preferences, Worldviews, and Policy Innovations. *Journal of Economic Perspectives* 28: 189–208.

Rodrik, D., A. Subramanian, and F. Trebbi (2004). Institutions Rule: The Primacy of Institutions over Geography and Integration in Economic Development. *Journal of Economic Growth* 9: 131–165.

Rousseau, J.-J. (1992 [1755]). *Discourse on the Origin of Inequality.* Indianapolis, IN: Hackett.

Rutherford, M. (1994). *Institutions in Economics: The Old and the New Institutionalism.* Cambridge University Press.

Sachs, J. and P. Malaney (2002). The Economic and Social Burden of Malaria. *Nature* 415: 680–685.

Salsburg, D. (2001). *The Lady Tasting Tea: How Statistics Revolutionized Science in the Twentieth Century.* New York: Holt Paperbacks.

Sappington, D. (1991). Incentives in Principal–Agent Relationships. *Journal of Economic Perspectives* 5: 45–66.

Schelling, T. (1960). *The Strategy of Conflict.* Cambridge, MA: Harvard University Press.

Schermerhorn, J. (2012). *Management,* 11th edition. Hoboken, NJ: Wiley.

Schlicht, E. (1990). Rationality, Bounded or Not, and Institutional Analysis. *Journal of Institutional and Theoretical Economics* 146: 703–719.

Schneider, F. and D. Enste (2007). *The Shadow Economy: An International Survey.* Cambridge University Press.

Schoeck, H. (1987). *Envy: A Theory of Social Behavior.* Indianapolis, IN: Liberty Fund.

Segal, J. A. and H. J. Spaeth (2002). *The Supreme Court and the Attitudinal Model Revisited.* Cambridge University Press.

Shelanski, H. and P. Klein (1999). Empirical Research in Transaction Cost Economics: A Review and Assessment. In G. R. Carroll and D. J. Teece (eds.), *Firms, Markets, and Hierarchies: The Transaction Cost Economics Perspective.* Oxford University Press, pp. 89–118.

Shirley, M., W. Ning, and C. Menard (2014). Ronald Coase's Impact on Economics. *Journal of Institutional Economics* 11: 1–18.

Simon, H. (1955). A Behavioral Model of Rational Choice. *Quarterly Journal of Economics* 69: 99–118.

Sinn, H.-W. (1997). The Selection Principle and Market Failure in Systems Competition. *Journal of Public Economics* 66: 247–274.

Smith, A. (1983). Nationalism and Classical Social Theory. *British Journal of Sociology* 34: 19–38.

Smith, V. (1994). Economics in the Laboratory. *Journal of Economic Perspectives* 8: 113–132.

Sokoloff, K. L. and Engerman, S. L. (2000). Institutions, Factor Endowments, and Paths of Development in the New World. *Journal of Economic Perspectives* 14: 217–232.

Spamann, H. (2010). The "Antidirector Rights Index" Revisited. *Review of Financial Studies* 23: 467–486.

Stone, A., B. Levy, and R. Paredes (1996). Public Institutions and Private Transactions: A Comparative Analysis of the Legal and Regulatory Environment for Business Transactions in Brazil and Chile. In L. Alston, T. Eggertsson, and D. North (eds.), *Empirical Studies in Institutional Change*. Cambridge University Press, pp. 95–128.

Studenmund, A. (2010). *Using Econometrics: A Practical Guide*, 6th edition. Harlow: Pearson.

Sugden, R. (1986). *The Economics of Rights, Co-operation and Welfare*. Oxford: Basil Blackwell.

Sumner, W. G. (1992 [1906]). Folkways. In R. C. Bannister (ed.), *The Essential Essays of William Graham Sumner*. Indianapolis, IN: Liberty Press, pp. 357–372.

Sutter, D. (1995). Potholes along the Transition from Authoritarian Rule. *Journal of Conflict Resolution* 39: 110–128.

Tabellini, G. (2010). Culture and Institutions: Economic Development in the Regions of Europe. *Journal of the European Economic Association* 8: 677–716.

Teerikangas, S. and P. Very (2006). The Culture–Performance Relationship in M&A: From Yes/No to How. *British Journal of Management* 17: S31–S48.

Thaler, R. and C. Sunstein (2008). *Nudge: Improving Decisions about Health, Wealth, and Happiness*. New Haven, CT: Yale University Press.

Tiebout, C. (1956). A Pure Theory of Local Expenditures. *Journal of Political Economy* 64: 416–424.

Tilly, C. (1992). *Coercion, Capital, and European States, AD 990–1992*. Oxford: Basil Blackwell.

Tocqueville, A. de (2003 [1840]). *Democracy in America*. London: Penguin Classics.

Tullock, G. (1967). The Welfare Costs of Tariffs, Monopolies, and Theft. *Economic Inquiry* 5: 224–232.

Tullock, G. (1987). *Autocracy*. Dordrecht: Kluwer.

Twight, C. (1992). Constitutional Renegotiation: Impediments to Consensual Revision. *Constitutional Political Economy* 3: 89–112.

Ullmann-Margalit, E. (1977). *The Emergence of Norms*. Oxford University Press.

Uslaner, E. M. (2002). *The Moral Foundations of Trust*. Cambridge University Press.

Vanberg, V. (1992). Innovation, Cultural Evolution, and Economic Growth. In U. Witt (ed.), *Explaining Process and Change: Approaches to Evolutionary Economics*. Ann Arbor, MI: University of Michigan Press, pp. 105–121.

Vanberg, V. (1994). *Rules & Choice in Economics*. London: Routledge.

Voigt, S. (1993). Values, Norms, Institutions and the Prospects for Economic Growth in Central and Eastern Europe. *Journal des Économistes et des Études Humaines* 4: 495–529. Reprinted in S. Pejovich (ed.), *The Economics of Property Rights II: The International Library of Critical Writings in Economics*. Cheltenham: Edward Elgar (2001), pp. 303–337.

Voigt, S. (1999a). *Explaining Constitutional Change: A Positive Economics Approach*. Cheltenham: Edward Elgar.

Voigt, S. (1999b). *Improving Welfare by Seeking Rents. Or: On the Ambivalence of Rent Seeking for Explaining Constitutional Change*. Jena: Max-Planck-Institut zur Erforschung von Wirtschaftssystemen.

Voigt, S. (2011). Positive Constitutional Economics II: A Survey of Recent Developments. *Public Choice* 146: 205–256.

Voigt, S. (2013). How (Not) to Measure Institutions. *Journal of Institutional Economics* 9: 1–26.

Voigt, S. (2019). Institutions. In R. Kollmorgen, W. Merkel, and H.-J. Wagener (eds.), *Handbook of Transformation Research*. Oxford University Press.

Voigt, S., M. Ebeling, and L. Blume (2007). Improving Credibility by Delegating Judicial Competence: The Case of the Judicial Committee of the Privy Council. *Journal of Development Economics* 82: 348–373.

Voigt, S., J. Gutmann, and L. Feld (2015). Economic Growth and Judicial Independence, a Dozen Years On: Cross-Country Evidence Using an Updated Set of Indicators. *European Journal of Political Economy* 38: 197–211.

Voigt, S. and D. Kiwit (1998). The Role and Evolution of Beliefs, Habits, Moral Norms, and Institutions. In H. Giersch (ed.), *The Merits of Markets: Critical Issues of the Open Society*. Berlin: Springer, pp. 83–108.

Voigt, S. and S. M. Park (2013). Not a Quick Fix: Arbitration is No Substitute for State Courts. *Journal of Development Studies* 49: 1514–1531.

Walker, M. (1988). *Freedom, Democracy, and Economic Welfare*. Vancouver: Fraser Institute.

Wallis, J. and D. North (1986). Measuring the Transaction Sector in the American Economy, 1870–1970. In S. Engermann and R. Gallman (eds.), *Long-Term Factors in American Economic Growth*. University of Chicago Press, pp. 95–148.

Weber, M. (1964 [1922]). *The Theory of Social and Economic Organization.* Ed. T. Parsons. New York: Free Press.

Weber, M. (1993 [1920]). *The Sociology of Religion.* Trans. E. Fischoff. New York: Beacon Press.

Weber, M. (2011). *Methodology of Social Sciences.* Trans. and ed. E. A. Shils and H. A. Finch. New Brunswick, NJ: Transaction Publishers.

Weibull, J. W. (1997). *Evolutionary Game Theory.* Cambridge, MA: MIT Press.

Weimann, J. (1994). Individual Behaviour in a Free Riding Experiment. *Journal of Public Economics* 54: 185–200.

Weingast, B. (1993). Constitutions as Governance Structures: The Political Foundations of Secure Markets. *Journal of Institutional and Theoretical Economics* 149: 286–311.

Weingast, B. (1995). The Economic Role of Political Institutions: Market-Preserving Federalism and Economic Development. *Journal of Law, Economics, & Organization* 11: 1–31.

Weingast, B. (2014). Second Generation Fiscal Federalism: Political Aspects of Decentralization and Economic Development. *World Development* 53: 14–25.

Whinston, M. D. (2003). On the Transaction Cost Determinants of Vertical Integration. *Journal of Law, Economics, & Organization* 19: 1–23.

Wicksell, K. (1896). *Finanztheoretische Untersuchungen.* Jena: Fischer.

Williamson, C. R. and R. L. Mathers (2011). Economic Freedom, Culture, and Growth. *Public Choice* 148: 313–335.

Williamson, J. (ed.) (1994). *The Political Economy of Policy Reform.* Washington, DC: Institute for International Economics.

Williamson, O. E. (1975). *Markets and Hierarchies: Analysis and Antitrust Implications.* New York: Free Press.

Williamson, O. E. (1985). *The Economic Institutions of Capitalism.* New York: Free Press.

Williamson, O. E. (1996). The Politics and Economics of Redistribution and Efficiency. In O. E. Weingast, *The Mechanisms of Governance.* Oxford University Press, pp. 195–216.

Williamson, O. E. (2002). The Theory of the Firm as Governance Structure: From Choice to Contract. *Journal of Economic Perspectives* 16: 171–195.

Williamson, O. E. (2010). Transaction Cost Economics: The Natural Progression. *Journal of Retailing* 86: 215–226.

Wintrobe, R. (1998). *The Political Economy of Dictatorship.* Cambridge University Press.

Wittman, D. A. (1995). *The Myth of Democratic Failure: Why Political Institutions are Efficient.* University of Chicago Press.

Wydick, B. (2007). *Games in Economic Development.* Cambridge University Press.

Zak, P. J. and S. Knack (2001). Trust and Growth. *The Economic Journal*
    111: 295–321.
Zweigert, K. and H. Kötz (1998). *Introduction to Comparative Law*. Oxford:
    Clarendon Press.

Index